Letters of Credit

Walter Tracy

LETTERS OF

CREDIT

A View of Type Design

D AVID R. GODINE · PUBLISHER

BOSTON

First U.S. edition published in 1986 by
David R. Godine, Publisher, Inc.
Horticultural Hall
300 Massachusetts Avenue
Boston, Massachusetts 02115

First published in the U.K. in 1986 by
the Gordon Fraser Gallery Ltd., London and Bedford
Copyright © 1986 by Walter Tracy

LIBRARY OF CONGRESS CATALOGING IN PUBLICATION DATA

Tracy, Walter.
    Letters of credit.
    1. Type and type-founding—History—20th century.
    2. Type and type-founding. I. Title.
    Z250.A2T73 1986   686.2′24   86–9767
    ISBN 0–87923–636–1

First U.S. edition
Printed in England
Typeset in Monophoto Sabon by August Filmsetting, Haydock, St. Helens
Origination by The Westerham Press Ltd, Westerham, Kent
Printed by The Roundwood Press Ltd, Kineton, Warwick
Bound by Hunter and Foulis Ltd, Edinburgh
Designed by Peter Guy

Contents

TO FRANCES

Preface and acknowledgements

In my apprentice days, when I aspired to be a typographer and was learning about type faces, I realised after a time that the accumulation of facts about them, squirrel-fashion, was not enough. It was necessary to acquire a sense of values and to develop the ability to make judgements about the quality of the type faces I was using. I was therefore grateful to Updike, Morison, Johnson and others who, in their writings, not only explained the history of type designs but expressed opinions about them. If I sometimes found it difficult to accept a particular comment I was at least pleased that the writer had made me think about the matter. Now, after more than fifty years of involvement with type, it has occurred to me that, without trying to emulate the scholarship of the writers I have mentioned, I should set down a few thoughts of my own, in the hope that they may be useful to a reader who is fairly new to the subject, has an interest in type and perhaps some acquaintance with it, thinks (as I do) that it is more important to be able to judge the quality of designs than to have an encyclopedic knowledge of them, but does not yet feel sufficiently equipped to make a confident assessment of the merits of a type. I have supposed that he or she may be bewildered by the number and variety of type faces now current, suspicious of the high-powered promotion of some of them, and disappointed that the journals that deal with typography do not provide the same sort of critical analysis of type designs as is given to new literature and the performing arts in the general press. So I have chosen to describe some aspects of the nature of type that have a bearing on the design of it, and then to offer a personal appraisal of the work of four twentieth-century designers, to which I have added a view of Stanley Morison's single, but very significant, venture in the field.

The pages that follow, then, are a compound of fact and opinion. I am sure the reader will have no difficulty in recognising one from the other, and would not wish me to say 'in my opinion' every time I have a comment to make. At the same time, I hope the reader will keep it in mind that an opinion is not an absolute truth, a gospel from on high. To quote from John Rothenstein's *Modern English Painters*: '. . . there exists no such quality as perfect detachment. All writers worth reading have an attitude towards their subject . . . If the reader knows where a writer stands, he will be able to make the necessary allowance for his bias.' For my own part, I take the view that typography, like most other sorts of designing, is essentially a means to an end; and the end is not the self-satisfaction of the designer but the contribution he or she makes to the effectiveness of whatever is presented to the public. The use of type is a matter of taste as well as sense; and the fact that typographic letter forms are an inexhaustible source of interest and pleasure is a thing to be grateful for.

In the course of this work I have realised again how fortunate I have been in the people I have known. I think of James Shand, excellent printer, adventurous publisher, and good friend, in whose company I discerned that taste is thought, not just fancy. I think with affection of Harry Smith, who was for many years in charge of Linotype's type drawing office at Altrincham and had himself drawn the production drawings of the admirable Granjon, Georgian and other faces under the keen eye of George W. Jones. It was from Harry Smith that I learnt about the process of translating a design into actual type. I think too of colleagues in the Mergenthaler Linotype office in New York, particularly Paul Bennett and Jackson Burke, who made me aware of people and events in the American typographic scene.

In the preparation of this book I have had the benefit of information and material from a number of friendly people, and I am glad to express my gratitude to them: to Abe Lerner and Kit Currie, for practical encouragement and much kindness; to James Mosley, for directing me to useful sources, and to the staff of the St Bride Printing Library for their unfailing assistance; to Matthew Carter, Sem Hartz, Ruari McLean, Vivian Ridler and Berthold Wolpe, for reading parts of the text and offering valuable comment; to Rollo Silver for helpful information and advice; to Fiona Ross for translations; to John Dreyfus for the loan of Nonesuch items; to Walter Greisner for the gift of Klingspor specimen books; to Gertraude Benöhr for information relating to Jakob Erbar; to Nicholas Biddulph for informing me of the Futura patterns; to Steve Byers of Mergenthaler New York for specimen books and for copies of some Dwiggins items; to Maurits Enschedé for his interest and co-operation, to Joh. Enschedé en Zonen for special settings of types by Jan van Krimpen, and to Bram de Does for supervising them; to Jerry Kelly and A. Colish Inc. of Mount Vernon for a setting of the World Bible Newstyle face; to D. Stempel AG for prints of digitised faces; to the Houghton Library at Harvard for permission to quote from *WAD to RR*; and to the University of Kentucky Libraries to quote from material in their C. H. Griffith archive.

A version of the essay on the types of Jan van Krimpen was published in *Fine Print*, in April and July 1981. The essay on Dwiggins's types was the basis for a talk given at the annual conference of the American Printing History Association in September 1983, and the study of the Times Roman type was drawn upon for lectures at Yale and Columbia Universities in the same month.

W.T.

PART I

Aspects of type design

1: The vocabulary of type

Some of the terms used in discussing type designs and typo-graphic practice are illogical, or have more than one meaning, or mean different things in different places. They have come into currency in the talk of master to worker, journeyman to appren-tice, through the five hundred years of the craft of printing – or industry, as it now is. Most of the terms are serviceable enough, so they continue in use even though the practice of making type and using it is now chiefly a matter of electronic and computer technology, optics and photographic chemistry, which have add-ed their own terms to the vocabulary of printing.

This book is determinedly non-technical; but because it is meant to be of use to readers in a wide range of interests and with different levels of experience, the definitions and explanations that follow may be helpful.

Alignment or *alinement* relates directly to the baseline, *q.v.* Char-acters are 'out of alignment' when they do not appear to stand properly on the line (letters with curves at the base, like a and e, and the triangular letters v and w, actually extend a little below the baseline). Faulty alignment was often seen in badly-set metal type but is rare in modern digital typesetting. The baseline of type faces and type sizes being fixed and common to all means that they all align with each other – which is useful enough in advertising typesetting, though the makers of the systems tend to exaggerate the importance of the facility.

Ascenders. The lowercase letters b, d, h, k and l have stems that extend up to the cap line or, preferably, a little above it. The part of the stem above the x-line is the ascender. In j, p and q the part of the stem below the baseline is the descender. The two features are sometimes called extruders, but that is a misuse of the word.

Baseline or *zee-line* is the level of the feet of H and x.

Bowl. The curved part of the letters B, P, R, b, d, p and q, and the lower section of a.

Cold type is type-set matter produced by a machine which out-puts the composition on to sensitised paper or film. If and when mechanical (hot-metal) typesetting disappears altogether the term cold type will no longer be necessary.

Colour. The term *weight* is used in a comparative sense. To refer to the tone of a type in mass on a page the word *colour* is sometimes convenient.

Counters are the 'whites' within characters, particularly the en-closed areas: the 'eye' of e, the two interior spaces in B. But the term is also used for the space between the uprights of H and n.

CRT stands for cathode ray tube, the electronic device in some high-speed machines which transmits the letter images, formed of lines or dots, on to the output film or paper.

Digitising. The process of converting the contour of a character, or the whole of it, into coded data for storage in a computer's memory. See chapter five for various methods of digitising.

Display. When used in regard to size, it means sizes of type over 14 point. When used about the design of type it means a face other than a traditional text face, a type of highly-developed individuality, or an inlined or shadowed version of a basic face, intended for publicity use.

Dot-less i. An extra character now included in most modern systems so that accents can be automatically 'floated' into position over it.

Electronic typesetting. A term of convenience used in this book for 'cold type' machine typesetting as distinct from metal type composition. See *filmsetting* and *photo-composition*, and particularly *image-setting*.

Face has the same meaning as type, but can be used more precisely. Strictly, a type face is one of the sets of characters in a type family: thus Baskerville roman is one face, the italic is another, the bold is the third. This point is important when the capacity of a typesetting machine is being considered.

Film advance. In electronic typesetting, the distance from the baseline of one line of type to the baseline of the next. Commonly this means that type of say 10 point nominal size will be set on film advance of 10 point (often called 'solid' setting) or larger, say $10\frac{1}{2}$ or 11 point – though the increment can be by quarter-point or even one-tenth-point steps, according to the make of machine. Since the face size and film advance are separately controlled, 'minus' film advance is possible. It is occasionally useful in the setting of headlines, but makes a bad effect in text setting, as the classified advertisement columns of some newspapers demonstrate.

Filmsetting. An inaccurate but convenient term for 'cold' typesetting.

Fitting is the manufacturer's spacing of the characters. See the separate chapter on the subject.

Fixed spaces. In justified composition the spaces between words vary in width according to the width of the characters in the line and whether or not the last word is breakable. Those spaces are 'variable'. Fixed spaces have a definite and unvariable width. The two basic ones are the em, which is usually the width of the type size, and the en, which is either one-half the em or as wide as the numerals in the font. (See the essay on numerals.) The other fixed space is the thin, generally related in width to the en. The full-point and comma are usually given that width in faces that are possibilities for tabular setting.

Font (in Britain it is so pronounced, but spelt *fount*) is a type founder's term of quantity: the total number of letters and other items needed for a particular purpose, capitals, lowercase, numerals, punctuation marks, ligatures, monetary signs, and so on. The font needed for the composition of a telephone directory, with its several kinds of numerals, is different from the font needed for the setting of a novel. Font is not another word for type face or design, as some writers have thought – Stanley Morison, for one.

The strip of negative film on which the characters are arranged in some photo-composition machines is called a font. The term is also used for the sets of digitised characters in more recent systems. Because of the international marketing of such systems the four-letter spelling of the word (which was the original form, according to an editor's note in Moxon's *Mechanick Exercises*, second edition 1962) is becoming familiar in Britain and Europe. It is used in this book.

Frisket. Sunday printers will know that the frisket was, and is, a metal frame with a sheet of paper stretched on it and cut away to the type area, the frame being affixed to the tympan of a hand press to hold in place the sheet to be printed. The word has been borrowed for the piece of transparent laminate, one side red in colour, on which an enlarged type character is cut out, so that this 'frisket' can serve as a ready-made negative for photographic transferal to a master disc or film font, or as the artwork in the digitising process. Most current type designs exist in frisket form.

Gothic. Traditionally, the word has been used for two quite different sorts of letter: the pen-made letters sometimes called 'black-letter' or 'Fraktur', and the sans-serif form. In this book gothic means only the first sort, as in the review of Rudolf Koch's types.

H and J stands for 'hyphenation and justification'. For a computer justification is a simple matter of addition and subtraction. Hyphenation is a different matter. In proper typesetting words are hyphenated at the ends of lines according to their syllabic structure. The computer must be provided with a comprehensive list of prefixes, suffixes and roots if it is to hyphenate the words correctly at the line endings as part of the justification process. It is sadly clear that in some electronic typesetting the 'dictionary' store is inadequate, or not working properly, or has been deliberately by-passed.

Hot-metal means composed type matter produced by a Monotype or line-casting machine. Anyone who has handled line-cast correction slugs straight from the machine knows that they are certainly hot. The term can hardly be applied to foundry-made type, which may have lain in store for a long time before being put to use by the hand compositor. *Cold metal* is the only appropriate term for it. The important thing about metal type is its physical nature, not its temperature at the time of composition.

Image-setting. The term describes the modern systems that deliver pictures and graphics as well as type matter.

Justification is the adjustment of the spaces between words so that all the lines of the text will be the same length, or 'squared up'. Unjustified setting, sometimes called 'ragged right', has uniform word spacing, with the variable excess at the end of the line. It does not, as some typographers used to think, obviate the need for hyphenation.

Kern. The top of the roman lowercase f, and the top and bottom of the italic *f*, are kerns which project into the 'air space' of adjacent letters. In metal type they had to rest on the shoulder of the next character, and often broke off. In the linecasting systems kerns were not possible, because it was matrices that were assembled, not type. In most electronic typesetting systems kerns present no problem. They do not, however, always make a good effect. See *ligature.*

Kerning. A kerning routine in a computer-aided typesetting system reduces the space on one side of a letter to enable it to stand closer to the adjacent letter. See the chapter on character spacing.

Ligature. A character consisting of two or more letters tied together for aesthetic effect. Strictly, the ligature is the particular part of the character that connects the letters. The most familiar ligatures are ff, fi, and fl. The ffi and ffl used to be standard in British and American metal type fonts, but they are often omitted from electronic systems. Some systems dispense with ligatures altogether, on the assumption that the kerned f and the dot-less i will make acceptable substitutes. But the conjunction of the ball of f with the following l (fl) is never as clean as in a properly designed ligature.

Linecasting. The general name for the Linotype and Intertype mechanical composing system, in which, from the operation of the keyboard, a line of character matrices is assembled. From that a line of metal type, called a 'slug', is cast automatically. In the Ludlow linecaster, which is used chiefly for headlines, the matrices are composed by hand.

Logotype. A whole name or word made as one piece of type, or one character, in a font. A directory printer can save time in composition by having 'Inc' or (in Britain) 'plc' supplied as one character, available at a single key-stroke.

Matrix. A piece of brass or copper into which a character has been stamped or engraved and from which type can be cast.

Mechanical composition, as distinct from electronic or photocomposition: any system comprising a keyboard and a hot-metal casting apparatus. In this book the term usually means the machines made by the Monotype and Linotype companies.

Monotype. The registered trade name of the mechanical system which produces composed type matter in the form of single metal types.

Photo-composition. As used in this book it means those typesetting devices that consist of a lens system, a light source, a font of characters in the form of a disc or film strip negative, and a means of selecting a character from it. Traditional photography provides the basic principle, as distinct from systems which employ CRT or laser for the transmission of the characters.

Pixels, from *picture elements:* the 'atoms' into which the digitising process converts a character.

Program (not programme). The set of instructions in a computer which it carries out in sequence. A typesetting program is special, and may have additions to it for the performing of particular functions, such as page make-up.

Resolution. The definition or resolution of characters produced by a CRT or laser-equipped typesetting system depends on the number of lines per inch at which it operates, and at which its character font was originally scanned. At 300 lpi the resolution is low, and is only suitable for work on low-grade paper, such as newsprint. On a firm-surfaced paper the curves and diagonals of letters at low resolution show the saw-edged effect of the scan lines or pixels. At high resolution, say 1000 lpi, the contours are clean. At low resolution the output speed is high; at high resolution it is much slower. Output resolution has introduced an extra factor into the concept of quality in printing.

Roman is a term of several meanings. It can mean upright as distinct from italic. It can mean normal weight as compared with bold weight. And it can refer to a seriffed face as distinct from sans-serif. The sense in which 'roman' is to be understood is usually clear from the context; but it is sometimes necessary to be explicit and to say, for instance, 'bold roman' if that is what is intended.

Set. To set type is to compose it into words, lines and pages. But set has another meaning, when it refers to the width of characters. For example, Perpetua is of narrower set than Baskerville. In traditional Monotype usage the set of a particular size of a given type face is the width of the em space in American points. One-eighteenth of that width is the unit of measurement for the characters in the font.

Small caps, as an additional alphabet useful for expressing a 'difference' in composition, particularly in book work, used to be standard in regular fonts of metal type and matrices. They were not simply the capitals reduced in size, but were specially drawn to a width and weight that would harmonise with the lowercase and capitals. Makers of CRT typesetting systems hoped at first that a 'small cap' routine in the computer pro-gram, by which the capitals would be automatically reduced in size, would produce a tolerable effect. It did not. The letters came out too cramped and too light. Manufacturers who take quality seriously now provide correctly drawn small capitals in selected book faces.

Stem. Some writers use 'stem' for any vertical stroke in a letter. In this work the term is used of one stroke only – usually, but not always, the one that a scribe would write first: thus, the upright in E and p, but not the vertical strokes in N, which are secondary to the diagonal stroke.

Swash letters are the fancy alternatives in the italics of some book types, Garamond and Caslon, for example – though in the latter the swash letters, according to *Caslon's Circular* for Summer 1890, 'do not belong to the original founts; the first Caslon deeming them superfluous, discarded them. They have been recently engraved . . .' They are generally more of an affect-ation than an asset. They were available in mechanical typeset-ting but seldom used, because they had to be inserted into the line by hand. They have almost disappeared in modern practice.

Titling. Capitals and numerals usually made to occupy all the body size. Thus the capitals of Perpetua Titling 258 are larger than those of Perpetua 239, size for size. The capitals of the Times Titlings are actually smaller than those of the normal roman and bold. See the essay on Times Roman.

TTS stands for teletypesetter, a method used chiefly in the American newspaper industry by which news agency reports are transmitted by wire or radio in punched code form, decoded by the receiver in an outlying newspaper office, and converted into punched tape which then drives the operating unit on a Linotype keyboard for 'no hands' typesetting. The method re-quires the use of type faces made to a simplified 18-unit system. Some of them appear in current lists of digitised type faces.

Unit system. A measurement formula to enable the widths of all the characters in a font to be expressed as whole numbers. The main unit is usually the width of the em of the type size, divided into smaller units: 18, 36, 54, 96 units to the em are some of the systems in use.

Weight. In this book the terms light, bold and heavy are used to express variations from the normal weight. They are reasonable equivalents to the German *leicht, halbfett* and *fett*, which occur in the essay on the types of Rudolf Koch. In modern practice Book, Medium and Black, with Extra and Ultra as supplemen-tary adjectives, are frequently used as additions to the scale of weights – not always appropriately. 'Book' is hardly the right term for Futura, a sans-serif face not used for book compo-sition. And help is needed to understand just what is meant by 'Erbar Extra Medium'.

x-height. The distance between the baseline and the x-line, the level of the top of the lowercase x. It usually refers to the height of the lowercase as compared with the capitals, though in a normal seriffed face nearly all the lowercase letters are slightly taller than the x.

The classification of type designs is an unresolved problem. In 1860, when the Miller & Richard type foundry of Edinburgh introduced the new face created by Alexander Phemister they said it was superior to 'old style' types (meaning Caslon's face in particular). Yet they named the new face 'Old Style', to the confusion of printers in Britain, who were forced to invent a new term, 'old *face*', for Caslon and the earlier book types. But all was not clear. John Southward, a respected writer in the printing trade, clarified the matter. In his *Practical Printing* (second edition 1884) he wrote, 'The words "Old Face" and "Old Style" are at times used indiscriminately to the faces imitating the ancient founts, and to those which are a modern modification of them. It may, however, be desirable . . . to call the one "Old Face" and the other . . . "Old Style".' And that has been the general

ABCEGHJKMPQRSTW
abcdefghijklmnopqrstuvwxyz

ABCEGHJKMPQRSTW
abcdefghijklmnopqrstuvwxyz

ABCEGHJKMPQRSTW
abcdefghijklmnopqrstuvwxyz

ABCEGHJKMPQRSTW
abcdefghijklmnopqrstuvwxyz

The three basic styles of seriffed faces.
Old style, represented by Bembo, *c.* 1495, and Janson, *c.* 1685;
Transitional, Fry's Baskerville, *c.* 1768;
Modern, Walbaum, *c.* 1810.

TYPE of the OLD STYLE of face is now frequently uſed—more eſpecially for the finer claſs of book work ; as however the faces which were cut in the early part of the laſt century are now unpleaſing both to the eye of the critic

The *modernised old style* cut by Alexander Phemister in Edinburgh, 1860; imitated by most British and American type founders.

practice in Britain: to refer to all text faces from those of Aldus through to the Caslon type as 'old face', and to reserve 'old style' for the more regulated faces that imitate the Phemister letter. The American way is more logical: 'old style' for types of the first group, and 'modernised old style' for the second. The American convention is used in this book.

Those terms being adopted, it is not surprising that the class of text face that was so different from the old style, the one that was created by Firmin Didot in 1784 and developed by his followers, including Bodoni, should have been called *modern*; and that the class that came between the old style and the modern, exemplified by the types of Fournier and Baskerville, should be called *transitional* – though A. F. Johnson thought that 'a vague and unsatisfactory epithet'.

The names of those basic classes of type were different in continental Europe, but equally imprecise and illogical. In France the equivalent of old style was 'Elzevir' and of modern 'Didot'; there was a variation of the latter actually called 'Didot type anglais'. In Germany it was possible to talk of 'moderne Antiqua'. To eliminate such absurdities and to provide a classification scheme that was fairly comprehensive Maximilien Vox, the distinguished French typographer, introduced in 1954 the plan that bears his name. It comprised nine groups, each with a newly-invented title. Vox said the names could be changed if people so wished; the groups were the important thing. The scheme was adopted by the Association Typographique Internationale and by the British Standards Institution, which in 1967 recommended the following list, in which three of Vox's names are retained.

I, *Humanist*, faces derived from the Jenson type, for example Centaur and Italian Old Style.
II, *Garalde*, for faces from Bembo and Garamond through to Janson and Caslon.

The above two groups cover all the kinds of design otherwise called 'old style'.

III, *Transitional*, e.g. Fournier, Baskerville, Bulmer, Caledonia.

IV, *Didone*, e.g. Bodoni. To replace 'modern'.

 V, *Slab-serif*, in place of 'antique' and 'egyptian'.

VI, *Lineal*, in place of 'sans-serif'; the group divided into four sections: *Grotesque*, types of nineteenth-century origin; *Neo-grotesque*, recent versions of that mode, e.g. Helvetica; *Geometric*, e.g. Futura; *Humanist*, e.g. Gill Sans.

VII, *Glyphic*, e.g. Albertus.

VIII, *Script*.

IX, *Graphic*, 'drawn' letters, e.g. Cartoon, but also black-letter faces like Goudy Text.

It was realised by those of us who produced the BSI scheme that to retain the use of 'transitional' and 'grotesque' was not really satisfactory, but it proved too difficult to find better terms. Garalde, though a reasonable label for Garamond, Bembo and Sabon is hardly suitable for Ehrhardt, Janson and Caslon; a sub-section would be desirable. And it has been suggested that black-letter types should have a group to themselves. The classification was due to be revised in 1981, but it has not yet been dealt with. Because of that, and because it has aroused little interest in the United States, it is not used in this book. The fact is, any classification is simply an aid to study, not an end in itself. Once the student has got the characteristics of the groups firmly in mind and can 'place' any type face without difficulty the actual names of the groups, and their precision and logicality (or lack of it) cease to be important.

2: Type measure

When printing began, the type foundry was part of the printing office; but towards the end of the sixteenth century punch-cutters and founders began to set up on their own, and to sell their types to printers all over Europe. The sizes in which they made their types were not organised on any rational plan. At first there had been the large sizes for folio volumes to be read at a lectern; then the middle and smaller sizes for portable books. For convenience the founders named the sizes after the works for which they had first been made: hence Augustin and Cicero in France, and pica, brevier and long primer in England. The cicero in Europe and the pica in Britain became the units of measurement for line length and type area. In England, where printing struggled against re-pression until the end of the seventeenth century, printers had to put up with what they could get. In France, where the trade was encouraged by patronage, it was possible for printers to express annoyance at the fact that type sizes were not always the same from one foundry to another, and that there was no reliable correlation between one size and the next.

An attempt to remedy this state of things by official decree was made in Paris in 1723, when in a set of regulations on the conduct of printers and booksellers there was included a rule that type founders were to make their type body sizes to a prescribed system of relationships. It was one thing to make regulations; it was another thing for a type founder to alter his 'standards', such as they were, and so risk damage to the continuity of his business. But for a man setting up in the profession *de novo* there was no obstacle. It was Pierre Simon Fournier's decision in 1737, when he was 25, to do just that – to start on his own, to cut his own punches and make his own matrices and even his own moulds. He thus created an opportunity to give reality to the regulations of 1723 – though in regard to the relationship of body sizes he did it on his own terms.

Fournier's system was simple enough. Using the familiar terminology of linear measurement he set up a scale of two 'inches' (*pouces*), divided these into twelve parts (*lignes*) and each part into six *points*. All the usual body sizes were to be made to a stated number of these 'typographic' points: nonpareil was 6 points, petit-texte was 8 points, cicero 12 points, and so on for the twenty type sizes he envisaged. The use of a definite base made it possible to fix a definite relationship between sizes.

Fournier's *pouce, ligne* and *point* were not precisely of the same dimensions as the divisions of those names in the French 'foot' (which itself at that time varied from one area to another). It is probable that Fournier thought it commercially prudent to produce body sizes not greatly different from those in common use.

The obvious advantages to the printer in a system of sizes which had a definite relationship to each other were widely recognised, and Fournier's great innovation was adopted throughout France and the Netherlands during his lifetime. But after Fournier's death in 1768 the wind began to blow from another direction.

The great Didot family began its rise to eminence in printing in the middle of the eighteenth century when François Didot, a successful publisher and bookseller, added printing to his other activities. He was joined by his son François-Ambroise who, by the excellence of his work, gained a notable reputation. About 1775 he started a type foundry as an adjunct to his printing office, and it was presumably then that he decided to revise the Fournier point system by making it directly relative to the official linear measure, the French 'foot' and its normal subdivisions. This was praiseworthy and logical, no doubt, and in accord with the spirit of the age of reason. But it resulted in a unit larger than Fournier's: the Didot point is .0148 inch (.38 mm), while the Fournier point was about .0135 inch (.34 mm).

The introduction of the Didot system was not universally acclaimed. There were those who found the 'largeness' of the Didot sizes too much of a departure from tradition to be tolerable; and there were others who, having adopted the Fournier system, disliked the thought of changing to the new one. But the great reputation of the Didot family – especially when the sons of François-Ambroise, Firmin the punch-cutter and Pierre the printer, achieved prominence in the 'classic' movement in typographical design – overcame opposition to the new point system, and it rapidly gained favour. And then logic defeated logic.

In 1791 an official committee was set up to devise a new system of weights and measures; in 1795 its terminology was established; and in 1801 the metric system was given legal status (one of the notable reforms of the French revolution). It thus obliterated the one advantage that had been claimed for the Didot point system in comparison with Fournier's – compatibility between the measurement of type, particularly in page width and depth, and the measurement of paper and other materials of printing. The annoyance this caused to printers could not be assuaged – the Didot point system was too solidly established. Indeed, in the course of the nineteenth century it extended itself throughout Europe and beyond, wherever French influence was dominant. Although Firmin Didot made an attempt in 1811 to revise the system instituted by his father so as to bring it into relation with metric measure, nothing came of it. The Continental printer was obliged to accept the fact that the typographic point and the metre, however unrelated, were here to stay.

These energetic (if unfortunate) efforts by French type founders aroused little interest among their counterparts in Britain. Though Johnson and Hansard, in their respective *Typographia*s of 1824 and 1825, refer to the need for regularity in type sizes, they have nothing to say about the reforms of Fournier and Didot. The first mention of either seems to have been made in 1841, in Savage's *Dictionary of the Art of Printing*, which describes Fournier's system at length. Although there was a growing desire for some sort of regularity – a desire which increased in the United States as the number of foundries multiplied – it was not until T. L. De Vinne began writing for *Caslon's Circular* in 1878 that American printers gave serious attention to the French systems.

The origin of the American point system has been described on more than one occasion – not always accurately. The system was first adopted by Marder, Luse & Co., the Chicago type foundry

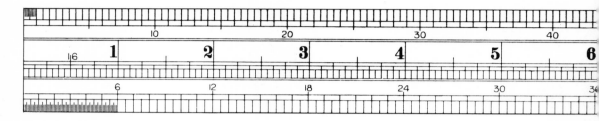

The Fournier, Didot and American point scales, with inch and metric measure.

vigorously conducted by John Marder, which did a large business in the western states. In 1871 the foundry was destroyed in the great Chicago fire. Marder immediately raised funds to rebuild and replace matrices and machinery. He saw an opportunity to put into practice a suggestion which had been made to him by Nelson Hawks, a Milwaukee printer. Hawks, who may well have known the Fournier and Didot systems, proposed that the pica should be divided into twelve parts, to be called 'points', and that each body size should be a definite number of points, so that regularity between sizes could be achieved. In 1872 the Marder, Luse foundry resumed business, and in the next few years made much in their advertising of what they called their 'American System of Interchangeable Bodies'. A few other foundries adopted the Chicago system, but some objected to it on the ground that the Marder, Luse pica was different from the pica most commonly used. This objection was sustained. On 17 September 1886 the twenty-four member companies in the United States Type Founders Association formally adopted the point system as standard, but selected as the basis of it not the Chicago foundry's pica but the pica of the Mackellar, Smith & Jordan foundry of Philadelphia – the largest and oldest foundry in the United States. A minority of members considered the new standard to have been 'capriciously and unscientifically selected, not based on any regular fraction of the foot or metre'. To counter that the Mackellar foundry claimed that eighty-three of their picas measured exactly thirty-five centimetres – an equation of very limited utility. The outcome, then, was a 12 point pica em measuring .1660 inch (4.21 mm), and a typographic point of .0138 inch (.35 mm).

In the United States the system was adopted fairly rapidly. No doubt the process of change from the old to the new was stimu-

Type measure

AMERICAN-BRITISH			DIDOT		
Points	inches	mm	Points	inches	mm
1	·01383	·35	1	·01483	·38
2	·0277	·70	2	·0296	·75
3	·0415	1·05	3	·0445	1·13
4	·0553	1·40	4	·0593	1·51
$4\frac{3}{4}$	·0657	1·67	$4\frac{3}{4}$	·0704	1·79
5	·0692	1·76	5	·0742	1·88
$5\frac{1}{2}$	·0761	1·93	$5\frac{1}{2}$	·0816	2·07
6	·0830	2·11	6	·0890	2·26
$6\frac{1}{2}$	·0899	2·28	$6\frac{1}{2}$	·0964	2·45
7	·0968	2·46	7	·1038	2·64
$7\frac{1}{2}$	·1037	2·63	$7\frac{1}{2}$	·1112	2·82
8	·1107	2·81	8	·1186	3·01
9	·1245	3·16	9	·1335	3·39
10	·1383	3·51	10	·1483	3·77
11	·1522	3·87	11	·1631	4·14
12	·1660	4·22	12	·1780	4·52
14	·1936	4·92	14	·2076	5·27
16	·2213	5·62	16	·2373	6·03
18	·2490	6·32	18	·2669	6·78
20	·2767	7·03	20	·2966	7·53
24	·3320	8·43	24	·3559	9·04
30	·4150	10·54	30	·4449	11·30
36	·4980	12·65	36	·5339	13·56
42	·5810	14·76	42	·6229	15·82
48	·6640	16·87	48	·7118	18·08

lated by the formation, in 1892, of the American Type Founders Company, which took over twenty-three foundries whose output amounted to eighty-five per cent of the total for the country. In Britain the full acceptance of the point system was delayed for some years because of acrimonious disagreement between some of the founders; but the American point system had become pretty general in the English-speaking world by about 1905 – though a catalogue issued by Stephenson Blake in 1919 had to say that the system 'cannot be said to have as yet secured such full adoption in this country as in America'. Even in 1930, in the firm I joined as an apprentice compositor, we had to be careful not to use 10 point spaces with long primer type, or 8 point with brevier.

There are, then, two typographic measurement systems in use: the American point system in the English-speaking world, and the Didot system in continental Europe and wherever French commercial influence was strong in the nineteenth century. Fifteen lines of American 12 point type will fit the depth of 14 lines of Didot 12 point. The American system is so nearly compatible with inch measure – thirty picas is only two hundredths of an inch less than five inches – as to be quite convenient in relating type area to paper area. The Didot system does not correspond at all well to metric measure. The advent of electronic typesetting has been thought by some people to provide the obvious opportunity to abandon both systems and to universalise type measurement by making it strictly and entirely metric. Enthusiasm for this view is not yet total. It is strongest in continental Europe, where the discrepancy between the Didot system and metric linear measure is, presumably, a nuisance to the designer of printed matter. In Britain, a consequence of membership of the European Economic Community has been official encouragement for the replacement of imperial measure by metric, but it makes only slow progress in the graphic arts. Some typographers are keen for metric type measure; others recognise its convenience in calculation but find the millimetre too small a unit for easy measurement on the layout pad by comparison with the pica em and the half-em. In the United States metric measure has as yet few advocates in the printing industry. It seems possible that the use of the Didot system will decline more rapidly than the American; but both systems are still quite deeply embedded in typographic practice and are likely to be with us for some years yet.

The point system of type measurement has been used in these pages rather than metric sizes because the books that have been quoted and the type specimen catalogues that the reader may consult have all used either American or Didot sizes. But for those who need to know the metric equivalents the table on the preceding page will be useful.

3: Types for study

Not long ago it was taken for granted that the people most interested in type faces were those who used them, or actually created them: typographers, publishers, printers and, of course, type designers themselves. But in recent years another set of people, quite different from those with direct involvement, have developed an interest in printing types. They are the academics – the mathematicians, computer scientists, psychologists, even philosophers – who have found it worth their time to theorise about the nature of letter forms as a human creation, one of the things that other animals do not have. Actually, the interest of some of them began a fair time ago, in the 1950s, when a good deal of work was done on the subject of legibility which echoed and amplified experiments done in earlier times. (It cannot be said to have had much influence or practical effect.) More recently, academic interest has broadened. Psychologists study the recognition of letters as an aspect of illiteracy. Philosophers examine the role of letters in the visual representation of meaning. And some scientists are now actually engaging their minds with the design aspects of letter forms, using a computer not simply to produce design variations more quickly but to create them *de novo* – if not by immaculate conception then by a sort of artificial insemination. Test-tube type faces, so to speak.

These studies and experiments now being conducted in universities and institutions may in time produce benefits to a wider field than the academic circles in which they are performed; but they are not the subject of this book, which is written from within the class of those whose profession it is to put information, opinion or persuasion into print or on to television screens and visual display terminals. Their knowledge of types usually begins with technical or design school training. It develops with working experience, and it is the range of that experience that nurtures the perceptions about types which become almost innate in the typographer and type designer, but which are not present in the academic observer, because of the difference of vocation. As some academic writings show, the absence of practical experience of type gives rise to a tendency to treat all types as equal and similar in nature, purpose and function. In short, there is a failure to recognise the different roles of type faces. In particular, there is sometimes a lack of understanding of the fundamental difference between types designed for display and types meant for text. The difference can be expressed as a maxim: text types when enlarged can be used for headings; display types, if reduced, cannot be used for text setting.

Croissant, Frankfurter, Pinball, Shatter and Stop are a few of the scores of display types which have been issued by the makers of dry-transfer ('rub-down') lettering sheets and headline type-on-film machines. In some of them ingenuity is the prime characteristic. They are the latest in a class of type that has quite a long history. The earliest I know is the so-called 'Italian' face which in

Battle of the Nile on Real Water.

An early use of the fat face, which began to be used on theatre posters in 1807.

England was first seen in the catalogue issued by the foundry of Henry Caslon II in 1821. T. C. Hansard thought the type was a 'typographic monstrosity', and a modern writer has called it 'reprehensible'. It has been misunderstood. It is not, as some have

ENGLISH ITALIAN FOR 1824.

The fat face turned inside out. The full point
defied the treatment.

said, a maltreated egyptian. I think it was an exercise in ingenuity
by a lively-minded person who, knowing that the 'fat face' –
which was the modern letter that had, as the song says, gone
about as far as it could go – had astonished the printers, decided
that the shock could be repeated if all the characteristics of the fat
face were reversed – the thick strokes made thin, the thin strokes
and serifs made thick, tapers inverted, and so on. The Italian face
was a *jeu d'esprit*, not meant to be judged in conventional aesthetic terms. Even more ingenious are the recent Block Up and
Bombere faces, which exploit the illusion of an extra dimension,

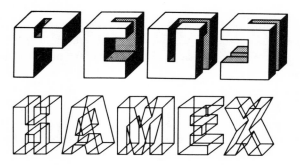

Block Up and Bombere.

and Stop, which is more subtle than it seems at first sight. But
such types are (literally) not typical. Most publicity types stay
closer to familiar letter forms, though novelty is usually their
chief *raison d'être*. They are meant for the come-on line in advertising work or the brand name on a package, or in the multitude
of items generally called ephemeral printing. Such types have no
certainty of a long life, because novelty is by definition itself
ephemeral. While they last they serve a turn, adding a visual fillip
to print just as the rustic, ribbon and bamboo types did a hundred
years ago. Some of these display types are skilfully designed.
Others are heavily-promoted but dismal souvenirs of the tail-end
of the nineteenth century, which do little credit to those who use
them and none to those who revived them. Others again are
inexcusably clumsy, and only see the light of day because their
promoters know that there are advertising typographers for
whom it is enough that a type is new. (The temptation to include
here a rogues' gallery of such types has been resisted.) Whatever
their merits, publicity types are of little help to anyone attempt-
ing to acquire a sound knowledge of typographic letter forms and
to recognise the criteria by which they should be judged. For that

purpose it is necessary to concentrate on a different area: to study those types which from their beginning were intended to be used in the composition of text matter – the 10 or 11 point of the typical book, or the 8 or 9 point of the magazine or newspaper; in other words, types designed for long stretches of reading, which prove their merits by subtleties of detail, not by novelties of form or flourish.

At first thought the obvious text faces to describe and analyse would seem to be the revivals and re-modellings of the types now regarded as the great classics of the past: Bembo, Granjon, Ehrhardt, Caslon, Fournier, Baskerville, to name a few. Certainly the student ought to make a careful study of the types of the past, in their original form through the writings of Updike, Johnson, Morison and Nesbitt, and also in the revivals and adaptations produced in the 1920s and 30s – cautiously keeping it in mind that type faces have not always been named accurately and that there are important differences between, say, Italian Old Style and an Aldine face, the true and false Garamonds, the original Caslon and Baskerville and the 'regulated' versions of them. However, the history and characteristics of those distinguished revivals will not be rehearsed in these pages; not only because that has been done sufficiently elsewhere, notably in Stanley Morison's *A Tally of Types*, but because those types were first created when printing was a craft, not an industry, when the powered press and machine-made paper were yet to come, and type faces were not so much designed as developed from a previous model. For those reasons, then, and particularly because type designing, as a professional activity outside the type foundry, began just about the beginning of this century, the types to be discussed in detail in the second part of this book will be the creations of some notable twentieth-century designers who took an individual view of type and recorded their thoughts about it.

To continue for a moment, though, about the revived classics: typographers seem to have an ambivalent attitude towards them. Like other design-conscious people they appreciate buildings, furniture and other objects made in the past but, rightly, frown at reproductions of them: neo-Georgian houses, Jacobean-style interiors, book club editions in pseudo-Renaissance bindings, and so on. They decidedly want things made *now* to show the fact, and not pretend otherwise. Yet they have a different attitude towards text types – willingly, even preferably, setting a modern novel or journal in a type that was created several centuries ago. This is a contradiction, no doubt; but it is a necessary one. There is an important reason why the revivals should continue to be used. On the basis of practical experience of them and on what has been written about them during the past sixty years it has been possible to form a corpus of ideas about letter design from

which a standard of quality has been developed and widely understood. Only by the existence of these reproductions of types of
the past could this awareness of what is admirable in type design
have been achieved. That was Stanley Morison's view. In his
introduction to *A Tally of Types* he wrote, in reference to the
state of type design in the early 1920s: 'The original twentieth-
century book type might come in due course. But certain lessons
had first to be learnt and much necessary knowledge discovered
or recovered. The way to learn to go forward was to make a step
backward.' That is sound enough as the reason for reviving
classic types in the first place. The question is: has the argument
much substance at this stage in time? It has – though it might be
expressed differently. The revivals, to which can be added some
of the twentieth-century text types which Morison predicted, are
still the essential source material for the understanding and
appreciation of all type designs. If they did not exist, or were
discarded, there would be no standards by which to verify our
ideas of what is good and bad.

Unfortunately, appreciation is not always as alert as it should
be. After more than half a century of existence the revivals are
now taken for granted; rather too much so, it seems. They are
regarded as constituting a body of classics not simply because
their origins were in the past but as though there is something
about them that puts them above critical scrutiny. The result is
that the typographer too willingly accepts the debased versions
of the classic faces now current in some modern electronic typesetting systems (as if the revered name of the type was itself a
guarantee of fidelity to the original), instead of demanding that
types of that class and kind should be available in modern typesetting to at least the same standard of quality as was present in
them when they were first made and admired in mechanical
composition. For that reason the wise student of typography
will keep on his shelves examples of well-produced books and
periodicals produced during the period 1930 to 1960; not for any
nostalgic reason but simply because it is in them that text type
faces, composed in metal and printed letterpress, are to be seen in
something like pristine form. They are therefore the only reliable
standards by which to judge the design quality of the versions
offered to us in these electronic times.

4: Legibility and readability

There are two aspects of a type which are fundamental to its
effectiveness. Because the common meaning of 'legible' is 'readable' there are those – even some people professionally involved

in typography – who think that the term 'legibility' is all that is needed in any discussion on the effectiveness of types. But legibility and readability are separate, though connected, aspects of type. Properly understood, and used in the meanings appropriate to the subject, the two terms can help to describe the character and function of type more precisely than legibility alone.

Legibility, says the dictionary, mindful of the Latin root of the word, means the quality of being easy to read. In typography we need to draw the definition a little closer; we want the word to mean the quality of being decipherable and recognisable – so that we can say, for example, that the lowercase h in a particular old style italic is not really legible in small sizes because its in-turned leg makes it look like the letter b; or a figure 3 in a classified advertisement type is too similar to the 8. So legibility is the term to use when discussing the clarity of single characters. It is a matter for concern in text sizes, and especially in such special cases as directories, where the type is quite small. In display sizes legibility ceases to be a serious matter; a character which causes uncertainty at 8 point will be plain enough at 24 point.

Readability is a different thing. The dictionary may say that it, too, means easy to read. In typography we can give the word a localised meaning, thus: if the columns of a newspaper or magazine or the pages of a book can be read for many minutes at a time without strain or difficulty, then we can say the type has good readability. The term describes the quality of visual comfort – an important requirement in the comprehension of long stretches of text but, paradoxically, not so important in such things as telephone directories or air-line time-tables, where the reader is not reading continuously but searching for a single item of information.

Legibility, then, refers to perception, and the measure of it is the speed at which a character can be recognised; if the reader hesitates at it the character is badly designed. Readability refers to comprehension, and the measure of that is the length of time that a reader can give to a stretch of text without strain. The difference in the two aspects of visual effectiveness is illustrated by the familiar argument on the suitability of sans-serif types for text setting. The characters in a particular sans-serif face may be perfectly legible in themselves, but no one would think of setting a popular novel in it because its readability is low. (Those typographers who specify a sans-serif for the text columns of a magazine may be running the risk of creating discomfort in the reader – to the ultimate benefit of a rival journal.)

Legibility and readability are the functional aspects of a type design. But there is more to a type face than the functional. A type designed for newspaper text may prove equal to, say, Bembo in a carefully conducted readability test; but it would not be chosen for the composition of a book. This is only partly because the newspaper text type was designed for high-speed production methods which do not allow for much finesse. A stronger reason is that in the editorial columns of newspapers we prefer the text and headlines to be set in plain matter-of-fact types, and in books we want faces of refinement and distinction. Set a novel in a newspaper type and the effect will be so uninviting that the success of the work will be jeopardised. Set a newspaper in a book type and we will not take it seriously. (There was once a newspaper which used Caledonia for its text. That excellent book type helped the paper to gain awards for good design but, ironically, contributed to its early demise.) So as well as the functional aspects of type design there is the aesthetic aspect; and it is the proper balancing of the functional and the aesthetic which we look for in the work of the type designer, just as we do in other fields of product design.

5: The making of type

Electronic typesetting has now had a dominant place in printing technology for a fair number of years, and there has been ample evidence of the high level of fidelity which a capable manufacturer can achieve in reproducing the subtleties of type faces (and, for that matter, too much evidence of what an insensitive manufacturer can perpetrate). Yet some writers on typography continue to assert that the change from mechanical typesetting to systems comprised of electronics for their power and photographic chemistry for their product requires some sort of change in the design of type faces, without specifying what kind of electronic typesetting they have in mind. It is true that low-resolution systems impose severe limitations on letter form and detail; but the high-resolution systems used for most of the printed matter we read allow the type designer as much freedom as he is likely to need, and can reproduce his work to a remarkably high standard.

The belief that the method of manufacture has an influence on the design of type is not new. There is little justification for it. In fact, the history of printing types is a tale of sophistication in letter design being achieved at quite an early stage, reaching heights of ingenuity in the nineteenth century, and not being affected to any noticeable extent by the techniques of manufacture.

To examine that point, and bearing in mind that a large number of types in use at the present time were created before the advent of electronic typesetting – and some of them even before the invention of mechanical composition – an outline of the successive methods of manufacture may be useful.

For four hundred years, from the middle of the fifteenth century when printing in Europe began, the making of type was a combination of four hand crafts: the cutting of letter punches, the striking of matrices, the casting of the type, and the dressing of it ready for use by the printer. Each of them was essential, but only the punch-cutter's work displayed itself to the critical world.

The punch was a short bar of annealed steel, the end of which was to be shaped to the form of the character. For any letter that contained an interior enclosed space, such as B, O, a, g, the punch-cutter would first make a counter-punch to the shape of the interior white area – hence the term 'counter' for that part of a letter. The counter-punch would be driven into the face of the punch, and then the outer profile of the letter would be formed by filing away the unwanted metal; slow painstaking work, with many pauses for the checking of the size of the letter and the thickness of its strokes with a variety of specially-made gauges.

The counter-punch.

When the letter was finished the punch would be held in the smoke of a lamp or candle flame until it was blackened, and then pressed on to paper so that its image could be compared with other characters of the font. If it was satisfactory the punch was hardened. It was then struck into a small bar of copper, which thus became a matrix. It had to be justified, its sides rubbed down to remove the displacement caused by the strike, its face lowered until the depth of strike was correct. The matrix was then passed to the type caster, a skilled workman whose tool was the mould, the ingenious device in which the matrix was fixed so that the letter was at the bottom of an aperture adjusted to the size of type required. Molten metal was poured in to form the piece of type. (As A. F. Johnson pointed out in his *Type Designs*, the mould was the essence of Johann Gutenberg's invention in printing, not punch-cutting or the press, both of which were already known in

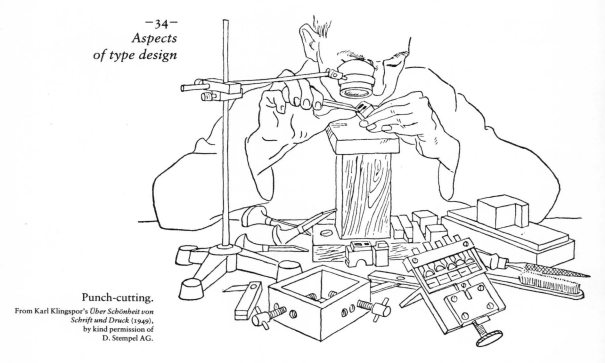

Punch-cutting.
From Karl Klingspor's *Über Schönheit von
Schrift und Druck* (1949),
by kind permission of
D. Stempel AG.

other crafts.) When a sufficient number of castings had been done
the pieces of type were assembled in line, their feet cleared of
extraneous metal and identifying nicks were grooved into the
shank. Note that in this series of tasks the punch, so laboriously
produced, was not an end but the means to an end: the matrix
was the indispensible item.

That was the method of type making used for types as diverse
as the textura of Gutenberg's work, the romans made for Aldus
(one of them we know today as Bembo), Robert Granjon's
remarkably elaborate Greek type, his Civilité, the delicately
complicated Union Pearl of about 1700, Firmin Didot's austere
modern face, and many of the nineteenth century 'fantasy' types
– to mention only enough to show what a variety of design was
achieved by the skill of the punch-cutter during the long period
when printing was done by hand and eye, and not by any sort of
machine. It is clear that, as a means of creating a letter, the act of
shaping a punch had no particular influence, and enforced no
limitation, on the style or shape or detail of the character. Letters
could be any width, angles and serif ends could be as sharp as
desired (because the metal was being cut away, not incised), and a
modification to the mould allowed letters to be provided with
kerns; in short, the skilled punch-cutter had fewer limitations in
his creative work than was later the case in the making of type
faces for mechanical composition, as we shall see.

It was the punch-cutter himself who, if he possessed artistic
sense as well as manual skill, was capable of influencing the
appearance of a type – indeed, of creating a new effect altogether.

Thus the types cast from the matrices struck from the punches cut by Claude Garamond owe their distinctive appearance to his creative sense, his vision of the style of face he wanted to produce. The same can be said of Kis and Caslon, Fournier and Firmin Didot, and many others. They were designer punch-cutters. Baskerville is a different case. He had the vision; but his punches were cut for him by John Handy, who can be called an interpretive punch-cutter. There have been others such: Edward Prince, who brought into being the ideas of Morris and Cobden-Sanderson; Charles Malin, who was engaged by Stanley Morison to cut punches of Gill's Perpetua design before Monotype took up the work; and P. H. Raedisch, who interpreted the designs of Jan van Krimpen. Most of the men who worked for the nineteenth-century American foundries were punch-cutters of the interpretive sort, able to receive a sketch or note for a new type and give its characters style and coherence. As William Loy wrote in 1898, 'Very few engravers of type faces work from their own designs; indeed, the qualifications are so dissimilar that one would hardly expect to find them in the same individual.' No doubt there was a third class of punch-cutter, the artisan kind, employed not for any ability as designer or interpreter but for manual skill and accuracy – which must have been considerable, to judge by the 'finish' of the faces shown in the later nineteenth-century type founders' catalogues. The seven or eight punch-cutters in the Mergenthaler plant in 1890 were probably of that sort – their task being to cut punches for newspaper text types in imitation of existing founders' faces, but more particularly, to replace the punches which broke so frequently.

In type founding as elsewhere the invention of steam power made mechanisation possible. A machine for the rapid casting of type was developed early in the nineteenth century. Towards the end of that period some type founders adopted, as an alternative to punch-cutting and matrix striking, the engraving of the character directly into the matrix blank – a method only suitable for fairly large sizes and for designs in which rounded angles, caused by the powered rotating cutting tool, were tolerable. (More of this later, when the work of Frederic Goudy is examined.) Yet another method, the electrotype matrix 'grown' from a pattern cut in 'soft' metal, was an easy way of producing a new type face, and one of the reasons why the last quarter of the nineteenth century was such a prolific period. The most significant event, though, was the mechanising of punch-cutting. It removed an obstacle to the progress of mechanical typesetting, and was thereby the indirect cause of the decline of type founding as a trade.

The unwitting instigators of the event were Linn Boyd Benton and his partner R. V. Waldo. They conducted the Northwestern Type Foundry in Milwaukee, where Benton devoted his energy

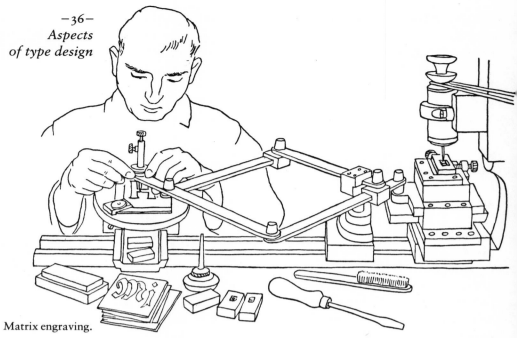

Matrix engraving.

to the creation of types in which all the characters and spaces would be on one or other of nine widths, instead of the many random widths of traditional type founding. This early unit system – basically the same as the system later employed by Talbot Lanston in his Monotype machine – was intended to expedite the work of the compositor; one of them, testing the type, admiringly called the system 'self-spacing'. To assist in the production of the type faces needed for the new system Benton invented a machine which was soon to have unexpected significance. Bullen called it a punch-cutting machine, but by his own description it was not intended to cut punches but simulations of type, in 'soft' type metal, from which electrotype matrices were grown. The machine was patented in 1885. Waldo mentioned the machine during his efforts to sell self-spacing type to the *New York Tribune* and in turn Whitelaw Reid of that journal told Philip Dodge about it. Dodge had assumed responsibility for making the Linotype machine a commercial proposition, but knew that one of the obstacles was that the cutting of punches by hand was far too slow and the breakage rate too high. Dodge hurried to Milwaukee and persuaded Benton to try his machine in the cutting of a steel punch. It worked. A leasing agreement was arranged, and mechanical composition took a long step towards viability.

Mechanical punch-cutting, one of the salient developments in the history of printing, played a central role in the rapid advancement of both the Linotype and Monotype composing systems in the early years of the present century. Actually, two machines were involved. One of them was a version of the pantographic routing machine which for many years had been used in the making of wooden type for poster printing. A drawing of the character, scaled up to about ten inches, was placed at one end of the machine's table. At the other end a wax-coated metal plate was locked in position. The operator carefully tracked the follower point along the lines of the drawing, and the cutter at the end of the pantograph arm imitated the movement, in reduction, on the waxed plate. The surplus wax being removed, the plate was electrolytically coated with copper. The copper shell was backed with lead, and the result was an accurate representation of the character, about one-quarter the size of the drawing, and in firm relief; it was called a pattern, or former. That was the original method, and the one always used, with technical refinements, by Monotype. The American Linotype company, using the same kind of tool, at first cut the pattern character in plaster and from that made a stereotype in metal; but later they adopted the process developed by the English Linotype company, by which the character was cut through the upper one of two metal plates, which were then riveted together before the surplus metal was removed. The differences in the method are not important. The significant thing is that for the first time the type design now existed on paper in the form of accurate drawings – because type making had changed from a manual craft to a species of precision engineering.

The punch-cutting machine itself also worked on a version of the pantographic principle. A heavy upright frame held the table on which the pattern was secured. The follower arm was mounted vertically above the table. At the top of the arm was a lathe head containing a revolving cutter. The steel punch blank was fixed in a chuck adjacent to the cutter. The operator attached a circular follower to the arm and tracked it around the profile of the character on the pattern, exchanging the follower for a smaller one after each pass. The motion was exactly imitated in miniature by the cutter on the punch blank, so that the character took shape gradually. The operator would check the progress of the work from time to time, and when the punch was completed it would be checked in a projectorscope against the original drawing. If it was approved it was then hardened, and was then ready for use in the matrix stamping press – at which point one of the differences between the Monotype and Linotype systems manifests itself, the Monotype font requiring only one matrix of the character, the Linotype font needing up to twenty.

The traditional punch-cutter was quite absent from this scene – to the regret of some writers on type design. Updike, for instance: 'I have sometimes questioned whether a machine can be so managed that it will ever produce those fine and imperceptible qualities of design given to it by the hand of a clever type-cutter . . . That there has been an improvement of late [he was writing in 1922] in type cut by machine is undeniable . . . This improvement, I learn, has come to pass through a more sympathetic and subtle manipulation of the machine itself, and by modification of rules by the eye of the workman who operates it.'

Jan van Krimpen, too, made much of 'the problems' of mechanical punch-cutting in his *Letter to Philip Hofer* (a sadly muddled work whose chief merit is that it caused John Dreyfus to write a very interesting commentary on it). Updike and other critics disapproved of the 'mechanising' of letter forms, by which they meant the eliminating of 'the slight irregularities which the human eye and hand always leave in manual work', which Van Krimpen thought were 'an important element of the charm of hand-cut type'. It may be that it was not so much the accidental imperfections of execution that these critics admired in the types of the masters of the past as the subtleties of style which the designer-punch-cutters had deliberately introduced into their faces. In their comments they show no sign that they recognised the different kinds of punch-cutter – though one of them, Bruce Rogers, had a sense of that when, speaking of his Montaigne type, he said, '. . . partly through the conventional training of the punch-cutter (who was nevertheless a most admirable and skilful workman), the desired quality was only partially attained'. And it seems, from the way the critics expressed themselves, that they had an imperfect understanding of the way type designs for mechanical composition were produced. The workmen who operated the pattern-making and punch-cutting machines did not, because they could not, alter the letter forms in any way. That was the province of the drawing office, where, from a projection of a character on a type proof or from a designer's original drawing, the 'ten-inch' drawing was produced. Insensitivity in that area was not unknown. In 1921 Goudy had cause to complain about the treatment of his Garamont design. 'Drawings like mine, which were made free-hand, were not the sort usually worked from at the [American] Monotype company, so there was a constant fight to see that the workmen did not "correct" what seemed to them to be bad drawing on my part. If I intentionally gave a letter an inclination of one degree, they straightened it up. My serifs, which had a definite shape, were changed to meet their own ideas, since "they had always made them that way".' But if the work of the type drawing office was under the supervision of someone with a good eye for a letter, as was the case, for example, in the Linotype companies and in the English Monotype office, the letter drawings would show either a faithful replica of the original or a modification of it in accordance with a premeditated view of the desired result. There is ample evidence of the care that was given to the reproduction of designs, old and new, to preserve the character of the face and to make it suitable for the requirements of modern printing. For example, when sending a proof of Linotype's version of the so-called Janson type to Carl Rollins for comment on 18 January 1932, C. H. Griffith wrote, 'I hope you do not mind my bothering you so much with this proposition, but I am so anxious to have the Linotype face worthy of its name. If I cannot succeed in satisfying myself that our interpretation of Janson will be worthy of the honored name it bears, we shall not hesitate a moment to scrap the whole work and forget it.' And there was the solicitous handling of Granjon and other revivals by Harry Smith at Altrincham in collaboration with G. W. Jones; and Fritz Steltzer's expert supervision of Monotype's Ehrhardt, a radical adaptation of the Janson face. Those examples could be multiplied. Stanley Morison was unfair to his colleagues when he wrote in *A Tally of Types*, 'Virtue went out with the hand-cutter when the mechanic came in with his pantograph and the rest of the gear.'

However, there were certain aspects of type face manufacture for mechanical composition which potentially had a bearing on the appearance of type. One of them was due to the punch-cutting machine itself. Since it worked on the pantographic principle and had the facility of fine adjustment it could produce several sizes of punches from a single pattern. In practice, though, the manufacturers had the sense to see that restraint was needed if their type faces were to compare favourably with foundry-made types, and they accepted the fact that they must continue the traditional practice of 'optical compensation': that is, the modifying of the lowercase x-height and letter widths to maintain legibility in small sizes and elegance in the larger ones – an important subject, to be enlarged upon in a following essay.

Optical compensation. A letter from the 12 and 8 point sizes of Caledonia, enlarged to the same type size.

There were constraints in the Monotype system which at first sight seem severe. The system had two parts: a keyboard whose output was a ribbon of perforated paper, the perforations representing codes for the characters and for the justifying of the lines; and a casting machine, driven by the ribbon, which contained a metal pot and a die-case – that is, a frame holding the matrices in rows, an equal number in each row. The first constraint was the fact that the width of every character, including its own side spaces, had to be equal to a multiple of one-eighteenth of the width of a selected em quad, five eighteenths being the minimum, eighteen the maximum. The second constraint was the limit on the number of characters which could be allowed to each of the fourteen available widths. In the early days these limitations had a disagreeable effect on the appearance of certain types but that was soon overcome by technical development. The layout of the matrix case became variable, and the number of matrix rows was increased. The 'set' – the width of the em quad – could be plus or minus a quarter, half or three-quarters of a point, which allowed a certain amount of optical compensation in the text sizes. By the earlier years of this century the system had enough flexibility to reduce the limitations to insignificance so far as character design was concerned, as the high quality of the types in the English Monotype list demonstrates.

In the case of the line-casting machines there was no need for a unit system of character widths, so a roman could be designed with complete freedom. The characters in the italic, however, had to be designed to fit on the same matrix as the roman, which meant that the italic came out too wide to be historically authentic in types like Granjon and Garamond, though the italic of a later period, like Scotch, was reasonably true to its original. On the other hand, a bold face duplexed with a light face, especially in a sans-serif combination, would sometimes look cramped. The other notable limitation derived from the fact that what was composed in the line-casting machine was a line of matrices. Kerning was therefore impossible. The measure of a designer of type for line-casting was his ability to design a respectable non-kerning f. G. W. Jones and Harry Smith at Altrincham managed it very well in the Granjon and Georgian romans.

Mechanical typesetting, the combination of keyboard composition and the automatic casting of metal type, has not disappeared; but it is plain that the last quarter of this century has become the era of electronic typesetting. It is the computer that made it possible.

The electronic computer was developed in the Second World War. It was a pretty clumsy affair; but the invention of the transistor in the late 1940s brought the computer down to the sort of size that made type-on-film a feasible proposition, so the established manufacturers of mechanical composing machines addressed themselves to the task of creating machines for converting keyboard composition into photographic, instead of metal, output. It was clear to them that the great stock of letter drawings they had accumulated since the beginning of the century was a valuable asset which should be used as it stood, as far as that was possible. But first, several problems had to be solved.

One matter which the manufacturers had to resolve was directly connected with the fact that the chief task of the computer in an electronic typesetting system (though it does many other things as well) is to relieve the keyboard operator of the time-

consuming business of organising the justifying of each line of
text. To perform this task the computer must be told the width of
every character and all the 'fixed' spaces in all the fonts in the
machine; and it wants this information not in the form of actual
dimensions, such as $3\frac{1}{4}$ points or .0449 inch or 1.14 mm, but in
whole numbers. So a unit system was necessary. Type specimen
books of the 1970s, still in use, show that Linotype adopted the
18-unit system, with which they were already familiar in the
manufacture of newspaper text types for teletypesetter use; and
they proceeded to refit their saleable type faces to character
widths of one-eighteenth of a square em. One unit was reserved
for kerning, and roman and italic f were redesigned accordingly,
as was capital W where the original was wider than 17 units.
Monotype's position was a little different. Their drawings were
already unitised in 18 units; but the ratio of width to height often
varied from size to size, so it was necessary for them to choose the
size of artwork that would give an acceptable effect over a number of type sizes in output.

In spite of disparagement by some present-day writers (who
cannot be acquainted with printed work of the first half of this
century), there is ample evidence to show that in the 18-unit
system it was perfectly possible to produce a satisfactory set of
characters; but because the unit was 'large' the amount of careful
trial and adjustment needed to balance the characters with each
other took a good deal of time. So in the late 1970s Linotype
changed their system to 54 units to the em; a convenient plan,
because any type already made in 18 units could be used in a 54-
unit machine without adjustment, and in the production of a new
design the unit was small enough to ensure that little or no re-
drawing was necessary. There were other systems in use. For
example, one manufacturer used 36 units. Photo-composition
machines with unitised characters are still in service here and
there.

The quality of a type design does not rise or fall according to
the system of width units used in its manufacture. It depends
entirely on the ability of the people responsible for its production.
If their understanding of the matter is insufficient, if their judgement of letter shape, proportion and spacing is uncertain and
variable, no system of width measurement, however accom-
modating, will compensate for low-grade workmanship or
supervision.

The technical problem of deriving a 'solid' version of a character from the pencilled outline of it on the existing pattern drawing
was easily solved. In one method the drawing was placed on a
light box and a sheet of red masking film, perforated near the top
edge with register holes, was secured over it. The draughtsman
traced the outline of the character with a point or blade and
peeled away the red surface from its colourless support, so that

the result was a perfect facsimile of the character, in clear on a solid background. Because red acts like black in black-and-white photography this 'frisket', as some people call it, served as a negative, which could be placed in a sophisticated version of a process camera and shot into a prescribed position on a film positive. When the full array of characters had been dealt with the result was a master font, from which copies would be made and supplied to the user of the composing machine. That, or some variation of it, was the method by which the established composing machine manufacturers made direct use of their tried and tested type face artwork in the transfer from metal to film – or hot to cold, as the phrase has it.

The first kind of electronic typesetting system was called a 'photo-typesetter'. The 'photo-type' part of the term is an indicator of both the physical form of the character array in the machine, the font strip or disc, and the way the characters were transferred to the film or bromide paper output material: that is, through a system of lenses in a version of traditional photographic practice. Note that the type faces made for such machines derived directly from the original letter drawings, and what appeared on the output was simply a sequence of photographs of the letters as they were drawn at the beginning of their existence. That is not strictly true, perhaps, because for a time there were those who believed and practised the idea that the angled corners of counters – for example, where the bar in H meets the uprights – should be notched, to compensate for the tendency of the photographic process to round off the angles (that is, when the lenses in use were not of the best quality). But that practice, which was soon discarded, was intended to preserve the original state of the design, not to modify it in any way. However, in the other kind of electronic typesetting system that established itself in the early 1970s the abrasion of the edges of characters became a new feature of typography and a cause for concern, especially in the appearance of large headlines.

Machines of the photo-typesetter kind are opto-mechanical; the font is a spinning disc, or there is a moving grating to select the character to be exposed, or there are other moving parts. Movement takes time, and puts a limitation on the scope and speed of a machine – and speed of output is what most printers want; hence the other sort of machine, in which the optical lens system was replaced by a cathode ray tube, a sophisticated version of the object that forms the screen in the familiar television receiver. In the first CRT machines the character font was still in the form of a photographic negative. The machine contained a scanning device, a light spot which traversed the characters, its responses to the profiles of the letters being recorded in the buffer in the computer. When the line of text was completed the signals were released and the characters were 'painted out' by the cathode ray tube – the letters being formed, so to speak, by slices of light. That is a very simplified account of a complicated sequence of events; but the point of it is that for the first time the profiles of the characters are being interfered with – or, as some would say, degraded. Scrutinised under a magnifying glass it is possible to see that the curved and diagonal strokes have become stepped, the size of the step being precisely that of the light spot. In enlargement the effect is displeasing, but the thing is entirely relative – the width of the writing spot and the type size being the deciding factors as to whether the effect is noticeable in print. With the machine working at, say, 1000 lines to the inch, when the light spot is only one-thousandth of an inch in diameter, the stepped effect is not visible to the reading eye even at quite large sizes. At 600 lines to the inch (when the output is very much faster) the 8 and 9 point text in a newspaper looks normal enough, though that is too coarse a resolution for headline sizes.

As soon as CRT became a feature of electronic typesetting systems 'resolution' became an important addition to the printer's vocabulary. It refers to the edge quality of the letters; and suitably qualified as 'high', 'medium' or 'low', it indicates the extent to which the contours of the letters look 'clean' to the eye, and therefore the extent to which the subtleties of the original design have been preserved.

Of the various sorts of writing spot in use CRT has continued to be the outputting method in most electronic typesetting systems, though some important machines use a laser beam. The introduction of CRT and laser into typesetting technology were considerable advances; but the replacing of the photographic font negative by the digitising of characters has been an even more radical step, and one that has produced problems as well as advantages. The motive for digitising is easily stated. By converting the type characters into little bits and recording the bits as electronic signals which can be stored on a disc as an adjunct to the computer, they can be called out in intelligible shape by the modern micro-computer at a speed which could not have been imagined a few years ago, and with an edge quality of considerable refinement – though that has to be paid for.

The method of digitising is the cause of one of the things that make type production, and in some cases type designing, much more complicated than formerly. Actually, there are several methods. In one method the frisket or enlarged solid image of each character is passed through a sensitive scanning device which reads and records the character on a grid, in which the size of the basic element is related to that of the writing spot that will paint out the character on the output material. What comes out of the scanning process is a 'sample'. It is only the beginning and there is much more to be done. When the full alphabet has been scanned the result is printed out. The characters must now be 'edited' by someone with an educated eye. He or she studies each sample letter carefully and marks out unwanted picture elements ('pixels') and marks in extra pixels where a curve or diagonal stroke needs improvement. The edited proof is handed to an operator who calls each character out of memory and on to a screen, and then proceeds to key the corrections. When all the corrected characters are back in font store they have to be tested at actual print size and, if necessary, revised again. The process is time-consuming and expensive in inverse proportion to the resolution. In a type digitised at 1200 lines per inch the em square of a 12 point master contains 40,000 pixels and the contour of the letter on the sample will be fairly close to that of the original design. The amount of manual editing and correction will be much less than for a type digitised at 600 lines per inch, where the 12 point em has 10,000 pixels and letters like a, s and w will show stepped edges which need a good deal of attention. In the case of a type intended for use in a small size, such as a newspaper classified advertisement type or a telephone directory face, digitised at 600 lines, the 6 point em has 2,500 pixels: that is, 50 by 50, which on the proof sheet makes a distinctly gingham effect and needs much work by the editor and corrector before the array of characters can safely be put into memory store as the master font ready for copying for the user. To reduce the labour time and the amount of data which has to be stored for each character, other methods have been devised. In one of them the letter is related to a pattern of lines equivalent to the tracks of the writing spot, and the beginning and end of each line where it meets the contour of the letter is plotted and recorded, the writing spot in the typesetting system 'filling in' the outline at the output stage. The analysis of the character shape takes more time than sample scanning, but the method reduces or eliminates editing and correction, and the memory requirement is much less than in the first method, though the processing is more elaborate. In another approach the profile is 'converted' to a sequence of vectors, and their junction points are recorded; the computer in the typesetter is programmed to connect the points and fill in the outline. In all such methods (and there are others) a good deal of time and effort by skilful people has to be put in to the editing and correcting of samples or the analysing of characters for special digitising to work with special programs, so it is not surprising that more sophisticated methods of scanning and automatic contour plotting are in active development.

The intention in editing and correcting a digital sample is, of course, to repair and restore the character; but the process itself can be thought of as manipulation – the adding or subtracting of bits to the edges of letters with, usually, a considerable amount of

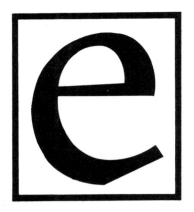

Digitising.

A letter in its natural form, as it would appear in metal type or on the film font or disc in an opto-mechanical photo-typesetter.

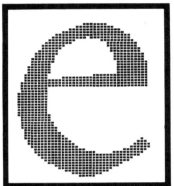

A simplified representation of the letter when it is automatically scanned and converted into digital pixels. Every pixel is stored as a code in the computer's memory.
(In reality, the pixels, and the lines in the next example, touch or overlap each other).

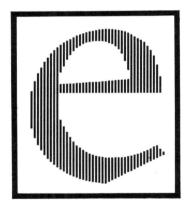

The amount of data to be stored is much less when the letter is 'run-length' scanned, as in this example. Only the start and stop of each scan line is recorded – an economical means of storing the data for large sizes of type, though processing the data is more complicated.

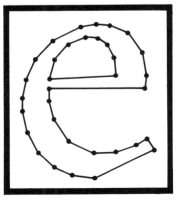

For even more economical storage the profile of the letter can be imagined as a series of vectors (line or arc), their connecting points being selected by an operator plotting them into store. A special routine in the computer's processor connects the points and fills in the letter shape at the output stage.

Those are simplified examples of basic methods of digitising. Computer technology advances so rapidly that the digitising of characters is now a highly sophisticated process which, at high resolution, leaves no trace of itself in the printed output.

freedom. Ingenious people have extended that thought to the creation of additional versions of a type, by recording its details in a computer memory and contriving a program by which the details can be manipulated at will, to produce further weights of a type, semi-bold, bold, extra-bold and so on. It is possible that by the time these words are in print that process will have been refined, linked to type sizes, and added to the software of the printer's electronic typesetter, so as to provide, automatically and from one digital font, the kind of properly graduated optical compensation which, as described earlier, was a valuable feature of type faces in mechanical typesetting.

The making of type faces is now a highly sophisticated technique in which elaborate computer programs and digital recording systems are central. Advances in the technology are described in journals devoted to electronics and the computer, and discussed in seminars and conferences. It is claimed that only now is type being produced in immaculate condition, unimpaired by the constraints of earlier methods. The typographer, and for that matter the general reader, may find the technology so fascinating as to lose sight of the fact that the technology is used in the production of bad designs as well as good ones, and that in the end it is what appears in print or on screen that counts.

Without dwelling on the technicalities, then, the point to grasp is that a type face in digital form is a fragmentation, the atomised form of the design as a series of discrete elements, according to the degree of fidelity allowed by the outputting machine for which it is intended. Whether we can actually see the effect of the process in print depends entirely on the resolution at which the face was digitised and the typesetting machine operates. To quote Charles Bigelow: 'Trained typographers claim that resolutions below 600 lines per inch seem crude or coarse; resolutions between 600 and 1200 lpi seem acceptable or adequate; resolutions above 1200 lpi seem as good as traditional analogue type' – that is, type in which the edges of the letters are natural and unchanged. Clearly, the quality of the subsequent plate-making, paper and presswork will be factors in the matter. Typesetting at a resolution of 1200 lpi may show no sign of its digitised genesis in printing of ordinary respectable standard, but may look not quite sharp when the presswork and paper are of the superior quality demanded for some sorts of publicity work; hence the very high resolution of 2000 lpi obtainable from some modern systems. Conversely, the jagged edges which may be discernible at 600 lpi or less on the output from the typesetter will not be visible if the presswork is low-grade and the paper surface fluffy, as is the case in newspapers and some government service work, where economy in cost is more important than aesthetics. That, though, is not an acceptable excuse for the poor appearance of recent editions of dictionaries and reference books once renowned for the quality of their printing. One cannot avoid the suspicion that the sogginess of the presswork is deliberately induced to disguise too crude a resolution in the original type matter.

A font of characters digitised at high resolution may require a large random-access memory (R A M) or expensive software for the micro-processor; and the speed at which the characters can be called out is very much less than is the case with a lower resolution. High resolution produces quality, low resolution is cost effective, and the printer contemplating the purchase of a system has to make his own evaluation of those two factors, according to the class of work he has to do. There is an obvious temptation to choose the cheaper and faster system. A printer of quality does not succumb to it.

To recall what was said at the beginning of this essay: up to the last quarter of the nineteenth century the creation of a type was a hand craft, and there was nothing in the method to restrict the style, shape or detail of the design so produced. When composing machines were introduced there were certain mechanical principles in the machines which imposed constraints on the proportions of characters, but the shapes, details and edge quality of them were not affected. It is not possible to make such simple statements about digital type designing and production for use in electronic typesetting systems. It is necessary to particularise.

When a face is digitised at high resolution, say 1200 lpi, there is usually nothing in the production method to inhibit the work or affect its quality, so long as there is an understanding eye to supervise it. However, if the same design is required for say 300 lpi or less it will certainly be affected. Its subtleties of stroke modelling and serif formation will have to be disciplined or eliminated altogether, to the extent that the distinctive character of the original may be lost. Times Roman has been a particular victim of that enforced erosion of its characteristics.

It has been suggested that that should be prevented from the beginning: that at the outset a new type should be planned to exist in a number of digital resolutions, the high-resolution version displaying refinements and subtleties which the designer will simplify or eliminate in the lower resolutions, though the general character will be maintained. As an aesthetic proposition it raises doubt. In practice it would probably mean that, to preserve the likeness through a range of resolutions, the details of the design would have to be 'averaged', the high-resolution version actually being denied some of the subtleties of contour normally allowable in modern digitising methods because to include them might separate that version from the lower grades. The limitations of low resolution would restrict freedom of expression where it is desirable and possible. The alternative view is preferable: that each resolution should have its own collection of faces, correctly designed to make the best of its limitations. This aesthetic argument would not be necessary if people would abandon the assumption that a type of high quality or popularity (not the same thing) should be available in its own name in any kind of outputting system, however degraded the result. I do not see that the matter is affected by a printer's requirement for a high-resolution face for final output and a low-resolution version of it to be used for high-speed proofing only. In that case the proofing version need not strive to be a look-alike; a 'rough' version is sufficient. Experienced editorial people are quite willing to work with a crude-looking proof, so long as the character count is identical with the type face actually to be printed.

6: Proportion

The point system of type measurement produced benefits of varying significance. One of them, the fact that types and spaces from different foundries could be mixed together in a line with impunity, diminished in importance as the use of mechanical composing machines increased and the printer became, in effect, his own type founder. What continued to be an important benefit was the fact that types of different sizes could be placed together on the basis of simple arithmetical adjustment: the initial letter at the beginning of a chapter, the price at the end of a two- or three-line description in a store advertisement, and so on. And there was another improvement. In the early years of this century the new-found pleasure in the benefits of regularity and dimensional stability induced the founders to re-cast their types on common alignments, so that all their romans and their clarendons, bold latins and antiques (the 'related bold' being yet to come) would line together accurately and so eliminate the former haphazard effects of uncalculated baselines. This offshoot of the point system was called 'point line', which meant, in the words of one founder, 'that the distance between the bottom edge of the face of the type and the bottom edge of the type body (in other words, the 'beard') measures a definite number of points, varying according to the size of the body'. The diagram accompanying that description showed that the benefit sought for was the easy justification of one size with another. It is clear, though, that the effect on the proportions of the letters must have been crude and ill-balanced – the length of the descenders in 8 point, for instance, being proportionately greater than in 10 point, the reverse of what is visually desirable. Bruce Rogers thought nothing of point line. Referring to the so-called Fry's Baskerville, which he ad-

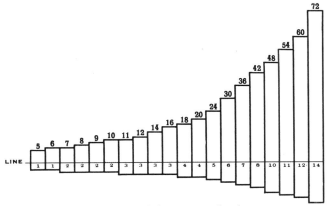

Point line. From a Stephenson Blake specimen book, 1915.

mired, in his *Report on the Typography of the Cambridge University Press* (1917), he said 'The present showing of it in the founder's specimen sheets suffers . . . from having recently been altered to standard line, a most pernicious practice when applied to any type and particularly the old style ones.' However, the significant thing is that the idea of standard alignment had been born. When the American Linotype company adopted the principle of standard alignment about 1913 each size was given its own baseline position to which all their subsequent type faces conformed. Unfortunately, the taste of the time being what it was, the standard alignments were fixed too low for the kind of descenders which came to be desired by book designers in the 1920s and 30s, when types of the past were being studied, appreciated and revived. Linotype therefore found it necessary to produce alternative 'long' descender characters (which really means descenders of better proportion than the regular sort) in such classic types as Garamond and Janson, and also in Dwiggins's Electra and Caledonia. George W. Jones, who was responsible for the English Linotype company's Granjon, Georgian and other distinguished revivals, would have nothing to do with the standard alignments, and insisted that the baseline in his types should be so placed as to ensure that the descenders were of satisfactory length.

This detail of typographic history, the location of the baseline, is relevant to the present. Some important type faces in current use owe a significant aspect of their appearance to rules of proportion established at a time when the scope of typographic knowledge was limited and the standard of design was low. The faces needed the attention of a discerning eye before they were transferred to filmsetting. Electronic typesetting systems measure 'film advance' – that is, type size plus inter-line spacing, if any – from baseline to baseline, which meant that the manufacturers of the systems had to decide at the outset just where to fix the baseline in the vertical aspect of the 'window' through which the type would be transmitted to the output material. The

The 'long' and the regular descender in Caledonia.

decision being made, the baseline became a permanent and unchangeable feature of the system; it is common to all type faces supplied by that manufacturer, and all functions, such as the placement of sized-down font numerals in the role of superior figures, are measured from it. With their considerable library of existing letter drawings to call upon Linotype chose to use their traditional standard alignments of the hot-metal era: 8, 12 and 18 point alignments where an existing type was available in display as well as text sizes. New designs were made to the standard 12 point alignment only, whatever range of sizes it was to be used in – a doubtful practice. Other manufacturers made choices to suit themselves – some of them to unfortunate effect on the proportions of their types, to judge from the evidence to be seen too often on the booksellers' shelves.

The length of the descenders is only one aspect of the proportions of a type design and, in regard to readability, not the most important. If the descenders are short the appearance of the letters g, j, p, q and y may be displeasing to the professional eye, but the reader's comprehension of the text will not suffer much. The case is otherwise with the ascender elements in b, d, h, k and l which, if they are shortened, cause the letters to lose some of their individuality and the words in which they occur to lose some of their familiar shape. Actually, though, ascenders are seldom shortened – certainly not when the baseline is fixed. When ascenders seem to be short it is usually because the x-height is larger than normal. An extreme example is the Antique Olive sans-serif type; an attractive face when used in a display line but not very legible or readable when used in advertising text matter – a consideration that evidently does not trouble some typographers.

The ratio of x-height to ascender height is an important factor in the style, and the quality, of a type. Francis Meynell's 'Nonesuch Plantin', which was Monotype Plantin 110 with the ascenders lengthened as well as the descenders, transformed the type to a remarkable degree, making it look not only more refined but as if it derived from another period: Fournier's, say, not

---

It was a delightful occasion, and began one of my most treasured friendships, which did not end until B.R.'s death in 1957. I found his personality a complete confirmation of his work as a typographer. His line of talk was as firmly gentle as his drawing of a border or typeface. He was a propagandist but he was kind; he admired a great tradition and showed how one could adapt it to modern use; he treated the young aspirant as a fellow-worker.

The lengthened ascenders and descenders in Monotype Plantin 110,
as used in the text of Sir Francis Meynell's autobiography *My Lives*.
The 11 point size of Monotype Baskerville was similarly treated.

Granjon's. For my own taste, if x to h is a proportion of about six to ten a face will look refined and be pleasant to read. If the x-height is much less than that the face may be stylish but will be unsuitable for a long text. A larger x-height conduces to dullness. Small x-height was a characteristic of types produced in the first quarter of this century; see, for instance, Goudy's Pabst Roman, the charming Nicolas Cochin, and the popular Astrée of the 1920s. A more notable example is Cheltenham Old Style, the first size of which, the 11 point, was made in November 1900. The design is always credited to the architect Bertram Goodhue, though Ingalls Kimball of the Cheltenham Press may have directed it. The insensitive modelling of the face was partly redeemed by the small x-height, which gave the type a degree of refinement. The recent large x-height version has eliminated even that small virtue. It is not the only type of the past to have been tastelessly re-proportioned by latter-day design studios.

The height of the capitals compared with the lowercase ascenders is another vertical relationship that has an effect on the appearance and quality of a type. The accepted opinion now is that in a type designed for book printing the capitals should be shorter than the ascenders. The amount of the difference in height has varied from one face to another. In Poliphilus, Bembo and Garamond the difference is clearly visible. In eighteenth-century faces such as Caslon, Fournier and Baskerville the capitals are nearly as tall as the ascenders. (At Francis Meynell's request Monotype made shortened capitals for Fournier 185 for use in the first Nonesuch Shakespeare.) Trump Medieval, a type of comparatively recent origin, has capitals that are unusually short – a characteristic favoured in Germany, no doubt, where the printed language uses capitals very frequently.

In sans-serif types 'short' capitals seldom occur. An interesting exception is Tempo, the Ludlow design, which was popular in British newspapers for many years. In the light, medium and bold versions (but not the heavy weight) the height of the capitals is

SIMONE HATS are extremely unusual in that they combine a noticeable Elegance of Style and a Superior Quality. Fifty Years of Experience goes a long way toward the making of such Hats.

SIMONE
MADISON STREET

The original Cheltenham Old Style, as shown in the November 1904 number of the ATF *American Chap-Book*.

The basic character in a type design is determined by the uniform design characteristics of all letters in the alphabet. However, this alone does not determine the standard of the type face and the quality of composition set with it. The appearance

The basic character in a type design is determined by the uniform design characteristics of all letters in the alphabet. However, this alone does not determine the standard of the type face and the quality of composition set with it. The appearance

Linotype Ionic was the progenitor of several faces, including Textype, shown here. The type size is the same, and there is hardly any change in the size of the capitals. The distinct difference in appearance is due to the lowercase x-height.

noticeably less than the height of the ascenders – though it could be argued that the capitals are normal and it is the ascenders that are unusually tall.

Shortening the capitals helps to prevent them from becoming obtrusive and disturbing the texture of the page. That was not always thought necessary. Some of the heavy versions of the modern face popular in Europe in the second half of the nineteenth century had capitals so emphatic that they must have been intentional. Those types were extreme, in every sense; but the same characteristic was present in some of the normal Scotch Roman faces, and when in time there was a change in taste and the disparity in the capitals and lowercase was thought to be undesirable those faces had to be modified – which is one of the reasons why some suppliers had a second version of Scotch Roman. By contrast with the imbalance of weight still to be seen in some current type faces the stems of the capitals in Eric Gill's Bunyan type (known as Pilgrim in the Linotype list) have exactly the same weight as those of the lowercase letters. Occasionally, in under-nourished printing on smooth paper, the capitals look a little weak. To produce the appearance of balance the strokes of capitals have to be slightly heavier than those of the lowercase, because of the greater area of the interior spaces. Again, it is a matter of proportion, and one that is decided by the eye and not by a calculator or computer.

The proportions of letters one to another within a font is one thing; the modulating of those proportions through a range of sizes is another. It is the process of 'optical compensation', of being aware that the ratio of lowercase size to type size that is satisfactory at one place in the range will not be so at others, and making the necessary adjustments accordingly.

It was recognised long ago that though the human eye finds it easy to read type of 12 point size, 8 point needs more effort and 6 point is often difficult. Type founders learnt to help the reader by adjusting the proportions of letters according to size. The 'pilot size' of a text type would usually be the 12 point or 10 point. For the 8 point size the baseline would be a little lower on the body, so the capitals could be slightly taller at the expense of the lowercase descenders. The lowercase x-height would be increased in relation to the capitals, and the characters would all be made a little wider and the space between them increased. For the 7 and 6 point the process would be carried still further. The motive was a functional one: to make the characters of the small sizes as legible as possible. The process was reversed for the display sizes, 18 point and larger, where legibility was not a problem and an aesthetic motive could apply. By refining the serifs, reducing the stroke weight, character widths and spacing, and increasing the length of the descenders, the elegance of the design would be enhanced.

This sensitive modulation of the proportions of characters according to type size was adopted by the makers of mechanical composing machines, as is shown by a letter of 28 April 1947 from C. H. Griffith, who was responsible for type face development at Mergenthaler Linotype, to W. A. Dwiggins, on the subject of the latter's Falcon type. 'The proportional scale of Falcon, 6 to 10 point, has puzzled me for the past year or so, and particularly the 6 and 7 point sizes. They simply did not seem to range smoothly. Repeated checking . . . disclosed no optical errors in

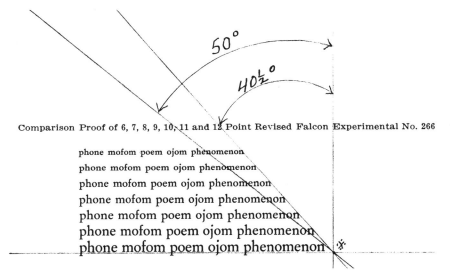

Comparison Proof of 6, 7, 8, 9, 10, 11 and 12 Point Revised Falcon Experimental No. 266

The graduations of the proportions in the Falcon type.

basic dimensions of height, width, stem, hairline, etc. Still, the 6 point appeared small and cramped and a feeling of looseness was indicated in several of the other sizes under certain conditions.' After describing the exhaustive re-checking of letter drawings and proofs of trial characters, to no avail, Griffith says he ordered the factory to make new matrices. 'The root of the trouble was a slight error by the factory in shaving the side bearing to drawing figures at a time when several new inspectors were being broken in.' He then graphically demonstrates the extent to which the proportions of the 12 point pilot size had been adjusted through the smaller sizes. 'While in a "mathematical" mood and with the feeling that the Falcon series presents an almost perfect proportional curve to the eye I thought I would find out just how our "eye" curve compares with the geometric curve which these "blowers up" and "blowers down" will probably have to use in their photo-composition machines that employ one master size of pattern. I am enclosing a proof of the series all cast on 12 point body as required by the rules of geometry. You will observe the curve of geometrical proportion produces an angle of 50 degrees, while the curve of our optical proportion has an angle of $40\frac{1}{2}$

degrees from the vertical. This means that 6 point in color and width is approximately 71 per cent of 12 point, and not 50 per cent. *And* the eye is the sole arbiter of proportion after all . . .'

When photo-composition became a reality in the 1950s the manufacturers of typesetting machines had to make an important decision: whether or not to carry forward into the new system the principle of optical compensation, when the plain and tempting fact was that the photographic part of the system was capable of producing a considerable range of type sizes from just one font. To abandon the principle altogether was to risk forfeiting a substantial part of a reputation for typographic quality. The manufacturers faced the problem by compromise. American Linotype produced film replicas of both the 8 and 12 point versions of text types, and of the 18 point where display sizes existed. To judge the effect of using 8 and 12 point as masters to produce other sizes the Falcon type, previously mentioned, can be used as an illustration. Ten point from the 8 point would have been about 10 per cent wider than the metal version; 10 point from the 12 point would have been about 7 per cent narrower than the metal. In fact, by comparison with the optical proportions described by Griffith, all sizes except the 8 and 12 point would have varied from the ideal – the sizes which were reductions from the artwork being weaker than the metal versions, and the sizes which were enlargements from it being clumsier. This compromise between the full scope of former manufacturing finesse and the geometrical progression inevitable in electronic typesetting can only be regarded as a loss of some of the refinement of types as they used to be. It was probably the only course possible at the time.

Ultimately, though, it was for the printer to decide whether he would buy more than one font of a type face to satisfy the typographic sensitivity of his customers. Unfortunately, it became clear that some printers preferred to sacrifice typographic quality for economy in capital expenditure. This encouraged some manufacturers, especially those who had entered the field without a 'bank deposit' of existing letter drawings, to think that if printers were willing to use a single font for all sizes of type then there was no need to bother with optical compensation. Some of them apparently thought that increasing the x-height of the faces would be an acceptable alternative. It is not. Although it assists the legibility of small sizes it vulgarises the larger ones.

To make a choice from a broad range of working drawings of just one size of artwork for a master font that will be used to compose a band of type sizes is an anxious business. Too much concern for the look of the display sizes may mean that the artwork size chosen, say the 12 point, produces a cramped result at 6 and 8 point. Nervousness about the small sizes may result in a

abcdefghijklmnopqrstu
vwxyzij

zichzelf te behoeden
wijt van eentonighe

Geen enkele drukker mag, om zichzelf te b
van eentonigheid in zijn zetwerk, tegen bet
in het veronderstelde belang van versiering,
logica en duidelijkheid door enige typografis

Geen enkele drukker mag, om zichz
verwijt van eentonigheid in zijn zetw
gedogen dat, in het veronderstelde b
weld gedaan wordt aan logica en duide

Geen enkele drukker mag, om zichzelf te behoeden voor h
zetwerk, tegen beter weten in gedogen dat, in het veronders
gedaan wordt aan logica en duidelijkheid door enige typogi
in een driehoek wringen, hem in een hokje persen, hem te
zandloper of een ruit heeft, is een zonde die meer rechtvaar

Geen enkele drukker mag, om zichzelf te behoeden voo
zetwerk, tegen beter weten in gedogen dat, in het verond
gedaan wordt aan logica en duidelijkheid door enige typ
in een driehoek wringen, hem in een hokje persen, hem te
loper of een ruit heeft, is een zonde die meer rechtvaardig

Geen enkele drukker mag, om zichzelf te behoeden voor het vei
tegen beter weten in gedogen dat, in het veronderstelde belang va
logica en duidelijkheid door enige typografische buitensporigheï
hem in een hokje persen, hem te martelen tot hij de vorm van een
die meer rechtvaardiging behoeft dan het bestaan van hetzij italiaan:
en zestiende eeuwen of de zucht iets nieuws te doen in de twintigs

Geen enkele drukker mag, om zichzelf te behoeden voor het verwijt van eenton
dat, in het veronderstelde belang van versiering, geweld gedaan wordt aan logi
sporigheid. Zijn tekst in een driehoek wringen, hem in een hokje persen, her
een ruit heeft, is een zonde die meer rechtvaardiging behoeft dan het bestaan v
tiende en zestiende eeuwen of de zucht iets nieuws te doen in de twintigste. Dit
en wij hebben er zo veel van gezien gedurende de voorbije 'wederopleving va

Monotype Bembo, 24, 12, 8 and 6 point: left, the metal version, right, a film version

choice that makes the larger sizes appear clumsy. The Bembo
face, an admirable example of optical compensation by the
Monotype drawing office, demonstrates the point. In the specimens of the metal version shown here the modifications of x-
height and lowercase letter widths up and down the size range
can be discerned by the sensitive eye. In the other version the 8
point is almost identical, but three of the sizes were obtained by
direct projection from the 8 point, instead of the separate masters
available. The 6 point is obviously less effective than the metal 6
point; and the 24 point, where the characters are precisely three
times the size of the 8 point, is distinctly less elegant than the
original. (The effect on the italic can be imagined.) It would be a
comfort to be able to say that that kind of thing never actually
happens. But a new work by a distinguished novelist, printed in
England as recently as 1983, has chapter headings in 24 point
Sabon italic which sprawl deplorably, for the same reason.
(Tschichold would have hated such ill-treatment of his design.) It
is not an isolated case.

Although there are few faces that have the modest x-height and
long ascenders and descenders of Bembo, automatic sizing inevitably impairs all faces to some degree. Modern designers, creating
faces for electronic typesetting, avoid the worst effects of it by
organising the proportions of their characters as a compromise
between the ideal and the necessary. But it is a compromise. Not
until the suppliers of high-resolution fonts adopt the principle of
separate masters, each proportioned for a narrow band of sizes,
will their claim that their faces are superior to the metal versions
be justified in all respects.

7: The forms of letters

It is a matter of constant interest that new text types continue to be created and added to the substantial list of those in current use – not to mention the many that have been relegated to history – yet in all of them the characters conform to certain rules of shape and structure which, it might be thought, would severely limit the possibility of new invention and individuality.

The capital letters are the obvious ones to begin with, though Herbert Bayer would not have done so in 1925 at the Bauhaus. He wrote: 'Why should we write and print with two alphabets? We do not speak with a capital A and a small a.' He was not the only one to confuse the nature of speech with the representation of it.

The quality of a capital A can be affected in two ways: by the spread of the limbs (if they sprawl the letter will look vulgar); and by the height of the bar (too low, and the letter will look dull; too high, and it may not print well in small sizes). So there is a desirable, even obligatory, arrangement of the three strokes if the letter is to be acceptable. Most of the other capitals have structural rules that are just as fundamental to their aesthetic effect.

The letter B looks 'natural' when the upper bowl is a little smaller than the lower one. Most designers agree about that; but Rudolf Koch chose to make the two parts of the letter almost equal in his Kabel, Koch-Antiqua and Marathon types and got dangerously near to unattractive distortion of the letter.

In capital E it is the length of the three arms in relation to the stem and to each other that gives the letter its character. The lowest arm is usually longer than the upper one. It is noticeably so in Baskerville; more so in Walbaum. The middle arm is generally shorter than the others, but not always: see Emil Weiss's Roman and Sem Hartz's Juliana. The position of the middle arm is usually optically central in the height of the letter; but Van Krimpen placed it well above the centre in his Lutetia roman.

In the letter K the leg is nearly always longer than the arm; and straight, too – though it is curved in the Bell type.

The letter M is one of the key characters in the recognition of a type. In old style faces up to the latter part of the seventeenth century its legs were slightly splayed; see, for example, Bembo and Garamond. Some of the Dutch punch-cutters then made the letter stand to attention. Caslon, who followed Dutch models, gave his M vertical legs; so did Baskerville and Firmin Didot. That style of M contributed to the formality of the 'modern' faces, though some designers of such types in this century, Tiemann and Reiner, for instance, have preferred the splayed style. The central part of the letter usually meets the baseline; but it stays well above it in some display faces: Albertus, for example, and, in different categories, the Memphis and Gill Sans faces.

In roman faces the tail of Q has often been used by designers to add individuality to a type. Most of Goudy's are good; but the Q in his Newstyle is eccentric. In the original Caslon italic the Q is an exuberant single-stroke flourish, a calligraphic form quite different from the roman. (It is also present in the italic of Van Dijck.) Goudy often used a modified version of it.

From the Caslon specimen of 1734.

The capital R is another key letter in the identifying of a type. It is remarkable that so much individuality can be contrived from just three elements: a vertical stem, a bowl, and a leg stroke. A long leg makes the letter look elegant, which is good when the letter is at the end of a word set in capitals but not when it is followed by another letter – which is why the short-legged version in Bembo is usually the one chosen, regretfully, in place of the original version. The leg is usually slightly concave in faces based on the Jenson letter, like Centaur, straight in old style faces, but arched with a looped terminal in moderns. In Ruzicka's Fairfield type the R has a distinctive 'Queen Anne' leg.

Capital S is too often a dull letter, especially in French 'classique' types after Firmin Didot. To my eye the letter looks most vital when the top and bottom halves are *apparently* equal and there is a slight forward movement, as in Berthold Wolpe's Pegasus type.

In most text types the W is visibly two Vs, either crossing each other in the centre, as in Garamond, or overlapping, as in Caslon. The simplified form of the W in Baskerville, in which the two middle strokes join without a serif, is an aid to clarity, especially in the lowercase and in small sizes.

Lowercase letters too have their rules of structure.

The letter a is interesting for existing in two forms. The familiar one, used in all normal seriffed faces, has a closed bowl in the lower half and an open loop above. The other sort has a single closed bowl joined to the stem. Both kinds are of ancient origin and were present in different varieties of black-letter in the early days of printing. In the first decade of this century, when many hybrid types, compounds of black-letter and roman, were produced by the German type founders, most of them had the two-storeyed a; but a third of the seventy or so faces listed as 'Neudeutsche Schriften' in the 1926 volume of the *Handbuch der Schriftarten* have the single-storey sort, which had been the standard form in the numerous fraktur types used in German printing in the previous four centuries. The round a was therefore well known to the German public, and presumably Paul Renner had no difficulty in getting it accepted in the 'geometric' Futura sans-serif he created in 1927. I suspect Edward Johnston and Eric Gill would have considered it as alien in a printing type, though Johnston used the round a in some of his calligraphic work. No one would welcome the round a in a seriffed type; but ironically

*Aspects
of type design*

Ad Lib

Lowercase letters derive from calligraphic sources. When they are carefully written it is natural, not a mere convention, for the stem to carry a serif on the *left*. The d in this hand-drawn feature title in a London newspaper breaks the rule, to no good effect.

the two-storeyed form becomes the least happy letter on those occasions when a roman face in a CRT typesetting system is slanted to simulate italic.

The significant part of the letter b is the lower end of the stem. In some old style types it terminates where the curve of the bowl flows into it. In others it ends in a short tapered element. Compare Bembo and Caslon. The 'rational' type cut by Phillipe Grandjean in 1693–1702 for the royal printing office in Paris introduced a new feature: a serif at the foot of the stem, as though the letter was simply a reversal of the letter d. The style was adopted by many of the later punch-cutters who produced 'modern' faces. It is in Bulmer, but not in Scotch Roman; in Bodoni, but not in Walbaum.

The design of the lowercase e in text faces produces strong feelings (or should do so). The slanting bar was a feature of the e in Nicolas Jenson's and other roman types before 1500. Then it was discarded in favour of the horizontal bar. It reappeared in the 'Basle' roman of 1854 used by Whittingham, and then in William Morris's Golden type and other private press types derived from the Jenson roman, including Bruce Rogers's Montaigne face of 1901. It was when Rogers's Centaur type of 1915 was adopted by Monotype in 1929 that the general typographer became aware of the letter. In that type, the most elegant version of the Jenson face, the slanting bar is perfectly acceptable. But to my eye the form sometimes has an unwanted restlessness. Goudy was over-fond of it; and some recent designers seem to have seen it as an easy option, a facile way of adding instant 'character' to a type face.

What was said about the lowercase a applies almost equally to the letter g: two forms, a two-storey one and a single-storey form with a tail; both of ancient origin, the single-storey g being the form present in the early German textura types used by Gutenberg, the other form occurring in the less formal type used by Schoeffer at the same period. It was the two-storey form that became the standard in roman text faces. By contrast, and showing their relationship with fraktur types, almost all the 'Neudeutsche Schriften' in the *Handbuch der Schriftarten* have the single-storey form of g. The same is true of the 'Grotesk' (sans-serif) types which were current in Germany in the first twenty years of this century. The case was quite otherwise in American and British sans-serifs, where the single-storey g was unknown – though familiar enough in traditional italic types. The single-storey form is therefore German in origin, though now universally accepted in sans-serif faces, including some not by German designers. It is (rightly) seldom seen in seriffed faces, other than egyptians; the classified advertisement type called Maximus, used at $4\frac{3}{4}$ point, is an exception.

The letter h in some italic faces is a matter for concern. Two kinds are current. The one whose lower half resembles the letter n – that is, its second leg is straight, with a short upward terminal to the right – first appeared in the italic of Grandjean's *romain du roi* of 1702. It was imitated by Fournier and then by Firmin Didot, and it became the standard form of the letter in 'modern' faces. Caslon did not adopt it, but Baskerville did. The other kind of italic h is the one that was present in all the italics from the first Aldine type up to Kis's 'Janson' and Caslon's italic. It has the right leg bent into the interior of the letter, which makes the h look very like the letter b in small sizes. Worried about this, some designers have kept the base of the letter fairly open, with the result that the right leg looks feeble. The h in the Sabon italic is an example; it is the only disappointing letter in this admirable type.

Small things matter in type designing: the dot of i and j, for instance. In a sans-serif type it is naturally centred over the width of the stem. But in a seriffed face it is optically more satisfactory when it is placed a little to the right of centre. In early faces the dot was quite small. Where that characteristic has been continued into the revived version of an early type, as in Centaur and Bembo, or respectfully imitated, as in Lutetia, the dot becomes vulnerable to the short light-flash in photo-composition and in offset-litho platemaking, and sometimes disappears in print.

If it is to remain fully identifiable the lowercase l cannot afford to give away any of itself above the level of the top of x. In faces of large x-height that part is, in effect, diminished, and the letter loses more of its identity than any other ascender character.

In old style types the bowl of roman p has a tendency to 'pull' the letter out of true, so the stem was often given a degree of angle to counteract the effect – a refinement that is discouraged when a type is to be digitised, for fear of a saw edge to the stem. An increase in the length of the right-hand foot serif helps to keep the letter in balance.

The letter t in old style romans has a bracket to the left side of its cross bar. In 'modern' romans the bracket is usually, but not always, omitted. In italic faces the distinction is not so clear-cut. In the Blado italic for Poliphilus and in the Bembo italic the t has the bracket; in the italic for Centaur there is no bracket.

Lowercase y frustrates the designer, who wishes the ball at the foot of the letter could be allowed to kern below the preceding letter – until he or she remembers that the preceding letter is frequently g.

Those are some of the natural features of type faces old and new. 'Natural' is the right word, because they are more than mere conventions. They may be ignored or deliberately flouted by the designers of publicity types, as a painter may discard the rules of perspective – reasonably enough, because a publicity type is required to be different from the traditional, and eccentricity of

One of the unusual variations from the normal which Pierre Didot introduced in his effort to make his types look different from those made famous by his brother Firmin.

form and detail may be the chief element of its novelty. But designers of text types have to obey the rules; not only because the aesthetic quality of each letter depends on that discipline, but because, to quote Updike, 'a test of the excellence of any type is this − that whatever the combination of letters, no individual character stands out from the rest − a severe requirement to which all permanently successful types conform'. How, then, do designers contrive to create new types that preserve the natural features of letters and yet are visibly different from others of their kind?

They may take advantage of the simple variations of structure already mentioned − the splayed or vertical legs of M, the treatment of the foot of b, and so on − but those modest choices are not themselves sufficient to produce the degree of originality that is the designer's objective. Distinctive identity comes from the characteristics that are additional to the structural ones; the flesh on the skeleton, so to speak. The most important is the relative thickness of the strokes that form the letters. If the 'thick' stroke (the second stroke of A, say) is actually not very thick, and the 'thin' stroke is fairly robust, and that is the case with all the letters in the face, then the texture of the type will be quite even, and perhaps monotonous, in the literal sense of the word. But if the stroke weights are organised the other way, the main strokes strong, the secondary ones fine-drawn, the contrast between them will be evident and the effect of the type on the page will be incisive and possibly dazzling − though not necessarily more agreeable to the eye. The amount of contrast produces the particular texture of a type, and it is the first aspect of a type face that the student takes note of in the process of identifying it. If the contrast is not particularly marked the type is not Bodoni and probably not one of the many other modern faces. If, though, there is enough contrast to make a moderately clear-cut effect the type is unlikely to be Pilgrim (Eric Gill's Bunyan), which is a very even-textured type; and it may not be Baskerville, which in some printing makes a fairly bland effect. Stroke weight and contrast, then, help to establish the general class of a type face.

The next feature to note is the stress or bias in the round letters, o, c and e, and those with round parts, b, d, p and q. If the maximum weight is at three or nine o'clock the stress is said to be vertical. It is a characteristic of the transitional types and the moderns. If the weight is at two or eight o'clock the stress is oblique, and that is characteristic of old style faces.

The other feature to which the designer of a text type gives a good deal of thought is the serif. The length of it is not really at his choice, because it is determined by the spacing, the 'fitting', of the characters − a subject to be dealt with a little further on. The shape of the serif is a matter of choice, and the range of possibility is considerable. It can be thick or thin. Its end can be sharply cut

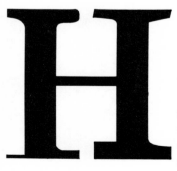

A medley of serif shapes.

or rounded off. It can be bracketed to the stroke, or unbracketed. It can even be wedge-shaped.

Stroke weight and contrast, stress and serif shape are three of the means by which the designer, combining and permuting them, achieves the particular individuality of a new type face.

8: Secondary types: italic, bold face

A. F. Johnson described italic as 'a sub-division of roman', because it derived from a similar source, one of the styles of writing practised by professional scribes in Rome at the end of the fifteenth century; this particular style being gracefully narrow in form and therefore well-suited to the printer's desire to contain a long classical text within a smallish book. Some of the early italic types were upright, though informal in character. So 'italic' refers to place of origin and, more particularly, style; it does not really mean 'inclined', though that is usually implied when we use the term nowadays. For the first quarter of the sixteenth century only the lowercase was italic; the capitals were roman. And it was not until the middle of that century that italic began to be used as an auxiliary to roman, for words in a foreign language, for emphasis, for the titles of other works, and so on. 'Secondary' was Stanley Morison's convenient term for that aspect of the function of italic. An italic font, then, can perform two roles: as a text type – in which case the secondary type, for the title of a quoted journal, say, is the roman; and as an auxiliary in a roman text.

In Germany, well into this century, italic was not regarded as essential. It was allowed that differentiation could be indicated by using roman but letter-spacing the particular words, a custom familiar to German readers from their experience of fraktur types, in which an inclined form was not a possibility. Ellic Howe records that the London *Family Herald* of 1822 did the same thing, but for a different reason: its text was composed on a machine that had no room for a second type. George Bernard Shaw, who had ideas about typography, specified letter-spaced roman lowercase for the emphasis in speeches in the early printed edition of his plays.

The distinguishing features of the traditional italic characters are, first, a general effect that they run together (which is why cursive is a more appropriate name for the style), and second, the slope of the letters, which may be as various as the 25 degrees of Caslon's italic and the near-upright 4 degrees of Eric Gill's Joanna italic. Stanley Morison saw those two factors as having distinctly different values. His article 'Towards an Ideal Italic', in the fifth volume of *The Fleuron* (1926), is one of the most remarkable of his writings. The first half is a valuable account of the history of the italic form, in which he records and illustrates the change from the calligraphic appearance of the early types, with their wealth of tied letters, to the disciplined italics of the eighteenth century. He mentions the italic of Grandjean's *romain du roi*, which A. F. Johnson said was the first example of a true secondary italic, designed for, and at the same time as, a specific roman. Morison speaks of an italic cut for F. A. Didot as being 'the best example there has been of a regular formal italic' but remarks that 'it is to be regretted that all trace of calligraphic originals has not been removed'. He then moves to the chief purpose of the article: to advance the proposition that the informality of italic as we know it is incompatible with the calm regularity of roman; that its single useful characteristic is its slope, which is all that is needed to provide differentiation; and that therefore the truest type to serve in the secondary role is a sloped version of the roman. He argued the case with his customary vigour. 'Certainly a type of conspicuously different colour and design from that of the roman cannot be tolerated, for it is clear that maximum repose will attach to a page where the roman and italic most nearly approximate.' He illustrated his proposal with a selection of characters from the Caslon face, in their roman form and also specially drawn to an angle of 15 degrees. What he did not do was to comment on any of the sloped roman types already in existence. For example, he could have referred to the catalogue of 'self-spacing' types issued by the Benton, Waldo

GLOBE JOB ROOMS---SAINT PAUL.

In January, 1886, I put in a font of Self Spacing and I am glad to state to you that from the total amount of composition of four compositors for sixty days, I estimate that the saving by increased composition was equal to the whole cost of the type.

The Benton-Waldo sloped roman.

type foundry of Milwaukee about 1886. All the 'italic' faces in it are actually sloped romans*; one of them was shown in the first volume of T. L. De Vinne's *Practice of Typography*, a work which Morison admired. And closer at hand, frequently to be seen in the printing of the 1920s, was the De Vinne type (the one

* In an article in *The Inland Printer* of October 1922 H. L. Bullen called them an 'innovation'; but there were others in existence, usually display types. The Milwaukee foundry probably made them by necessity, the urgent need to get their self-spacing types on to the market, and that may have been the reason why Benton invented his 'Delineator' machine, which enabled him to use one set of roman drawings to produce, very rapidly, variations of the design, including slanted versions, for the making of the patterns for electrotype matrices.

created by the Central Type Foundry, not the American Linotype text face). In my early days in a London composing room it ranked in popularity with Cheltenham Bold. It could not have escaped Morison's attention. Its italic was a sloped roman, with no concession to calligraphic influence. If Morison had paused and glanced at it, and at the Milwaukee faces, he might have hesitated to press his sloped roman theory in so uncompromising

Spanish=American War Parfumerie Hygiénique

Gustav Schroeder's De Vinne 'italic', 18 point.

a way. It is a little confusing to find, in *A Review of Recent Typography* (a revised edition of an earlier work) published the year *after* the 'Ideal Italic' article, Morison describing the Tiemann Kursiv face as a 'handsome letter, *flowing as an italic should be* . . .' (my italic). Presumably the passage had not been revised as thoroughly as the rest of the book. In the last volume of *The Fleuron*, issued in 1930, he wrote approvingly of a new suite of types by Lucian Bernhard who, said Morison, 'is the first type designer to put into practice the principles laid down in successive articles in *The Fleuron* as to the relation of roman, sloped roman and script − the trinity in which, it was forecast, contemporary type faces must henceforth appear'. Bernhard's types were hardly the best sort of support for the dogma Morison was asserting, being 'fancy' types only suitable for advertising work.

Morison had tried to put the sloped roman idea into effect in the italic of the Perpetua type, a new arrival which provided an

abcdefghijklmnopqrstuvwxyz

30 point Perpetua italic.

important item in the same volume of *The Fleuron*. The type was described by Beatrice Warde in an article on the typographic work of Eric Gill. With more loyalty than accuracy she wrote: 'Perpetua italic . . . interestingly carries out the prediction first made in the fifth number of *The Fleuron* that, if the italic is to develop into a contemporary form, consistency demands that it should no longer retain the calligraphic peculiarities derived from a school of writing quite different from that of the roman; that it must, in fact, become frankly the italic *of* the given roman, with only slope, and the modifications necessary to slope, to distinguish it from the upright version'. But the specimen that accompanied the article shows that Perpetua italic was not the uncompromising sloped roman of Morison's 'ideal'. It contained three significant characters, a, e and g, which were not simply inclined versions of the roman but calligraphic and 'informal' in style. When they were joined a little later by a flowing f their effect on the appearance of the italic was much stronger than their number. They contributed to the face just enough of the stylistic contrast which must be present in addition to the slope if a secondary type is to be attractive as well as effective. Morison himself came to see this when he instigated the Times Roman faces in the following year and included an italic which was in no sense a sloped roman, and, as he said later, 'owed more to Didot than dogma'.

Perpetua italic is a hybrid. Most of the lowercase letters are sloped versions of the roman, those letters with vertical strokes, like m, being equipped with seriffed feet planted firmly on the baseline. The alphabet, though, is vitalised by the four characters, together with the k added later, that relieve what would otherwise be a dull set of letters. It is a modified sloped roman, and should be so classified. Gill's Joanna italic and the italic devised by Linotype to work with the Pilgrim roman (Gill's Bunyan) are other examples. So too are the italics of Melior and Trump Medieval. The modified sloped roman is better than the

abcdefghijklmnopqrstuvwxyz

20 point Trump italic.

undiluted sort; but most people would probably prefer an authentic italic.

The mistakes of great men are as interesting, and often as instructive and valuable, as their achievements. Morison's evangelising for sloped roman has been recalled here for two reasons. It temporarily influenced Van Krimpen and Dwiggins, whose work is to be discussed in later pages, and it provides the ground for a judgement of the sloped romans that are being produced today – not by type designers, who rightly show little interest in the idea, but by typesetters, who bring sloped romans into existence at the touch of the 'slant-on' button. The face that emerges is not a new design, and it has no physical existence; it is simply an acceptably distorted image of the roman.

When the first CRT typesetting machines came into use in the early 1970s they had the high rate of output desired for newspaper work, but limited font capacity. So some production people took advantage of the facility in the CRT system by which the angle of the traverse of the light spot can be changed, usually 12 degrees either side of the vertical (the slant to the left gives a new look to Hebrew and Arabic composition). Having discovered that the effect of sloping a roman was accepted, some of them have continued the practice, even when the typesetting system has been replaced by one with larger font capacity. Acceptance, to the typographic eye, depends on the kind of roman type, and where it appears. To express a personal view: sloped versions of book types invariably make a poor effect; but types which tend towards the egyptian form can be tolerable – though hardly admirable. Thus a sloped Excelsior makes an acceptable stand-in for the actual italic of the type, as some German newspapers have discovered. (The custom in European newspapers of using italic for some news items is better than the British habit of using bold type for text matter – there being very few good-looking bold companions to news text faces.) The capitals of a machine-slanted face may look a little wide, and the roman lowercase a always looks, literally, taken aback; but these defects are less important in a newspaper than elsewhere, because though we expect the text of a newspaper to be readable we don't demand that it be elegant. And the same is true of the utilitarian kind of reference work, such as a trade directory – but not a dictionary, which ought to be typographically well dressed, though some publishers evidently think sloped roman is good enough for it.

There is, then, a class of printing where, it seems to me, the sloped roman is tolerable, if the typesetting system has limited

Register of Electors

Times Roman machine sloped.

font capacity and the omission of the 'real' italic allows room for another useful face. But for printing in which the type matter is intended to have visual as well as verbal interest – most publicity, and all book work – only the traditional styles of italic are acceptable. Which style – the narrow, deliberately graceful 'chancery' style of the first half of the sixteenth century, or the broader, less expressive form of Fournier's italics, or something in between – depends chiefly on the style of the roman, but also on the designer's awareness of the nature of italic and his ability to harmonise the italic with his roman. Even quite eminent designers have sometimes produced an uneasy alliance instead of a perfect marriage.

The other kind of secondary type, the related bold face, is a twentieth-century creation. Although the use of bold type for emphasis in text began when display advertising became a feature of the family magazines of the mid-nineteenth century, the bold types themselves were clarendons, ionics and antiques quite unrelated to the old styles and moderns used for the text. As late as 1938 the *Monotype Recorder*, a distinguished British journal of typography, could say, 'The "related bold" is a comparatively new phenomenon in the history of type cutting.' (One reason for that was Monotype's own Series 53, a bold roman in the old face mode which had for many years served as an excellent companion to such plain text types as Caslon, Imprint, Old Style 2, and even Modern 7.)

In its secondary role the bold face, like italic, is used for emphasis, in text books and official documents ('Failure to comply with this regulation . . .' looks more menacing in bold type than in italic). And in that role the effect is usually best if the bold type is visibly derived from the design of the roman. But bold type can perform another function more effectively than italic: as the introduction to an entry in a reference book – the key word in a dictionary, the subscriber's name in a telephone directory, or the first word or two in a classified advertisement. The bold type is then serving as a signal. To ensure that it is sufficiently strong and clear a bold sans-serif is often preferred, even when the text is in a seriffed face.

The practice of producing more than one weight of bold face in a seriffed type family was not common before the 1930s; the Cheltenham and Bodoni families were exceptions. In the thirties the German type foundries, actively stimulating the advertising typographer's appetite for novelty and variety, exploited the structural nature of the sans-serif and the egyptian to produce a range of bold, and indeed, light versions of the basic face. Thus the Bauer foundry's Futura face was offered in five weights (the American Linotype version, Spartan, actually ran to seven weights). The normal seriffed type, though, was usually supplied with just one bold companion – except for the occasional 'semibold', which in some cases it had been necessary to produce because the bold face itself had been overdone. That has changed in recent years. For commercial reasons the type design studios which have entered the typographic field have taken advantage of such electronic aids as the Ikarus system to multiply the weights of faces that were once thought of as essentially text types. Thus there is a version of Garamond which exists in four weights. Whether or not four weights of a roman type are really necessary is a less important question than another: which version should the student examine in his or her efforts to recognise the true nature of the design? In the case of a classic type that has undergone the slimming or fattening treatment – the 'normal' version itself probably revised to enable a suitable scale of emphasis to be achieved – there is only one reliable course: to search the libraries for a specimen of the type in its original form, or as it was first revived by a good manufacturer. The important thing is to study a metal version. There are respectable qualities in many types on film or in digital form; but fidelity to a classic origin is seldom one of them.

9: Numerals

The letters of the 'roman' alphabets used in printing, as distinct from the black-letter forms, are Mediterranean in origin; the lowercase derived from written script, the capitals from carved inscriptions on monuments. The numerals we use come from a different source: from the Arabs who, in their conquest in northern India in the eighth century A.D. observed that astronomical tables there were written in a special set of symbols, realised that they were much more convenient than combinations of letters, and adopted them forthwith, without much change in their shape and none in their arrangement. This is why, in Arabic writing and printing, dates and quantities in figures are read from left to right (the Indian practice) while the words are read from right to left. The difference in origin between roman letters and 'Arabic' numerals does not mean that the numerals are in any sense alien to us (though they were once so regarded); after all, if they had not been acquired they would certainly have had to be invented. They were taken up by European commerce and assimilated into professional writing at an early stage; they were known in Spain by the end of the tenth century – long before the advent of printing. 'Roman' numerals continued in use, though, perhaps because the Arabic figures were associated with trade and the sciences and were considered insufficiently dignified for literary work, especially when it was written in the Latin language. In fact, roman numerals are still favoured by some people, for no sound reason. Most television viewers in Britain must surely find 'Copyright MCMLXXXVI' at the end of a BBC programme quite incomprehensible.

Where numerals differ from letters is in their function. Although a few letters can perform a solo role in text matter (a and I in English, e in Italian), when they represent units of language, most letters have no function until they are added to others to make a word. But each of the figures, even the zero, is viable in its own right, and may function solo as well as in a group. A group of letters may contain an error which can be mentally corrected by the reader with the help of the context; thus we know quickly and without doubt whether the last letter in the misprint 'thep' should have been m or n or y. But there is no way of knowing whether any of the figures in an entry in a telephone directory are correct as printed, since any figure is as much a possibility as another. The point has been laboured here not just to repeat what was said on an earlier page about legibility, but as an approach to the design of numerals, in which there are some considerations that do not apply to letters.

By the second half of the fifteenth century, when printing had started to develop, numerals had discarded most of the signs of their Eastern origin and had assumed the shapes with which we are familiar. Type founders followed the style used by professional scribes, who had chosen to form the figures in a mode

1234567890

The old style numerals used for Monotype Bembo
and Van Dijck.

similar to that of the lowercase letters. So 3, 4, 5, 7 and 9 were descender characters; 6 and 8 were ascending; and 1, 2 and 0 were of normal x-height. The zero was usually made as a circle without modelling, to prevent confusion with the lowercase o – a practice which was not noticeably affected when, to facilitate the spacing of columns of figures in printed tables, type founders regulated the width of all the numerals to the width of the en space, one half of the em.

These numerals of varying heights are called 'old style' or 'non-lining'. They are hardly ever seen in sans-serif types, though De Vinne referred to a light 'gothic' face (presumably the Bruce foundry's Gothic No. 4) as having old style figures that were 'often selected for tables in which the greatest distinction is desired'.

Old style numerals remained the only kind in printing until the second half of the eighteenth century, when inventiveness in typographic letter forms became vigorous, and numerals were included in the type founders' experiments. The French raised the 3 and 5 to stand on the baseline – a reform that was even applied to Baskerville's types about 1782 after they had been removed to Kehl on behalf of Beaumarchais. That particular reform did not travel beyond France, but it persisted there for a long time; the first version of Perpetua, cut by Charles Malin in Paris in 1927, had 3 and 5 in the full-height style. A more thorough and significant change in the design of numerals occurred with the regulating of all of them to a common size, standing on the baseline. They were first seen in Britain in 1780, in William Caslon II's specimen of large types. Stower, writing in 1808, thought these 'lining' figures an improvement. T. C. Hansard disagreed strongly. He thought, rightly, that some of them were capable of confusion, and wrote with feeling of an imaginary navigation officer,

H 1234567890 m

The lining numerals of Monotype Bell are shorter than the
capitals, so they blend well with the lowercase.
The 'angle' of some of the figures suggests that Richard Austin,
who cut the punches in 1788, faithfully followed a written
example, not an engraved or printed one.

poring over tables of logarithms (which had in fact been set in lining figures since 1785) in the dim light of the ward room, trying to calculate the ship's reckoning, and fearful of making what might be a fatal error. Hansard had a point; but no doubt some of his readers took pleasure in remarking that throughout the book in which his criticism appeared – his excellent *Typographia* of 1825, produced in his own printing house – all the numerals were of the lining style.

'Lining', which simply means that the numerals stand on the baseline, is preferable to 'ranging', which suggests they are the same size as the capitals. To my eye, lining figures look best when they are somewhat shorter than the capitals; see, for example, the figures in Chappell's Trajanus type.

Lining numerals became a permanent feature of type face design, and will continue to be so. They are necessary; but they are not invariably better than the old style kind, which are always legible, for the same reason that lowercase letters are legible, the variations in size being a valuable factor in the process of recognition. In non-lining form the 3 and 8, though of similar shape, cannot be confused with each other, even in low-grade printing. And old style figures are aesthetically satisfying when they are in the company of lowercase letters in normal text matter, and blend into the texture of the page in a properly unobtrusive way. But, unfortunately, they are far from satisfactory in a line of capitals, when a date like 1972 can look incongruous – which is why the printer of *A Tally of Types*, in which the typesetting is impeccable, thought it necessary to use the lining numerals of Goudy Old Style for the dates in lines of Centaur capitals and Times Roman figures for the capitals of Poliphilus.

It is certainly beneficial to have lining numerals to accompany capitals, but the design of them tends to suffer more from the tabular width condition than does that of old style figures. In particular, the zero becomes a condensed oval, out of keeping with the proportions of the other characters in the font. The 4, too, becomes narrow, and a potential ink-trap in small sizes. The effect was ameliorated a little when, in the latter half of the nineteenth century, type founders (the American more than the British) made the numerals to the width of two-thirds of the em, a change which also improved the legibility of fractions. Linotype obtained the effect in a different way. In types up to 10 or 11 point the numerals were made to the en width of the next size up, with 'fixed' spaces to match. Monotype's practice – at least in Britain – was to stay with the en width. Perhaps it was dissatisfaction at the effect of this on the zero in lining numerals which explains the circular zero, the only non-lining figure, in the early fonts of Gill Sans.

In an ideal world manufacturers of typesetting systems would, of their own volition, offer both kinds of numerals in old style

1234567890

The upstanding 3 and 5 in Deberny & Peignot's Baskerville.

1914-1918

The descending 8 in the original version of Schneidler Medieval, 1936.

1234567890

The small zero in the early fonts of Gill Sans.

and transitional faces meant for text composition. Indeed, in the days of metal type they frequently did so. But now it is not so easy. The typographer or conscientious printer who tries to obtain old style figures has a hard task to face. And now that electronic typesetting is the common thing the manufacturer claims to have a clinching case for supplying only lining numerals, even in types of the classic old style sort. The reason is this. As well as their function in the representation of whole numbers, figures are the components of fractions (which continue in use in spite of the metric system). Tidy-looking fractions cannot be made from old style numerals, with their variations in size; so fraction figures obviously have to be of the lining form. It is now common practice in CRT and laser typesetting systems for a 'fraction routine' in the computer program automatically to 'create' the numerator of the fraction by miniaturising the font figure and elevating it to ascender level (as a superior figure, in fact), and to make the denominator by similarly reducing a figure but keeping it on the baseline, a bar being set between the two parts of the fraction. It is a trick that clearly requires the numerals in the font to be of the lining style.

The typographer or printer with a strong desire for visual harmony in letters and figures is obliged to accept that that ingenious facility is necessary, but has to try to persuade manufacturers to recognise that old style numerals are aesthetically important for certain type faces in good quality typesetting, and should be readily available as conveniently accessible additions to the font. Manufacturers with long involvement in printing understand this. With others, who may see the thing only as a pointless fancy, persistence is needed.

10: Character spacing

'It is difficult to appreciate without seeing a demonstration how completely a letter is altered by having more or less space about it. The success or failure of a type is very much a question of getting a good balance of white inside and outside the letters'. Thus Harry Carter, who had a much better appreciation of type than most of us. The interior areas of letters are fixed by the shape of the letters, but the spaces at each side of them are at will: at the will of the type designer, if he is doing his work thoroughly; at the will of the manufacturer's drawing office, if the designer has abdicated his duty to organise the spacing of his characters; at the will of the printer or his customer, who (unfortunately) can nowadays change right to wrong with impunity. The 'fitting' of letters – the allocating of the correct amount of space to each side of them, so that when they are associated into words they have a balanced relationship, without unsightly gaps or congestion – is a process fundamental to the success of a type design; but it is not always managed with total satisfaction. Harry Carter was critical of the revived Van Dijck type. 'The greatest defect of the 13-point size is that it is on too narrow a set. If it were more

> William Caslon cut his types on the Dutch pattern, and undoubtedly took van Dyck's romans and italics for his models. For a long time the fount of English used for printing Selden's *Works*, 1726, has been ascribed to Caslon, but Mr. A. F. Johnson has recently proved that the italic of the fount in question was the work of van Dyck and that the roman was also a Dutch importation.

13 point Monotype Van Dijck.

loosely spaced it would be much more comfortable to read and the letters would look much handsomer'. I think the same may be said of certain sizes of Monotype Bell, which evidently follow the tight fitting of the original face of 1788. By contrast, William Morris's Golden type was too loose. So was the metal version of

> ❡ Travaile, in the younger Sort, is a Part of Education; In the Elder, a Part of Experience. He that travaileth into a Country, before he hath some Entrance into the Language, goeth to Schoole, and not to Travaile. That Young Men travaile

The Golden type.

Gill Sans, which was spaced, I suspect, as if it were a seriffed face.

The type designer should be as concerned about the texture of his type *en masse* as about the shapes of the individual characters, and he or she ought to regard the fitting of them as an inescapable part of the design task. But some designers have left it to others. Eric Gill, for instance, who, from his experience as an inscriptional letter-cutter, had an expert sense of the spacing of characters, was content to say, in a letter to Stanley Morison about a proof of trials of Perpetua roman, 'The space between letters wants alteration, but as you say, that can be done independently of me.' (Barker, *Stanley Morison*, p. 233.) Reynolds Stone, another accomplished letter-cutter, left the fitting of his Minerva design to the Linotype drawing office staff at Altrincham. The fitting of the types designed by W. A. Dwiggins was dealt with by the Linotype office in New York, under the direction of C. H. Griffith; but at least Dwiggins took an interest in the process. In his *WAD to RR*, written in response to Rudolph Ruzicka's request for advice on type designing, he said, 'Each type letter, wherever it goes, carries along with it two *fixed* blank spaces, one on each side. And of course, each one of the 26 is likely to be placed alongside any one of the other 25 with *their* fixed blank spaces . . . the letter shapes occur in groups of similars: when you have solved for n alongside of n you are close to a workout for h i j l m and for the stem sides of b d k p q − a proper fitting for o gives you a line on the round shapes . . . a, c, e, on their open sides, and f g r t are hard to fit . . .' He went on to say, 'There isn't any fitting formula worked out yet. G. [Griffith] says there can't be any: that it is a job for the eye alone. I have a hunch that a "coarse" formula could be worked out, because there is certainly a "right" interval for a given weight and height of stem, varying as these dimensions vary'.

Griffith was right in his belief that the eye is the final judge of character spacing; but Dwiggins was also right to suspect that the fitting process could be expressed in the form of a system, a combination of formula and optical judgement − though I have never seen such a system described in print. The one that follows is based on the principles I learnt from Harry Smith of Linotype over thirty years ago. I have found it reliable, and I think Dwiggins would have accepted it.

In the roman alphabets, capital and lowercase, most of the letters are formed of straight strokes or round strokes, or a combination of them; and the direction of emphasis is vertical. The letters can be grouped like this:

letters with a straight upright stroke:
> B D E F H I J K L M N P R U   b d h i j k l m n p q r u

letters with a round stroke:
> C D G O P Q   b c d e o p q

triangular letters
> A V W X Y   v w x y

the odd ones:
> S T Z   a f g s t z

The fitting of the alphabets is best done when the letters have been sketched but before they are 'finished', because the fitting process may require adjustments of the character widths, especially if they are to conform to a prescribed unit system.

For the spacing of the capitals the basis is the H. The designer will have tested it with a few other letters and satisfied himself that the weight of its strokes, the width of its interior space, and the shape and length of its serifs are all in accord with his purpose. Four black-on-white copies of the H are needed. The width between the uprights of the letter is measured and half that amount is marked on each side of the letter on all four copies. When they are set together in a row, their eight upright strokes are equally spaced. That spacing will probably look correct if the type is a bold face, the verticals emphatic and the counters narrow; but for faces which have strokes of normal weight and fairly broad interior whites – ordinary text faces, in fact – the crossbar of H acts as a ligament drawing the uprights together, so the side spaces must be reduced until they look equal to the interior spaces. Creating this illusion is a task for the eye and careful judgement (a reducing glass is a useful aid). Time is needed to get the balance right. It is time well spent, because much depends on it. The length of the serifs must not be a controlling factor; they must be shortened as necessary. The spatial relationship of the verticals is the important thing.

The serifs at the four corners of H make a linking effect with adjacent letters. Because they are absent in a sans-serif type the side-spaces of a sans-serif H have to be narrower than those in a seriffed face.

When the four Hs look harmonious, the spaces between them not too open, not too cramped, the distance between them is measured. A half of the amount is now the appropriate allocation for each side of H, and for all other capitals having a straight vertical stroke.

The next letter to deal with is O, of which two copies are needed. One copy is placed between two pairs of correctly-spaced Hs, and the spaces on each side of it are reduced or increased until all five letters seem to be in balance. The space is then measured. The amount belonging to H is subtracted, and the remainder is therefore the amount due to O. But another test is needed. The two copies of O are marked with the side space just arrived at, and are placed side by side between the two pairs of Hs, thus, HHOOHH. This test may show the need to revise the fitting of O – and even the H, because it is a new test of that character too. When that has been done the process has reached the stage when the ideal spacing of the two most useful capitals, the 'standards', has been achieved.

At this stage, and not before, the letters must be adjusted to the unit system (if there is one) of the typesetting machine for which the type is intended. A unit system finer than 54 to the em will require little or no change in the side spacing. At 54 units at 12 point size the unit is .078 mm. In the 36 unit system the unit is

.117 mm. The capital H and O as so far designed and spaced are either an exact number of units, or up to half a unit astray; that is, the adjustment to be made to each of the side spaces cannot be more than .02 mm in 54 units or .03 mm in 36 units. The amount is small; but it is better to alter the width of the letters themselves (not a difficult task) as well as the side spaces, so as to regain the ideal fitting of the standards.

With the spacing of H and O now known precisely, it is possible to finish the drawing of the rest of the alphabet, by taking note of the groups of letters listed earlier and spacing them as in-

a Same as H
b Slightly less than *a*
c About half of *a*
d Minimum space
e Same as O

$_dA_d$ $_aB_c$ $_eC_c$ $_aD_e$ $_aE_c$ $_aF_c$

$_eG_b$ $_aI_a$ $_dJ_a$ $_aK_d$ $_aL_d$ $_bM_a$

$_bN_b$ $_aP_e$ $_eQ_e$ $_aR_d$ $_dT_d$ $_aU_b$

$_dV_d$ $_dW_d$ $_dX_d$ $_dY_d$ $_cZ_c$

S must be spaced visually, between standards

dicated above − modifying the letter widths (but not the side spaces) to the unit width values as necessary.
As the work proceeds the designer's eye becomes 'educated' to the relationship of the capitals one with another; but even a designer with long experience in the fitting of characters will not rely solely on the formula, but will check a letter between the H and O standards whenever uncertainty occurs.

The same method is used for the fitting of the lowercase, the standards being the n and o. (Fournier specified the m; but since that is often untypical, being designed after the n, with narrower interior spaces than those in n, h and u, the n seems a better choice for the standard.) The width between the uprights of n is measured, and a half of that amount is given to the left side of the letter and slightly less on the other side, because the arched corner seems to add to the space. Thus if the left side is given 10 the right hand side will be 9 or $9\frac{1}{2}$. The four copies of n are marked up and set in a row. If the type is a bold face the strong verticals and narrow interior may mean that the side spacing needs no alteration; but it if is a normal roman face the spaces between the four letters will have to be decreased (and the serif length adjusted) until the eight uprights look equally spaced. Then the lowercase o can be dealt with, and checked in combinations with n, like this:

nnonn   nnonon   nnoonn

If the type is a sans-serif that test will often reveal that n is too tightly fitted.

When the two letters look well regulated they are measured against the units gauge and the widths of the letters and their side spaces modified so as to maintain the ideal balance of black to white. With the n and o established as standards, the rest of the alphabet is organised by this scheme:

$_a$b$_e$ $_e$c$_f$ $_e$d$_a$ $_e$e$_f$ $_c$h$_b$ $_c$i$_a$

$_a$j$_a$ $_c$k$_d$ $_c$l$_a$ $_a$m$_b$ $_c$p$_e$ $_e$q$_a$

$_a$r$_d$ $_b$u$_b$ $_d$v$_d$ $_d$w$_d$ $_d$y$_d$

a Same as left side of n
b Same as right side of n
c Slightly more than left side of n
d Minimum space
e Same as o
f Slightly less than o

a f g s t z   must be spaced visually, between standards

The essential thing is that the space between letters should never be greater than the space inside n or m. (Some versions of Times Bold show the unhappy effect of that error.)

To see how well the spacing of roman type was done in the past I recommend a study of the excellent photographic enlargements reproduced in Philip Gaskell's article in the *Journal of the Printing Historical Society* No. 7, 1971.

The fitting of an italic type follows the same principles and method, and the same four letters, H, O, n and o, are prepared first, as the standards by which the rest of the alphabet will be controlled. The measuring of the side spaces must always be done at the precise centre of the vertical aspect of the letters. As in the roman, the side spaces will be derived from the interior spaces. The italic capitals, which are usually simply sloped versions of the roman capitals, though not so wide, present no difficulty. The lowercase may not be so easy if its letters are narrow, as in many of the old style italics; the two side spaces of n may then have to be nearly equal to a half of the width of its counter – which is a strong reason for making the serifs quite long, to hold the letters together.

Numerals are a different case. Almost any type, seriffed or sans-serif, of normal weight and appearance, may be required at some time to be used in the setting of text matter which includes columns of figures, and it is essential that the figures are properly positioned below each other. That means, of course, that they must all occupy the same width, in spite of their differences in shape and proportion. In the days of foundry-made type the common practice was to make the em space as wide as it was tall – a square of the type size, in fact – and the en space exactly half of that width. Numerals were made to the width of the en space, so columns of figures could be justified with em and en spaces according to the number of figures in each line. Monotype followed that principle, though the em space was not necessarily a square of the type size. This meant that in the text sizes of most Monotype faces the numerals were 9 units wide (the em being 18 units). That width is adequate for non-lining (old style) numerals; but it is really too narrow for lining numerals – the zero in particular often looking unhappily pinched amongst otherwise normal characters. In recognition of this, and because lining figures have always been preferred in America, Linotype's custom of placing the numerals on the width of the en of the next size up, in type faces up to 10 or 11 point, gave a little more advantage to the appearance of the 4 and the zero.

There are very few types (Galliard is one of them) where the designer has been allowed to design an alternative set of figures, each with a width and fitting suited to its shape. In most types the designer is obliged to conform to the rule that numerals must be 'tabular', uniform in width – only the figure 1 sometimes being allowed to be on a narrower width. This means that the designer must space the numerals individually, centring them visually in the width prescribed by the manufacturer.

Punctuation marks, too, are special cases. The modern habit of placing them on the narrowest width possible is not a good one. They are essentially functional, and need enough space to be clearly visible. The comma and period can very well be centred on a half of the figure width (if the unit system allows that). American usage requires the colon to be centred in its area, for use in numerical indications of time, so the colon should be spaced like the period. But when the colon is used as a punctuation sign it ought to be set slightly apart from the word it follows – a matter for the typographer and printer to take care of. The same applies to the semi-colon. Bruce Rogers pointed out in his *Paragraphs on Printing* that exclamation and question marks should also be set off from the last word because they often form disagreeable and confusing combinations with the last letter, especially if it is l or f. The designer should therefore place them off-centre on sufficient width to keep them clear of the preceding letter.

Like the other signs, quotation marks, single and double, make their full effect when they stand slightly apart from the letters. The double opening quote, which is often followed by a capital, especially in conversational wording, should be given a unit or two of space on its right-hand side. If there is also a single opening quote in the font it should be treated in the same way; but if the single is the only one it should not have the extra space because a pair of them, set in response to a demand for double quotes, will look too loose. The closing double quote usually follows lowercase letters; so does the apostrophe, in its own role and when it acts as the closing single quote. No extra space should be applied to the left-hand side in the manufacture. A keyboard operator who takes an interest in the appearance of his work will add a little space if the quote follows a tall letter.

The process just described must sound like a suitable case for a computer program, with modifying factors written in to take care of the variables between type faces. I do not think it could ever be wholly reliable. The features that make one type different from another have an influence on the fitting of the characters in a way that is not calculable, because the matter is one for aesthetic judgement, not arithmetic. Software might facilitate the task of spacing, but the designer's eye must be the arbiter.

In the spacing process the designer, working with his drawn letters, will have been using his imagination to visualise the characters and their fitting in actual type size. This is not easy, and no one expects the result to be right first time. So when the manufacture is completed a trial proof is produced for the express purpose of scrutinising the fitting, the characters being composed between standards at an appropriate type size, usually 12 point if the type is a text face. Some designers use only the capital H as the controlling standard, on the ground that it is entirely symmetrical in shape and spacing. The method has the disadvantage that lowercase letters seen like this, HaHbHcHdHeH, are not in a natural context. There is another method: to set the alphabets with their own standards, thus: HAHBHCHDHEH and OOAOBOCODO and so on, and nnanbncndnen and ooaoboco . . . That is a good way to disclose inequalities of spacing. But something more is needed – something life-like. Actual words must also be composed, to show all the letters in normal relationships; not only with other letters, but with themselves, because in most languages letters are frequently doubled (in English, the only letters which almost never double are a, h, i, j, q, u, x and y). A lowercase l with too little side spacing, as in some versions of Helvetica, makes an unfortunate clotted effect in such a word as 'million'. And an m too condensed in comparison with n, as in Goudy's Californian roman, would probably have been revised if the designer had checked it in a test setting that included words like 'common' and 'minimum'.

Letters do not live in isolation. They are the elements of meaning, the components of visible language, and their spatial relationship with each other is crucial, not only for the rapid recognition of words by the reader but for the regularity of texture that is essential if the reader's comprehension is to be maintained for a long period. Considering the amount of careful judgement that goes into the fitting of a type face it is unfortunate, not to say absurd, that in the 1970s some typographers, aided and abetted by trade typesetters, developed the habit of specifying the reduction of inter-character spacing in the text of advertising copy, with an effect that they would have rejected if a new novel by their favourite author had been set in the same way. The detrimental effect on the texture of type matter could have been predicted: emphasis of the white interiors of n, u, c and o and the white triangles of v, w and y, but a darkening where i and l occurred next to letters with vertical strokes. Nevertheless, the manufacturers of electronic typesetting systems willingly became accomplices in the act by producing 'advertising typesetting' computer programs which included a selection of automatic spacing routines, usually 'normal' (for which read 'correct'), 'tight' and 'tightest'. This use of 'minus spacing' is a spurious sort of sophistication. (Typographers involved in package designing, an activity just as important as publicity work, seldom indulge in it, no doubt because they are keenly aware of the need for clarity.) The practice can only be due to a compound of ignorance and indifference. Ignorance of the process of character fitting as described earlier is forgivable; it is an esoteric subject not part of the typographer's normal education. But ignorance of the essential role of character spacing has shown itself in the words of people who should know better. For instance, there are those writers who seem to believe that character spacing as we know it is a mere convention and that metal type allowed no alternative − and this in spite of Fournier's clear indication that the type founder could and would debase a type if required: 'Certain printers occasionally ask for type thinner in set than normal, to get in more letters to a line. This is perhaps prompted less by taste than by economy. In these circumstances it is necessary to make the m as thin as the extremities of the strokes will permit, so that no shoulder remains, and to regulate the set of the other letters in relation to it.' And there is the London typesetter who was heard to say, 'Before the introduction of the adjustable spacing program filmsetting looked like metal setting' − as if the printing of the past, from Aldus and Estienne to the Elzevirs and on to Whittingham, Rudge of Mount Vernon, the Doves Press, Nonesuch and Curwen, to omit many, lacked a desirable but unattainable improvement. And quite recently the manufacturer of an electronic typesetter issued an item of print composed in a face designed for the system, in which the colophon said, 'The standard inter-character space has been reduced by 2 units throughout' − as though they now thought that the fitting they had given the face in the first place was unsatisfactory. Perhaps the naïve belief that character spacing is simply a matter for choice is due to unthinking enthusiasm for computer programs ('the program allows choices, therefore we should use them'). No doubt the practice of reducing the character spacing in text will cease when typographers adopt a cool attitude towards the computer and a rational view of the qualities of readability and legibility.

However, there is one case where inter-character space reduction is reasonable and necessary: in a headline set from a font actually made for text sizes. In that case a judicious closing up of the letters improves what would otherwise be a loose and feeble effect. It is to be hoped, though, that before long electronic typesetting systems will be equipped with a complete modulation program so that all the aspects of a type – its x-height and stroke weights and its internal as well as its external spaces – will be automatically adjusted according to type size, so as to maintain a proper balance of all the elements of the design.

The advertising typesetting program includes one feature that alters character fitting to its benefit – or would do so if it were correctly organised. This is the 'kerning' routine, which allows a letter to intrude into the 'air space' of another when the circumstances make it desirable. The closing up of T, V, W and Y with non-ascender lowercase letters is a familiar example. Unfortunately, some manufacturers have got it wrong. Too often the program reduces the space between the letters by too much, diminishing the identity of the letters and causing a clot of congestion. One reason for this may lie with a precedent – the logotypes To, Tr, Ye and so on which Linotype used to make for some of their book types. It must have been those that Bruce Rogers had in mind when he said, '. . . the cutting [mortising] of such letters as V and W to make them set closer than their natural width is usually very much overdone. The new logotypes cut for this purpose are equally faulty in this respect. The resulting effect is more noticeable and more objectionable than the natural setting of the type would be.' If it is properly done the programmed kerning routine can have a mildly beneficial effect on the appearance of type in action (though thrusting the comma or period into the angle of w or y has the contrary result). However, the kerning of the triangular capitals A, V and W with each other produces as many awkward effects as it cures. It improves the appearance of the word AVAIL if the first three letters have a unit or two subtracted from the space between them; but the same process will have a bad effect in AVILA, because of the two uprights in the middle of the word and the unalterable white area in LA. There is only one reliable way to balance capitals with each other: it is to add space between them according to their shapes. Not so long ago, in the days of metal type, the art of visual letterspacing was understood and practised by most typographers and many typesetters, and headlines in capitals worked well and looked well. Now the art is in abeyance – except where a serious typographer makes the effort to refit the output by hand.

LAWYERS

Rub-down kerning out of control.
From an advertisement in an English newspaper.

If the kerning of capitals with capitals was deleted from 'refinement' programs the capitals would at least present themselves naturally; sometimes awkwardly, no doubt, but not ridiculously, as is too often the case.

11: The slab-serif

There are two classes of type faces which, though they are not used in book printing, frequently perform as text types and therefore deserve some examination. They are the egyptian and the sans-serif; occasionally used for the text of magazines and for features in newspapers (chiefly in the European press), but more often for the 'copy' in sales catalogues, promotion material and press advertising.

It was advertising that brought them into being in the early years of the nineteenth century, when the promoters of lotteries and entertainments and coaching services wanted their placards to shout to the passer-by with a louder voice than had been delivered by the display sizes of the Caslon and Baskerville style types previously in use. The egyptian and the sans-serif, with the fat face which came first in order of invention, were the three radical innovations in type design which removed the typography of ephemeral printing from the influence of the book and enabled it to acquire a visual style of its own. At first the fat face was the most potent. Its basis was the 'modern' face, with its characteristics carried to the extreme – its thick strokes made as broad as possible while the thin strokes and serifs remained hairlike. Fat face types, in roman and italic, were staples in display typography until the last quarter of the nineteenth century. As a species the fat face was revived in the 1930s, and it has continued in mild favour; Poster Bodoni and Ultra Bodoni are well known, though Falstaff is a better design than either. The fat face is the ultimate of a class, not a class in itself; and because it is not usable in continuous text it is outside our area of study.

Vincent Figgins was the first type founder to show the egyptian

or 'slab-serif', in a supplement (*c.* 1817) to his specimen of 1815,
where it was called 'Antique'. The design consisted of capitals
only; no doubt there were numerals too. The characters were full

HISTORIANS have informed us it happened that about the year 1706

An 'Antique' from a Figgins specimen book of about 1887.

face titling in four sizes, approximating 12, 22, 48 and 60 point,
and were presumably intended to be used in a subsidiary role to
the fat face types, which Figgins offered in a range of sizes up to a
stentorian 192 point. (It may be, though, that independent wood
letter makers were already producing the 'Antique' letter in sizes
larger than Figgins's.)

Not everyone admired the new design. In his *Typographia*
(1825) T. C. Hansard was scornful. 'Fashion and Fancy commonly frolic from one extreme to another. To the razor-edged
fine lines and ceriphs of type just observed upon [the fat face],
a reverse has succeeded, called "Antique" or "Egyptian", the
property of which is, that the strokes which form the letters are
all of one uniform thickness! − After this, who would have
thought that further extravagance could have been conceived?'
(He went on to fulminate about the 'Italian' face, the 'reconstruc-
ted' fat face mentioned earlier in these pages.) And in 1834 the
Journal für Buchdruckerkunst of Brunswick showed that it was
paying close attention to Hansard by describing the new type as a
'Monstrosität' − which now seems altogether too severe for what
we regard as a plain serviceable letter.

About the name: at the time of its creation there was great
public interest in Britain in the relics of antiquity, especially in the
accounts of what was seen during Napoleon's expedition in
Egypt. The 'antique' was fashionable, and type founders probably saw commercial advantage in naming their new designs
according to the vogue. Robert Thorne was the first to use the
term 'Egyptian', and in the course of time that came to be the
accepted term for the slab-serif class. The 1926 volume of the
Handbuch der Schriftarten − the volume that encapsulated the
range of types available in Germany before the great surge of new
designing in the 1930s − shows forty-five types called 'Egyptienne', in various weights and widths. In its English and French
forms the name is present in modern digital type face catalogues.

As said earlier, the fat face, extraordinary as it looks by comparison with traditional book types, was really the idea of the
bold version of an established text type, the 'modern', carried to
the extreme. It is not difficult to imagine a punch-cutter responding to a demand and cutting an exaggerated version of a style
with which he was familiar. On the other hand, it is very difficult

to believe that a punch-cutter – essentially an artisan, not an artist – could have thought up the egyptian, a letter form without a precedent in type. It has been suggested that the design was an imitation of lettering that was already being used by the painters of shop signs. That seems quite plausible. And it may be that the egyptian was the first type to be *designed* in our sense of the word: that is, each character carefully drawn on paper before manufacture, perhaps by a professional sign painter commissioned by the type founder to provide a pattern for his engraver to follow.

The special characteristics of the egyptian are two. The first is the apparently equal weight of all the strokes. In a good design there is actually a difference in the weights of main and secondary strokes and some modelling of the curves. The difference is slight, but just enough to give the type more vitality than one that lacks the modulation. The other characteristic is the thick square-cut serif, which is usually a little less thick than the main stroke. It is the strong slab-like form of the serif, not the fact that it is un-bracketed, that is of the essence in this class of type. (With those two characteristics in mind it is hard to accept the suggestion that the egyptian form was in Eric Gill's mind when he designed the Solus type, which is really no more than a Perpetua-like roman unhappily fitted with a thickened version of the serifs of Monotype Bodoni 135, recommended to Gill by Stanley Morison.)

The serif is the clue to a variation in the egyptian that was developed in the middle of the nineteenth century. In the true egyptian the serif forms a clean right-angle with the stroke. Then a bracket was added, and a little of the weight was taken off the secondary strokes and the serifs, though they remained substantial. The result was named Clarendon by one founder, Ionic by another. These modulations brought the design a little closer to the style of the then current text types, and Clarendon and Ionic

NORMANTON
Antique Suites

An extended Clarendon.

became popular as 'emphasisers' in text matter. The sturdiness of Ionic was the reason for its being chosen as the basis for the newspaper type of that name that was developed by Linotype in the 1920s, the progenitor of a series of newspaper text faces which have an important place in the history of twentieth-century typography.

While Clarendon and Ionic acquired a continuing existence as bold (though unrelated) companions to roman in text setting, the egyptian as a display face declined in favour for many years, supplanted by types of a more expressive kind. Then in the early

1930s, when creativity in type designing became vigorous, there was a revival – not of the actual nineteenth-century egyptians but of the idea of the slab-serif. It began in Germany where, as mentioned above, the 'Egyptienne' was well known, if not actually popular. Memphis Bold was the first of the new designs to appear, in 1929, soon followed by the Beton face. Both designs became popular, Memphis because it soon became available for Linotype machine composition in America and later in Britain, and Beton because it took the fancy of advertising agency typographers. Karnak, Cairo, Stymie and Rockwell were others of the ilk. The similarities in these new egyptians were greater than the differences. All of them were true slab-serifs in the sense that the serifs were unbracketed, and all of them get their character (such as it is) from the application of 'geometry' to the letter forms, so that curves are arcs of a circle (or appear to be so) and all the strokes are of regular thickness, with serifs to match. The 'mechanical' effect that this produces has caused some writers to rate the egyptians of the 1930s as inferior to those of the nineteenth century – which is reasonable, though only up to a point. In the older faces the quality was in their capitals which, in the heavy versions, presented a powerful blocky effect and, incidentally,

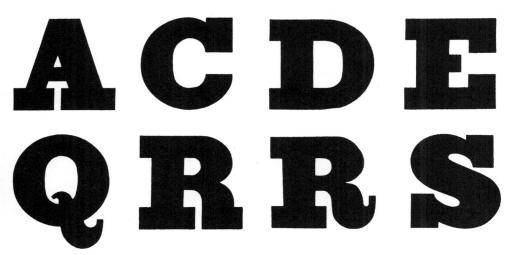

Some letters from Charles Hasler's type face for the Festival of Britain, 1951.

provided a good ground for engraving and shadowing; and in the light 'skeleton' versions the clear linear structure of the capitals provided a high degree of legibility, a fact which is recognised today by some designers of TV graphics. But the lowercase letters in the older egyptians were seldom as good as the capitals, particularly in the bold versions. The characteristics of the 'modern' roman prevailing when the egyptians were created were a dominating influence; and in some letters they conflicted with the form of the slab-serif. The lowercase b was a particular case. Its head serif obviously had to be wide as well as thick, or it would have been a stub, not a slab; and that determined the space at the left side of the letter. The stem of the letter had no foot serif. The result of those two features was often a noticeable gap when b followed other letters, especially a, with its upturned terminal. In fact, uneven fitting was a frequent defect in the old egyptians. The lowercase k sometimes looked too heavy, because of the number of strong serifs. And there were other characters, g and s for instance, that often looked unshapely. The new egyptians of the 1930s avoided these defects because their designers were not influenced by letter forms of another class. On the other hand, the German and American designers were trammelled by the compass and set square. If in the older types some of the letters have a 'blacksmithed' awkwardness, at least they seem to have come from a human hand. The faces of the 1930s suggest the product of a formula and a machine. George Trump's Schadow type (which is only just an egyptian) is an exception, in having a good deal of subtlety in its shapes and edges: and more recently some designers in Europe have succeeded in producing egyptians which retain the 'monoline' armature of the letter form and its rectangular serifs while avoiding the mechanical appearance of the types of the 1930s.

When an egyptian is used for text matter the evenness of its strokes and its prominent square serifs produce a canvas-like texture which in a long text soon becomes tiring, with the possibility that the reader's comprehension may suffer. Its readability is not high. On my personal readability scale of one to ten the egyptian rates about five. But in short passages, as in a catalogue or travel brochure, it can be effective; and when it is necessary to superimpose text matter on a tint or reverse it from black to white, it is actually more effective than a traditional text type. In fact, there are times when the unsubtle sober quality of the egyptian is more serviceable than the elegance of types of greater reputation.

12: The sans-serif

As an identifying term 'egyptian' expressed an idea – the noble past – rather than a species. It was even applied to the first sans-serif type, though 'antique' was more favoured, until that was displaced in Britain by 'grotesque', with 'gothic' and 'doric' as alternatives. There was no good reason for any of those names, but they continued in use until the beginning of this century, when it became customary to give a specific name to a new type rather than a number. The French adopted 'antique' as the generic name for sans-serif faces. The Germans called them 'Grotesk'. American founders settled on 'gothic' – a misleading term, as De Vinne said, which is otherwise given to black-letter types. To refer to these terms in the past tense is not really correct. A catalogue of digital type faces current in 1985 showed that this fine confusion of terms is still with us. It includes Antique No. 3, an egyptian, and Antique Olive, a sans-serif; Doric Bold and Doric Black, also sans-serifs; numerous Gothics, from Copperplate to Franklin; but nothing actually called 'sans-serif'. Gill Sans is the nearest – though on the original Monotype specimen sheets it was properly called 'Gill Sans-serif'. The term sans-serif, coined by Vincent Figgins in 1832, is at least accurate, even though it expresses a negative characteristic. 'Lineal', recently recommended in Britain, is a little more descriptive, but it has not become popular.

'The sans-serif is in fact an egyptian with the serifs knocked off, and it is probable that that was the manner of its creation.' It is to be hoped that that uncharacteristic flight of fancy by A. F. Johnson has not misled anyone. P. M. Handover's explanation is equally untenable. Her contention that Figgins emphasised the serifs of the fat face and thereby produced the egyptian, while William Caslon IV eliminated the serif of the fat face to create the sans-serif, shows a curious disregard of the structure of the three kinds of design. In fact, the sans-serif letter was in use in other fields long before the type founders began to produce it. Nicolete Gray has described its presence on fifteenth-century inscriptions in Florence. James Mosley has written of the architects and sculptors who, at the end of the eighteenth century, used the letter for its classical associations (it is significant that a number of the nineteenth-century German sans-serif types were called 'Steinschrift'). Mosley quotes James Callingham's assertion in *Sign Writing and Glass Embossing* (1871) that 'the credit of having introduced the ordinary square or San-seriff letters . . . belongs to the sign-writer, by whom they were employed . . . before the type founder gave them his attention . . .' It seems possible, though I have not seen it suggested, that it was the makers of large-size wooden type who first imitated the sign-painters' 'block' letter and supplied it to the printers of posters as a strong alternative to the fat face and the egyptian. If that were so, one could assume that as soon as the new letter appeared in print it may well have caught the eye of an enterprising type founder; in particular, one who had a commercial interest in the supply of large sizes of metal type. William Caslon IV, for instance. In 1810 he had successfully developed a special kind of matrix for the production of large type. As it is, though, the first sans-serif type we know, the one that appeared in his specimen book of 1816, is a puzzling thing; a single line of capitals, fairly broad in shape, no more than medium weight, and in one size only, about 20 point. It is, in fact, a type of very little value to a jobbing printer. My guess is that the face had originally been cut, from a design supplied to the type founder, for a special order – for a printer of labels for some sort of merchandise, say – and that Caslon then included it in his specimen book, calling it 'Egyptian' to suggest antiquity, in the hope that the face would take the attention of someone else with a similar need. Evidently it did not, because the style was not developed, either by Caslon's successors or their competitors, for a considerable time. My surmise, then, is that Caslon's type was not a highly original creation by the type founder which just happened to be ahead of its time. If that had been the case the face would surely have been altogether more powerful – as was, indeed, the next sans-serif type, Vincent Figgins's, which appeared sixteen years later. (Two faces offered by the Schelter & Giesecke foundry of Leipzig, one of them attributed to Conner of New York, are shown in the *Handbuch der Schriftarten* and dated 1825 and 1830. On stylistic grounds those dates are about forty years too early.) Figgins's sans-serif of 1832 was heavy and large, and in the following year he had ten sizes of sans-serif to offer. He made the style a reality, and his jobbing printer customers must have recognised the new design as a useful running mate to the fat face and the egyptian.

Unlike the egyptian, and particularly the clarendon, which soon assumed the role of companion to roman text faces, the sans-serif was evidently thought of as only suitable for titling display lines. Not until the 1860s did sans-serif types begin to appear in the weight, width and size appropriate to text setting. An example is the Gothic No. 4 that was shown in the catalogue issued in 1865 by the Bruce foundry of New York. Four sizes were available, equivalent to 6, 8, 10 and 12 point; there was a lowercase, and the numerals were non-ranging, a clear indication that the face was intended not only for single display lines but for text matter in many sorts of jobbing work, though not the extensive text settings with which we are now familiar. The use of sans-serif for that purpose did not occur until well into the present century, when the process of putting words into print ceased to be a matter for the editor or compositor with an 'artistic' touch and became the occupation of a new specialist, the typographer.

It is noticeable that up to about 1914 the type founders had become quite competent at producing bold condensed sans-serif types (Stephenson Blake, for instance, had several with much more character than any types of that sort produced since that date), but they seemed unable to instil any quality into faces of normal weight and width. The capitals were dull, because there was too little variations of width. The lowercase generally lacked the balanced proportions that had gone into the modelling of the bold version. The letters a, g, k, r and s were often ill at ease. It would not have troubled Bruce Rogers if the lowercase had never arrived. Speaking in 1938 and referring to the sans-serif form he said, '. . . it has been reproduced lately in almost innumerable versions, none of them fit for the printing of books. Indeed, the lowercase, by reason of the principle of its construction, is unfit for reading *anywhere*.' Not many people would have agreed with those last four words at that time; even fewer now. The interesting phrase in his statement is 'principle of its construction', by which I assume he meant the common weight of all the strokes as well as the absence of serifs. Those are in fact the two essential characteristics of the normal sans-serif face. There are types without serifs but with a visible difference in the weight of the strokes; the Britannic face, designed in Britain about the turn of the century, is an example. So are Koloss and Radiant, the distinctive Peignot, and more recently, the excellent Optima. And there are types of monoline stroke weight and serifs – usually very small. The Lining or Plate Gothics (called Spartan in Britain) are types of that sort. All of those variations of the sans-serif form are outside the area of these present notes. It is the regular sans-serif letter form that is under scrutiny here; and to consider how and why it became not only acceptable as a text face but, in the minds of some people, the only proper type for that role, it is necessary to look at two very different lines of development in Britain and Germany in the 1920s.

The first was Edward Johnston's sans-serif design in 1916 for the London public transport system. In spite of its being a 'private' type, not available for general use and therefore unknown outside the London area, it has a place in the history of type design for a reason that will emerge shortly. The design has always been accorded something like reverence by writers on typography in Britain. In 1974, when the transport authority was in doubt as to its continuing utility and asked some of us for an opinion, I too expressed warm respect for the original intention and admiration for the design itself – except for a few characters which I was then encouraged to redesign. Even so, on further thought I find my respect for the original project intact but my admiration for the design somewhat diminished.

Edward Johnston revived the craft of calligraphy, and in his own work he raised the craft to the quality of art. He is still regarded as the greatest calligrapher of the twentieth century. Calligraphy is writing. The calligrapher writes words. He does not draw letters. Johnston's involvement in the creation of an italic type for the Cranach Press had been an unhappy experience for all concerned, because, as John Dreyfus's absorbing account of it makes clear, Johnston was temperamentally incapable of producing letter drawings for someone else (the punch-cutter) to translate into metal, with satisfaction to himself as well as to others. But the sans-serif project was a task of a different sort, which he later spoke of with great pride.

ODBEFHIJKLMN

PQURSTVWCG

QU WA &YXZJ

obdcepqoug as

aahijklmnrs ek

tvwxyz   gg

1234567890

qupqjyg

Edward Johnston's drawings of the type for the London public transport system. Note the three versions of a and g, and the lowered centre of w.

He said that his 'block' letter was based on classical Roman capital proportions. Certainly his capitals avoid the squareness of earlier sans-serif faces, though E and F are wider than classical models and the short-centred M and the meat-hook S are hardly traditional. The lowercase is a different matter. Johnston started by deciding that the 'o' must be circular, and he evidently thought that the bowls of the other letters should be a section of the same circle. (There was a good deal of 'geometry' in the capitals, too.) The idea is reasonable, though a circle is always duller than an oval. The widths of all the other lowercase letters related to the o. The x-height was moderate. These proportions resulted in an open face of ample width. (P. M. Handover was wrong to call it 'exceptionally economical'. What Johnston was given to understand was that his type was so much more legible than earlier faces that it could be used in a smaller size with equal effect.)

Johnston established the stroke weight of the face by a method that is natural to the professional calligrapher, for whom the size of letters derives from the breadth of the pen. As the note on his drawing shows, the relation of stroke thickness to capital height was to be strictly 1 to 7. (Ibn Muqlah, the great calligrapher who lived in Baghdad in the tenth century, used the same ratio in his development and regulation of the Arabic script.) If Johnston had studied type founders' specimen books, as he had said he intended to do, he would probably have realised that unlike his scriptorial work, which was an end in itself, his drawing for the sans-serif was the means to a particular end – the manufacture of type for printing, which meant that he was at liberty to establish the stroke weight independently of the capital height. More importantly, Johnston should have learnt from observation of examples of type that where curves flow into stems, in sans-serif as well as seriffed types, the curves have to be made thinner if the illusion of evenness is to be maintained and a clotted effect at the joint is to be avoided. If he had been aware of that fact he might have made his b, d, p and q better integrated, the g more graceful, and the crotch of n and other letters more incisive.

It has been said that he took great care of the spacing of the letters, but his tests for that purpose have not been described. If he had tested his lowercase characters in word combinations, with due attention to their appearance when doubled, he would surely not have been satisfied with the gappy effect of his letter l (el) with its over-wide curved foot. The foot itself was a good invention to differentiate the letter from the capital I; but it was so broad that the letter stood aloof from the one that followed.

It might be argued that those features of the design are really the idiosyncrasies which give the type its distinctive character, and that they had no ill effect in the large sizes in which the type was used for its first five years or so, on station sign plates and as litho-printed letters on paper to be pasted on to the art work of

Ibn Muqlah's letter alif, to the height of seven rhombic dots.
From Y. H. Safadi, *Islamic Calligraphy* (1978).

the illustrative posters for which the transport authority was famous (a task I sometimes had to perform at the Baynard Press – where, incidentally, the bold version of the face, a titling, was drawn by Charles Pickering to notes provided by Johnston in 1929). The Johnston sans-serif did not actually become type – wooden for the sizes 6-line pica up to 36-line, metal for the 36, 48 and 60 point – until about 1922, when it was needed for letterpress-printed information notices. It was in the lower sizes that the defects in the lowercase were liable to become visible and, to some eyes, irritating. In the late 1970s the Johnston face was substantially reworked by a London design studio; but because of the variety of sans-serif types that now compete with it on station poster sites the type no longer has the distinction it had when it was introduced in 1916 and made such a superior contrast to the plebeian 'grotesques' of the time.

The particular attitude to the task that Johnston adopted – the belief that the letters should be based on the classic letter forms developed in Rome – is more significant to the student than the type itself, which remains a 'private' design, localised in the London area. That attitude was given further expression in a type that was by no means 'private' and so far from being localised actually achieved a world-wide reputation, if not popularity. This was the sans-serif type designed for Monotype by Eric Gill, a friend of Johnston, and introduced in 1928. Gill's original drawing for the type contained several unusual features. There was the flat bottom to the lowercase d (it is also present in his Perpetua roman), a feature that was repeated at the head of p and q. And there was the shearing of the ends of the vertical strokes at an angle – a device we shall meet again from other hands. Those features may have been not just personal fancies but signs of a conscientious desire to avoid imitating the Johnston face. They disappeared in the course of development. (The design as it finally emerged owes a good deal to the Monotype drawing office.) The letters and numerals of the Gill sans-serif in its basic weight are decidedly more stylish than those of the Johnston type. The bold version is dull; but the extra-bold deserves its popularity. Its numerals are particularly good. In its metal form the basic Gill Sans had one slightly unsatisfactory feature. As noted in the essay on spacing, its fitting was a little too loose for a sans-serif. In some filmsetting versions the character spacing has been slightly reduced, with a consequent improvement in the texture of the type in text sizes.

The Johnston and Gill sans-serif did not come into existence as the outcome of an artistic movement or campaign, but were instigated, separately, by two remarkable men: Frank Pick, the imaginative manager of the London transport system, who commissioned Johnston two years before the formation of the Design and Industries Association; and Stanley Morison, who saw typo-

**ad
pr**

Some characters from Eric Gill's first drawing for the sans-serif type. They were revised in manufacture.

ABCDEFGHIJKLMN
ABCDEFGHIJKLMN
OPQRSTUVWXYZ
OPQRSTUVWXYZ
abcdefghijklmn
abcdefghijklmn
opqrstuvwxyz
opqrstuvwxyz

Johnston and Gill Sans compared.

graphic possibility in Gill's sans-serif lettering on a shop front. The causes and effects of sans-serif development were different in Germany, where as early as 1907 two important events in the history of industrial design occurred. The first was the formation of the Deutsche Werkbund, an association of architects, craftsmen and (significantly) manufacturers. It held a notable exhibition in Cologne in 1914. The second event, also in 1907, was the appointment by AEG, the great electrical combine, of Peter Behrens as their design consultant, the first of his kind. From those two sources of design activity, and from the non-representational theories of the constructivist movement amongst Russian artists, there arose in 1919, the Bauhaus, that remarkable attempt to synthesise the values of art, craft and the machine. In its printing workshop constructivist principles were applied to typography:

the use of precise grids, the limitation of decoration to the 'pure' elements of geometry, the line, the square and the circle, and sans-serif as the type best suited to express the ideals of the modern creed. There were many sans-serif types to choose from; the 1926 volume of the *Handbuch der Schriftarten* shows well over three hundred of them in current manufacture. But most of them were dull and lifeless, inadequate to express the spirit of the age. The form must be re-created. The type founders recognised a promising field for enterprise, and the type designers responded to the challenge. The fundamental elements of geometry, the straight line, the circle and the arc, would provide the basis for the new types which, purified of any traces of the past, would speak for the aspirations of 'our time'.

Three of the new German sans-serif faces became internationally famous: Jakob Erbar's eponymous design, Paul Renner's Futura, and Rudolf Koch's Kabel (which will be discussed at length in later pages). All three of them are frequently in use at the present time.

The Erbar face was first in the field. Jakob Erbar had already designed a serifless type in 1919, though it was not a sans-serif in the full sense. Its main and secondary strokes were visibly different in thickness, because the type was meant to reflect the action of a broad pen – hence its name, Feder (quill) Schrift. (Erbar knew something of calligraphy; he had attended the class conducted by Anna Simons, one of Johnston's pupils.) The Feder type was undistinguished; Erbar's later Koloss, a heavier face on the same lines, was a much better design. There is no obvious connection between those faces and the sans-serif design that later made his name internationally known. He wrote that he did the first rough

WEIN KARTE

Jakob Erbar's Feder-Grotesk.

ÄBCDCEFGHIJKLMNO

PRSTÜVWXYZ

abcdefghijklmnöpqrst

úvwxyz   +!?".; *   &

Erbar:
the 1922 drawing.

1234567890 ſʒ

*Erbar
Sept. 1922*

drawings for a modern sans-serif type as early as 1914, but his
service in the First World War interrupted the work. A set of
capitals was drawn in 1920, and another drawing of 1922 shows a
complete font, on which the letter forms are not greatly different
from the type as it appeared in 1926. 'My aim,' he wrote, 'was to
design a printing type which would be free of all individual characteristics, possess thoroughly legible letter forms, and be a pure-
ly typographic creation.' He went on to say that it was clear to
him that the task would only be accomplished if the type face was
developed from a fundamental element, the circle. The letters c
and e, and the bowls of lowercase b, d, g, p and q all relate to the
circular o, which was fairly small compared with the capital O. In
the supplement to the *Handbuch* for 1927 the new type is shown
in full alphabets in light, medium and heavy weights, the light
and medium having an alternative lowercase of reduced x-height,
which was not exported. The type was introduced in 1926,

ABCDEFGHIJKLMNO ABCDEFGHIJKLMN
PQRSTUVWXYZ abcde OPQRSTUVWXYZ
fghchijkcklmnopqrsſßtu abcdefghchijkcklmnopqrsſßtß
vwxyz äöü 1234567890 uvwxyz äöü 1234567890

Erbar: the normal and small x-height versions.
From the *Handbuch der Schriftarten*.

though the related inlined bold version, called Grotesk Lichte
Fette but known as Phosphor in Britain and America, had already
been available for three years, if the date given is to be believed. In
the same supplement three weights of the Futura face were shown
in one-word samples.

Paul Renner evidently found the creation of a sans-serif on a
geometric basis a stimulating task. In the light version of Futura
as it first appeared his lowercase m had a flat roof (there was an
existing Grotesk called Roland that had the same feature). The r,
made of a pillar and a separate ball, is a typical *art deco* device;
and in the bold version the a is an ingenious play on the traditional shape. The g, a lively exploitation of geometric forms, was
one of two such inventions, as the pattern plates shown here
reveal. (I prefer the other.) The pattern plates are interesting for a
particular reason. Futura is taken to be representative of the
'Germanic compasses-and-set-square school', as one writer has
it. But these plates show four versions of the familiar single-
storey g. They differ by the amount of modelling in the curves of
the bowl as they enter the stem – a sign of refined perception in
the person responsible. That is not all. The three cancelled versions have a 'compassed' counter in the upper section; but in the
permitted version, the one finally adopted, the counter is not
circular but oval, as in the p and q – and it is all the better for it. In

The early versions
of these characters
are shown overleaf.

If this form had been issued
it might have influenced
later designers.

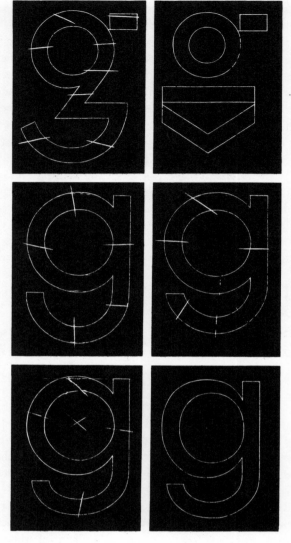

Futura: experimental forms from pattern plates made for matrix engraving.
By courtesy of Fundicion Tipografica Neufville, Barcelona.

Hamburgers   **Hamburgers**

First versions of Futura light and bold, before the design settled down.

Verlagsdruckerei
ZEITSCHRIFTEN

Futura as issued.

fact, Futura is just as sensitive a design as Gill Sans; it is simply that it does not refer to models of the past for such letters as G, R, a and t.

The Erbar and Futura designs were imitated by the other German foundries very quickly, but those two faces, with Kabel, were the ones that were exported and became well known. Futura was for many years the most popular sans-serif type in the United States because it was available for mechanical composition from Intertype under its own name and from Linotype under the name Spartan. In Britain during the 1930s both types were popular with advertising agency typographers, though they lost favour as Gill Sans gained it.

By about 1940, then, the sans-serif types considered to be usable for text setting consisted of two species. One of them was represented by Gill Sans; solely represented, actually, because it seems to have been inimitable. It was much admired in Britain, partly because of the interesting people involved in its creation: Eric Gill himself; Stanley Morison, the most distinguished figure in British typography, who had instigated the design; and Beatrice Warde, who publicised the type (and the people) so skilfully. It may be, too, that the traditionalist strain in the British character responded to the type's air of academic probity and did not object to the slightly mannered effect it presented in text composition. Gill Sans meant nothing to American typographers, and very little to European ones – a state of affairs which Monotype tried to remedy by producing an alternative version of four of its capitals, nine lowercase letters and seven numerals (but not an alternative name) to enable the type to be converted into a close imitation of

ABCDEFGHIJKLMNOPQRSTUVWXYZ
abcdefghijklmnopqrstuvwxyz

ABCDEFGHIJKLMNOPQRSTUVWXYZ
abcdefghijklmnopqrstuvwxyz

1234567890   *1234567890*

Gill Sans transformed.

Futura, which was the chief representative of the other species of sans-serif then current. Just where one's preference lay depended on where one stood. Stanley Morison had expressed his view in a curious way. In a letter to Robert Blake in May 1936 he had described Futura and Kabel as 'romantic', in contrast to the 'common-sense' quality of, and absence of 'trickiness' in, Gill Sans. If he meant 'romantic' as the opposite of 'classical', can the term really be applied to Futura? Gill Sans certainly reflects some characteristics of letter forms of the past, and to that extent it has a classical aspect, in the associative sense of the word. But might not Futura, in which the devices of geometry were employed to create 'pure' shapes, also be called 'classical', in the aesthetic sense of the word? 'Romantic', which implies the imaginative and personal, hardly seems appropriate. On the other hand, if Morison was taking the view that it was not very sensible to design a type according to a theory rather than to tradition, it could be argued that though the genesis of a type is interesting it has nothing to do with its visual quality and its functional efficiency.

Sans-serif faces tend to induce this kind of philosophising about classification, merit, preference and prejudice – considerations which had exercised the mind of Jan Tschichold, another influential figure in typography, a few years before Morison had made his remark.

Tschichold taught typography in Munich from 1926 to 1933, the period when the Bauhaus was active at Dessau. He was keenly interested in the work done by the graphic designers there, and by the typographic work produced elsewhere by El Lissitzky, Piet Zwart and others. He formulated a doctrine of graphic design, firmly non-traditional in its attitude, and expounded it in a book, *Die Neue Typographie*, which was published in 1928. Its statement on type is particularly interesting. 'Amongst all existing type faces only Grotesque fits spiritually into our time . . .'* The phrase 'our time' expresses both the rejection of the artistic conventions of the past and acceptance of the influence of modern science and technology. Tschichold's advocacy of sans-serif as the appropriate style of letter to express the spirit of the time in print was not a mere fancy or fashion; it was a serious and central element in his doctrine, and it consciously elevated the sans-serif from its former utilitarian role to a status at least equal to that of any of the classic seriffed faces.

He went on to speak of the kind of sans-serif he had in mind. 'The existing forms of the Grotesque do not, as yet, entirely satisfy the demands for the perfect type face . . . Most, but especially the latest "artist-designed" Grotesques (e.g. Erbar-Grotesk, Kabel) show modifications which fundamentally put them in the same category as other "designed" type faces (this makes them inferior to the anonymous Grotesques of earlier times) . . . One step in the right direction is the Futura designed by Paul Renner . . .' (That last remark seems to be little more than a politeness; it was Renner who had obtained the Munich teaching post for Tschichold.) Tschichold's rejection of the new 'designer's' types, and his belief that only sans-serifs of an impersonal form were acceptable was demonstrated in the choice of type for the text of *Die Neue Typographie*. It was a plain light-

*Quoted by kind permission of Ruari McLean from his unpublished translation of the work deposited in the St Bride Printing Library.

weight sans-serif which since its origin in about 1909 had become a staple jobbing type in German printing. The *Handbuch der Schriftarten* shows it as being available, under various names, including Akzidenz-Grotesk, from ten different foundries in 1926. And the text of Tschichold's second book, *Eine Stunde Druckgestaltung* (1930), was set in another face of the same kind, the Bauer foundry's Venus, which had been introduced in 1907. I

Hebrew type and its letters
Read the true experiences
LIFE IS EASIER FOR YOU

Venus Light, 1907.
The straight-sided y was replaced by the orthodox form in exported fonts.

think it was not so impersonal as Tschichold wished. Some of the capitals of Venus have interesting similarities with the expressive lettering of C.R.Mackintosh and Josef Hoffmann done a few years before.

An English version of *Eine Stunde Druckgestaltung* appeared in the July 1930 issue of *Commercial Art*, London, as a sort of manifesto for the new typography. Tschichold's view of type was now less dogmatic: '. . . it is permissible to use every traditional and non-traditional face . . .' though he went on, 'Of the available types, the New Typography is most partial to the 'grotesque' or 'block' type . . .' His view was even more relaxed in his third book, the *Typographische Gestaltung*, which was published in 1935 in Switzerland, to where Tschichold had moved when the political climate in Germany had become harshly repressive. That work (the text of which was set in Bodoni, with headings in Trump's City Medium) showed that Tschichold was now willing to use a varied typographic palette; it included the formal 'visiting card' style of script for purposes of contrast, and in regard to sans-serifs did not exclude Futura and Gill Sans – types which he had earlier rejected as possessing unwanted personal characteristics. Indeed, there is even a criticism of the types formerly preferred: 'The old sans-serifs are tiring to read because their letter forms are insufficiently differentiated.'* The book was very influential in Switzerland where, during the later 1930s and early 40s, graphic designers perfected a style of type-and-picture arrangement in which asymmetry, the 'grid', unjustified text and low-voiced headings were the factors of a design formula that produced pages of controlled rectitude. When the Second World War ended in 1945 and people and ideas were again able to circulate, this style of typography – called the 'Swiss' style, to Tschichold's disapproval – was widely adopted by typographers who, I suppose, experienced both a sense of release from conventions that had become stale and a welcome initiation into a new

Part of a poster by Josef Hoffman, Vienna, 1905

*Page 89 of the English-language edition, *Asymmetric Typography*, 1967.

intellectual discipline. Although the sans-serif letter was no longer held to be a fundamental article of the creed it was much favoured for its linear nature. In Britain Gill Sans was popular until about the middle 1950s; but then – perhaps because Swiss typographers had looked back to *Die Neue Typographie* and approved of its severe view of the aesthetics of sans-serif types – typographers developed a taste for two faces that had first been made in Europe in the early years of this century and were then produced by Monotype in the 1920s as Series 215, a face very similar to the medium weight of the Venus type used in Tschichold's second book, and Series 216, its bold companion.

ABCDEFGHIJKLMNOPQRSTUVWXYZ
abcdefghijklmnopqrstuvwxyz 1234567890
ABCDEFGHIJKLMNOPQRSTUVWXYZ
abcdefghijklmnopqrstuvwxyz 1234567890

ABCDEFGHIJKLMNOPQRSTUVWXY
abcdefghijklmnopqrstuvwxyz 12345678
ABCDEFGHIJKLMNOPQRSTUVWXYZ
abcdefghijklmnopqrstuvwxyz 123456789

Monotype Series 215 and 216.

American typographers will recognise them as similar to the various Trade Gothics which at that time were brought out of obscurity and granted the favour that they still enjoy.

These 'industrial' faces, as P. M. Handover usefully called them, form a third species to be added to the two classes of sans-serif already mentioned. The demand for types of this sort was considerable. In 1957 the Haas foundry of Basle stimulated it by redesigning one of their existing Grotesks and issuing it under the name Helvetica. Typographers everywhere developed a consuming appetite for it. Its range of weights and widths was increased; it was adopted by every sort of mechanical and electronic typesetting system; and its popularity became so great that it rivalled the Univers sans-serif, a type of the 'industrial' class but more original and subtle in its modelling than Helvetica and, because its character spacing was properly done, a better performer in text composition.

This essay has attempted no more than a sketch of the course of events that has led to the several species of sans-serif types that are now familiar: the original nineteenth-century grotesques or gothics; the improved version of that style designed since the middle of this century and called neo-grotesque or, as here, 'industrial'; the geometric faces of German source or inspiration; and the humanist sans-serif which draws upon the classic letter forms of the past. Only a few faces have actually been named here, and then only because they are exemplars. In fact, the number of sans-serif types currently available is so considerable that any attempt at a review would certainly be invidious.

The sans-serif letter form is restricted, or apparently so, in the scope it allows the type designer; but that is a challenge that serious designers like to face up to at least once in their lives.

PART II

Some designers
and
their types

A designer's attitude to his or her work is revealed as much in the work itself as in the life, letters and relationships. In the essays that follow, the sketch of the designer's life and times is meant to do no more than indicate the circumstances in which the work was done. The concentration is on the work itself – all the types in the case of Dwiggins and Van Krimpen, a selection only of the work of Goudy and Koch. The intention is to show their motives, and how they responded to the tasks they were given or created for themselves; how they observed the fundamental features of printing types as set out in the first part of this book; and finally, to offer a personal valuation of their achievements.

Although by character and circumstance they had little in common, there are similarities to note. Goudy and Dwiggins each interested themselves in substituting uncial letter forms for some lowercase characters. Dwiggins and Van Krimpen were both influenced by Morison's sloped roman idea. And Van Krimpen and Goudy each acquiesced in the revision of one of their types by another hand.

13: The types of Jan van Krimpen

In his lifetime Jan van Krimpen was one of the most distinguished figures in the world of typography. His designs for books were notable exercises in symmetry and scale, with every detail of type, spacing and choice of material fastidiously organised. He designed a number of books for the Limited Editions Club of New York, and in Europe the classic style and impeccable quality of his typographic work had considerable influence. He was even better known as the designer of the types to be discussed here.

In a thorough evaluation of twentieth-century type designs (should such a thing ever be attempted) the book types designed by Van Krimpen will be difficult to place. All of them display a degree of refinement hardly matched elsewhere, not excluding Gill's Perpetua; and they were much esteemed at their introduction. Yet none of them has achieved full admittance to that select list of types that are known to be effective in the practicalities of everyday printing. The reason is this. Each of the types, when closely examined, has a feature – amounting, in my opinion, to a defect – which has diminished its chance of unqualified welcome into the printer's typographic resources.

The circumstances of Van Krimpen's working life (except for the war years) could hardly have been better. In his youth he had studied art, and he became particularly interested in lettering. From that it was a natural step to typography and the designing of books. In 1923, when he was thirty-one, the firm of Enschedé in Haarlem printed a series of commemorative stamps for which he had drawn the lettering. Impressed by the quality of his work the firm invited him to design a type for them, to be cut and cast in their own foundry. Pleased with the result, Enschedé persuaded Van Krimpen to join their staff, to supervise the design and printing of fine books, to design specimens to demonstrate the firm's remarkable collection of historic types and, in time, to create further new types for them. This was wholly excellent for both of them. Enschedé acquired a person of knowledge, ability and taste. Van Krimpen had a secure and privileged future in one of the oldest and most eminent printing houses in Europe, with an expert punch-cutter in a working type foundry to co-operate with him in the realisation of his type designs. Enschedé benefitted from Van Krimpen's influence on the quality of their work. He had the benefit of their appreciation and encouragement for the thirty-five years he worked for them.

For his first type Van Krimpen began by drawing the text of a poem in roman capitals and lowercase. Enschedé admired the

In August 1861 I wrote another novel for the *Cornhill Magazine*. It was a short story, about one volume in length, and was called *The Struggles of Brown, Jones, and Robinson*. In this I attempted a style for which I certainly was not qualified, and to which I never had again recourse. It was meant to be funny, was full of slang, and was intended as a satire on the ways of trade. Still I think that there is some good fun in it, but I have heard no one else express such an opinion.

A B C D E F G H I J K L M N
O P Q R S T U V W X Y Z
abcdefghijklmnopqrstuvwxyz
12345 fffiflffiffl 67890

A B C D E F G H I J K L M N
O P Q R S T U V W X Y Z
abcdefghijklmnopqrstuvwxyz
12345 fffiflffiffl 67890

Lutetia roman and italic. The original version.

sample, and Van Krimpen then proceeded to design the full set of roman characters. His letter drawings were ready by the middle of 1924, and he went on to draw the italic. The type was made first in the 16 point size and was used in a book produced for an exhibition in Paris in 1925: hence its name, Lutetia (the Roman name for Paris).

In Britain the roman was reviewed in *The Fleuron* v in 1926 by Stanley Morison. He observed that the type was not derived from any historic predecessor or school, that the designer 'has kept himself free from current English, German or American fashions' (were there any?) and that the 'design is an exceedingly handsome one, its proportions . . . most agreeable'. He did not care for the e with the sloping bar, and would be pleased if the E could be reduced a little in width. But he clearly regarded it as a remarkably fine design. During the next two years the Enschedé foundry completed seven sizes of roman capitals and lowercase, three of titling capitals, and five sizes of italic (some of the punches being cut in Germany). They were shown in an inset in *The Fleuron* vi in 1928, and this time the italic was reviewed. It was noted to be a true 'chancery' letter, and the most legible of its kind so far; but the reviewer made the comment that it is 'so good in itself that it cannot combine, with the proper self-effacement, with its roman'. (Presumably by 'good' he meant 'distinctive' or 'expressive'.) The *Fleuron* inset shows some of the swash alternative letters made for the italic; and it must be said that they prettify the text only at the expense of comfortable reading. Swash letters were made for the roman, too; they can be seen in the Enschedé specimen books of 1930 and 1932. Many years later, when Van Krimpen wrote a survey of his type designs for The Typophiles, he had changed his mind, and expressed disapproval of such extraneous aids to elegance.

There was wide but not unqualified admiration for the Lutetia design. Oliver Simon, who visited Holland in 1928 and met Van Krimpen, ordered Lutetia for the Curwen Press. In America the Grabhorn Press installed the type and used it frequently, though when they tried the 18 point size for an edition of *Leaves of Grass* they found the face (not surprisingly) unsuitable for Whitman's reverberant verse. Another distinguished printer who changed his mind was Alexander Stols of Maastricht. The *Book Collector's Quarterly* for July–September 1934 noted that having composed Holbrook Jackson's *Maxims on Reading* in Lutetia, Stols disliked the result and re-set the book in De Roos's Erasmus Medieval – a type whose 'system of ornamentation' had been criticised by Van Krimpen in *The Fleuron* vii as 'rather tiresome'. The Merrymount Press had Lutetia but used it sparingly; Updike preferred a limited typographic palette. Bruce Rogers used the 18 point for Frederic Kenyon's *Ancient Books and Modern Discoveries* in 1927; but he did not care for the lowercase e, m and n, and substituted for them the letters from a font of Caslon, as noted by William Glick. This 'improving' of Lutetia was carried further by another hand.

Porter Garnett, an expert in printing, had been in charge of the Laboratory Press at the Carnegie Institute of Technology in Pittsburg since 1923. The Press was awarded the task of designing the catalogue of the Frick art collection, a monumental work of great prestige. In 1928 Garnett visited Van Krimpen to say that he wanted to use Lutetia for the work, but would Van Krimpen agree to certain characters being redesigned? His published reason was 'to amend such characters as seem to fall short of perfection'. He may have had another reason: to tell the governing body of the Frick collection that the type to be used in the printing of the catalogue would be, in a sense, original. Van Krimpen willingly agreed to the changes because, as he wrote nearly thirty years later, they accorded with the changes he would have made himself if it had been possible to do so.

Irascimini, et nolite peccare: quæ
dicitis in cordibus vestris, in cubilibus vestris compungimini. Sacrificate sacrificium iustitiæ, et sperate
in Domino. Multi dicunt: Quis
ostendit nobis bona? Signatum est
super nos lumen vultus tui Domine: dedisti lætitiam in corde meo.
A fructu frumenti, vini, et olei sui
multiplicati sunt. In pace in idip-
sum dormiam, et requiescam; Quoniam tu Domine singulariter in spe
constituisti me.

CC EE FF GG LL QQ
ee hh ii jj mm nn ss 88
?? !! .. ,, ;; :: () () -- " " [] []

Lutetia roman: the revised characters.

A study of the revisions is instructive. The e with the level bar is
more appropriate for this type, which owes nothing to Jenson. (It
was the only one of the changes to be adopted by Enschedé for
their own use of the type.) The wider h, m and n are in better
balance with o and other round letters. The new s, though, is too
narrow. In the i and j the dot, which was too small and isolated in
the original (even more so than in Bruce Rogers' Centaur), is in
better relationship with the stroke. The stronger punctuation
marks are more effective. Instead of revising the figure 8 it would
have been better to increase the width of the 2, 3, 4 and 5, which
are oddly cramped. The short-tailed Q was less likely to suffer
breakage than the elegant original. The shorter vertical in G was
evidently to Van Krimpen's taste; it appears in all his later designs. The revised C seems hardly different from the first version.
The changes in E and F are particularly interesting. The excessive
width which Morison had noticed, and the high middle bar, had
not been a feature of Van Krimpen's drawn lettering; but they
were characteristic of De Roos's types, which Van Krimpen
knew well (for that matter, they appear in several of Goudy's
early faces). The Garnett versions are certainly better.

Most of the revisions are distinct improvements, elevating a
good roman into a positively distinguished one. It is a pity that it

was not found possible to incorporate them into the standard Lutetia fonts, especially when Monotype, by arrangement with Enschedé, began to produce the face in 1928. When the completing of the printing of the Frick catalogue was taken on by the Thistle Press of New York about 1945 the proprietors offered to release the revised sorts for general use. Van Krimpen declined the offer, believing that by that time it would have caused confusion to introduce alternative characters.

In any case, the italic remains a problem. It was not a good working companion for the roman: too narrow, too dazzling and too dark. Van Krimpen said he took a long time to decide whether to design the face as a conventional italic or as a chancery letter. This suggests that he was thinking of it as a separate entity, and that he had not grasped the fact that an italic intended for use as a secondary letter can be successfully designed only by first trying out groups of tentative letters within a sample passage of the roman, with harmony of style, proportion and weight as the object to be achieved. But the empirical attitude and the practical method were not, it seems, Van Krimpen's way – either then, when he was without experience in type designing, or later, when the lesson should have been learnt.

To the growing number of people who were taking an interest in typography at that time, Lutetia was clearly unlike the recently revived Garamonds, the ubiquitous Caslon, and the familiar old styles and moderns. It was original, yet it was refined and unassertive. It made Van Krimpen's reputation as a type designer, and the types he created during the following twenty years were received with the greatest respect.

Mention should be made here of the attractive decorative alphabet produced by P.H.Raedisch, the punch-cutter in the Enschedé type foundry (one of the last of that ancient craft), by engraving a white line in the 36 and 48 point sizes of Lutetia

ABCDEFGHIJK
LMNOPQURS
TVWXYZ

Lutetia Open.

capitals, under Van Krimpen's direction. And there was also the Greek type, called Antigone, which Van Krimpen designed in 1927 as the first part of a scheme to create a complete set of characters and symbols for mathematical text books. In the event only the alphabets were produced. The capital delta and ksi look too large and the phi too small. But these are minor faults; the Antigone type is one of the best of Van Krimpen's designs. The

οὐ βραδύνει κύριος τῆς ἐπαγ-
γελίας, ὥς τινες βραδυτῆτα ἡγο-
ῦνται, ἀλλὰ μακροθυμεῖ εἰς ὑμᾶς,
μὴ βουλόμενός τινας ἀπολέσθαι
ἀλλὰ πάντας εἰς μετάνοιαν χω-
ρῆσαι. Ἥξει δὲ ἡμέρα κυρίου ὡς
κλέπτης, ἐν ᾗ οἱ οὐρανοὶ ῥοιζηδὸν

Α Β Γ Δ Ε Ζ Η Θ Ι Κ Λ Μ Ν
Ξ Ο Π Σ Τ Υ Φ Χ Ψ Ω

αβγδεζηθικλμνξοπρσςτυφχψω

Antigone Greek.

ABCDEFGHIJ

KLMNOPQRSTU

VWXYZ

ΓΔΘΛΞΠΣΦΥΩ

Open capitals, roman and Greek.

lowercase is distinctly calligraphic, so the type is nearer to Wiegand's type for the Bremer Presse of 1923 than to Scholderer's New Hellenic face of 1926; it is better suited to literary than to mathematical texts. To work with the Antigone Van Krimpen added ten Greek letters to the handsome set of open capitals he had already designed for use in title lines.

The house of Enschedé possesses a remarkable collection of punches and matrices. Many of them were acquired by purchase during the eighteenth century. Others were created by punch-cutters who worked for them, including Fleischman and Rosart.

Amongst the collection there had been a roman and italic
attributed to Christoffel van Dijck, 'greatest of Dutch letter cut-
ters', as Harry Carter described him. The faces were included in a
type specimen book issued by Enschedé in 1768, but only the
punches and matrices of the italic had survived, in the 16 point
size only. It was decided to create a roman to work with the italic.
It is not clear who made the decision. Van Krimpen himself,
writing in 1957, said that he had never been in favour of the
copying or adapting of historic type faces. If that had been his
view in 1928 he was probably in no position to oppose the plan.

There is only one way to accomplish such a task easily and
successfully. It is to use the method suggested by Emery Walker
and adopted by William Morris for his Golden type and by Bruce
Rogers for his Centaur: that is, to make bleached-out photographic enlargements of passages from books composed in the
type to be imitated, to paint over the characters, modifying them
as little or as much as seems desirable, and to give the resulting
collection of enlarged characters to the punch-cutter. Photographic enlargements of the Van Dijck roman were indeed
studied by Van Krimpen, but he did not work over them. Instead,
he *drew* a roman – and did little more than retain the proportions
and some of the features of the original. The result, as could
surely have been predicted, was a roman which, as a companion
for the existing Van Dijck italic, was 'a distinct failure', as Van
Krimpen frankly admitted. Considered by itself, the Romanée
roman has great merit. Except for the w and y, which are rather
cramped, the lowercase letters are in better proportion to each
other than in the original version of Lutetia. This second type is
therefore an advance on the first. This may be due to the influence
of the Porter Garnett revisions of Lutetia; but that cannot be said
of the punctuations and the dots on i and j, which are too light to
be effective. The r and g look well enough, though they have been
criticised by others. The ligatures are excellent (they were not
always so in Van Krimpen's types). The numerals are the best he
ever designed. The capitals, always his strong point, are very fine,
except for W, which is a little obtrusive. In all the characters the
thin strokes are fairly firm – no doubt because the designer was
attending to a model, the print of the lost seventeenth-century
roman. The reviewer in *The Fleuron* vii said, 'The general form,
proportion and relation of upper to lowercase remind us of
the Bembo . . .' This is going a little high – Romanée is rather
bland in comparison with Bembo – but the type is certainly a distinguished design, and it makes a fine effect in the text of
Typefoundries in the Netherlands (1978), Harry Carter's edition
of Charles Enschedé's great work. It is ironic that when about ten
years later the Monotype Corporation decided to make their own
version of the missing roman (Van Dijck Series 203), it was Van
Krimpen who, doubting now that the roman and italic in the old

Romanée is shown overleaf.

In August 1861 I wrote another novel for the
Cornhill Magazine. It was a short story, about
one volume in length, and was called *The
Struggles of Brown, Jones, and Robinson*. In this I
attempted a style for which I certainly was
not qualified, and to which I never again
had recourse. It was meant to be funny, was
full of slang, and was intended as a satire on
the ways of trade. Still I think that there is
some good fun in it, but I have heard no one
else express such an opinion.

A B C D E F G H I J K L M N
O P Q R S T U V W X Y Z
abcdefghijklmnopqrstuvwxyz
12345 ff fi fl ffi ffl 67890

abcdefghijklmnopqrstuvwxyz
12345 ff fi fl ffl ffi 67890

Romanée roman and italic.

Enschedé specimen book were by the same hand, discovered an
edition of Ovid, printed in 1671, in which the Enschedé italic
could be seen, with a roman which Van Krimpen judged to be a
true relation to it.

In spite of the lack of harmony between the Romanée roman
and the original Van Dijck italic four sizes of the roman were cut,
and it was the existence of these, and the fact that the Van Dijck
italic remained in only one size, that made Van Krimpen, twenty
years later, decide to create a new italic to work with his roman.
To keep these notes in historical sequence a comment on that
See page 117. italic is given at the end of this survey.

After the Romanée roman there was an interval until 1932, when
Van Krimpen conceived the idea of a family of types for book
printing, to comprise a roman, an italic, a script type, bold and
condensed romans, at least four weights of sans-serif, a Greek,
and possibly more – all to be related in style and consistent in
alignment. He was therefore intending to create a larger family of
types than had Lucian Bernhard, whose roman, italic and related
script had been remarked upon by Morison two years before, in
The Fleuron vii.

In August 1861 I wrote another novel for the *Cornhill Magazine*. It was a short story about one volume in length, and it was called *The Struggles of Brown, Jones, and Robinson*. In this I attempted a style for which I certainly was not qualified, and to which I never had again recourse. It was meant to be funny, was full of slang, and was intended as a satire on the ways of trade. Still I think that there is some good fun in it, but I have heard no one else express such an opinion.

ABCDEFGHIJKLMN
OPQRSTUVWXYZ
abcdefghijklmnopqrstuvwxyz
12345 fffiflffiffl 67890

ABCDEFGHIJKLMN
OPQRSTUVWXYZ
abcdefghijklmnopqrstuvwxyz
12345 fffiflffiffl 67890

Romulus roman and italic.

In his account of his designs Van Krimpen remarked that Romulus, as the new roman was called, was related to Lutetia. 'The lowercase of Lutetia being on the whole on the narrow side, it was to be expected that Romulus should be wider . . . A number of the capitals of Lutetia were, against the classical Roman tradition, too wide . . . their width has been reduced . . .' As letter shapes the alphabets of Romulus are exemplary. They are most satisfying in the display sizes; less so in the text sizes, where the limited contrast between the thick and thin strokes makes the face look rather lifeless.

The 'italic' was a departure from historical practice. The doctrine propounded by Stanley Morison in 1926 in *The Fleuron* v, that the logical form for the auxiliary face to a roman was a sloped roman, seemed at the time a revelation of truth, and it was taken seriously. Van Krimpen accepted the theory, though he was aware that Morison himself had not only been obliged to allow the introduction of a few informal letter forms into the 'italic' of Perpetua but had evidently thought that a traditional italic was the only kind that would be tolerated in the Times Roman newspaper type made under his supervision in 1931–2.

Van Krimpen began to draw the Romulus sloped roman in the autumn of 1932, though the face was not made until late in 1936. The width of the letters is very similar to that of the roman, and all the letters without exception follow the roman shape – though the t lost most of its crossbar. After it was introduced, reviewed and tested in the field Morison and Van Krimpen decided that the doctrine of the sloped roman was not valid. But there is no evidence of any later attempt to modify the monotony of the Romulus sloped roman by substituting an informal form of a, e and g, as had been done in the Perpetua italic – though there is an alternative italic-style f in the Monotype version. Van Krimpen would probably not have agreed to such a compromise with principle. In any case, he was much occupied with, and no doubt investing great hope in, the script type that, according to plan, was to be the third member of the Romulus family.

Van Krimpen had evidently discussed the script in correspondence with Morison, who, in August 1932, offered the suggestion that the scriptorial quality ought to manifest itself in the first and last letters of the words (that is, in swash letters), and in the capitals; and the script should possess both cursive and formal qualities. In fact, it should be a *cancelleresca bastarda* – and that was the name adopted for the type.

In the full Cancelleresca font there are indeed swash and other alternative characters – more than a hundred of them; and a number of the regular capitals do have an informal, though not particularly calligraphic, treatment of the serifs. It is the lower-case that contains most interest. The curves are much rounder than those in the Lutetia italic and so they bring the characters nearer to the kind of italic letter forms which work best with roman. The ascenders and descenders, though, are another thing: noticeably long and, in the case of the f, obtrusive and distracting. The type has been described as 'beautiful' and 'entrancingly graceful', and it has been favoured by a number of eminent printers for books intended for collectors. Used as Vicentino did with a similar type in the early part of the sixteenth century, in select books of verse designed as objects of beauty, the type makes a stylish effect; but for my taste it is mannered and pretty rather than beautiful, lacking the vigour of the Blado chancery italic revived by Monotype in 1923 – and, for that matter, Van Krimpen's own handwriting. Twenty years after its introduction Van Krimpen expressed disapproval of the exercise – not of the principle of *cancelleresca* as the third companion to a roman, but to the technical basis he had devised for its design and manufacture.

To furnish the script with the extra-long ascender and descender strokes he thought desirable he decided to place the face on a body one-quarter larger than that of the corresponding face size of the Romulus roman. Thus for 16 point roman the appropriate size of Cancelleresca would be 20 point, and for 8 point roman it would be 10 point. A one-quarter increase of 12 point would result in 15 point, an 'unnatural' size, so the Cancelleresca to work with 12 point would be cast on 16 point body. Those three sizes were therefore produced in the Enschedé foundry

Cancelleresca Bastarda.

according to that plan. But the plan would not work for the important 10 point size, the one-quarter increase of which results in $12\frac{1}{2}$ point. Since 13 point was out of the question and 14 point was not a popular size in Holland at that time, the 10 point Romulus could not be given a Cancelleresca companion. Van Krimpen came to regard this as a serious flaw in the plan, in which he and Morison (who had presumably approved it) were culpable. And he also expressed doubts about the rectitude of such a wealth of swash and ligatured items, which gave the type too 'playful' and personal a character. Perhaps he had realised too that to set Romulus roman and Cancelleresca in the same line the compositor would have had to add compensating spacing material above and below the roman words – a tiresome business for more than a few lines. Alternatively, a font of roman would have to be cast on the Cancelleresca body size, at due expense. In fact, as designed the Cancelleresca could only function as an individual face, not as a fully versatile member of the Romulus family. The practicalities of metal typesetting defeated an artistic ideal.

It is not possible to say much in favour of the other members of the family. The Semi-bold sprawls in a most ungainly way. The Semi-bold Condensed is a better design; the letters balance well with each other, and the fitting is correctly related to the character widths. But it is difficult to understand its purpose. It could hardly be used as a mate for any other member of the family; and that, after all, was the object of the scheme – as was emphasised in the rationale of the Romulus Greek. Van Krimpen thought highly of the principles that governed the design of this Greek,

Irascimini, et nolite peccare: quæ dicitis in cordibus vestris, in cubilibus vestris compungimini. Sacrificate sacrificium iustitiæ, et sperate in Domino. Multi dicunt: Quis ostendit nobis bona? Signatum est super nos lumen vultus tui Domine:

A B C D E F G H I J K L M N O P
Q R S T U V W X Y Z

abcdefghijklmnopqrstuvwxyz
12345 ffffiffllfifl 67890

Romulus Semi-bold.

In finem in carminibus; Psalmus David: Cum invocarem exaudivit me Deus iustitiæ meæ: in tribulatione dilatasti mihi: Miserere mei, et exaudi orationem meam: Filii hominum usquequo gravi corde? ut quid diligitis vanitatem, et quæritis mendacium? Et scitote quoniam mirificavit Dominus sanctum suum: Dominus exaudiet me cum

A B C D E F G H I J K L M N O P Q R
S T U V W X Y Z

abcdefghijklmnopqrstuvwxyz
12345 ffffifflfifl 67890

Romulus Semi-bold Condensed.

even if he was not finally satisfied with some of the character shapes. His ruling principle was that between the roman and the Greek there should be as little differentiation as possible. (An echo of the sloped-roman fallacy.) He decided that not only should the Greek be upright and the lowercase equipped with serifs, but letters such as lowercase zeta, kappa and nu should be similar to or even identical with letter shapes in the roman. It is a fallacy. In the very book in which Van Krimpen is explaining this – the account of his types that he wrote for The Typophiles – the occasional phrases in French and Latin are in italic, in accordance with the traditional and sensible custom of providing the reader with a visual signal of the sudden change of language. And the same should apply to Greek. To make Greek letters look like roman, and to give the lowercase zeta and ksi unfamiliar forms

on the ground that all calligraphic characteristics must be
eliminated, is to assume that letters can be reformed by 'logic'; in
short, it is to allow theory to overset practical sense. (Eric Gill
had followed the same cul-de-sac in designing his own Greek

Α Β Γ Δ Ε Ζ Η Θ Ι Κ Λ Μ Ν Ξ Ο Π Ρ Σ
Τ Υ Φ Χ Ψ Ω
A B C D E F G H I J K L M N O P Q R
S T U V W X Y Z

αβγδεζηθικλμνξοπρϛστυφχψω
abcdefghijklmnopqrstuvwxyz
fb ff ffi ffl fl fh fi fk fl
1234567890

ου βραδυνει κυριος της επαγγελιας, ως τινες βρα-
Non tardat Dominus promissionem suam, sicut
δυτητα ηγουνται, αλλα μακροθυμει εις υμας, μη
quidam existimant: sed patienter agit propter vos,
βουλομενος τινας απολεσθαι αλλα παντας εις μετα-
nolens aliquos perire, sed omnes ad pœnitentiam
νοιαν χωρησαι. Ηξει δε ημερα κυριου ως κλεπτης,
reverti. Adveniet autem dies Domini ut fur: in quo
εν η οι ουρανοι ροιζηδον παρελευσονται, στοιχεια
cæli magno impetu transient, elementa vero calore
δε καυσουμενα λυθησεται, και γη και τα εν αυτη
solventur, terra autem et quæ in ipsa sunt opera,
εργα ευρεθησεται.
exurentur.

Romulus Greek with roman.

type.) It would have been much more in accord with Van
Krimpen's original plan if he had designed an upright Greek, in
familiar style, with an italic Greek as a companion. The printer
would have been well served. For a Greek phrase interpolated
into a text in, say, English, he would use the italic Greek. For a
Greek text book the upright version would be used, with the italic
in a secondary role; and the other-language commentary, which
is usually in a separate paragraph, would be set in roman or italic
as required by clarity or emphasis. As it is, Romulus Greek mixed
with Romulus roman does not harmonise with it; it becomes
confused with it.

There remain the sans-serif members of the family. Punches
and matrices were made in 12 point in the Enschedé foundry.
Specimen settings of the four weights make it clear that the work
was terminated at an early stage of experiment. The light face
made a better effect than the others; but criticism now would be
unjust. If the work had proceeded Van Krimpen might have seen
the need to increase the height of the lowercase in all the versions
– slightly in the light weight, considerably in the heaviest, and
proportionately in the middle weights. This would have made it

See overleaf.

possible to enlarge the interior spaces in the bold lowercase. And no doubt he would have adjusted the weight of the capitals.

ABCDEFGHIJKLMNOPQRSTUVWXYZ
abcdefghijklmnopqrstuvwxyz
12345 fbffffifflfifhfkfl 67890

ABCDEFGHIJKLMNOPQRSTUVWXYZ
abcdefghijklmnopqrstuvwxyz
12345 fbffffifflfhfifkfl 67890

ABCDEFGHIJKLMNOPQRSTUVWXYZ
abcdefghijklmnopqrstuvwxyz
12345 fbffffifflfhfk 67890

ABCDEFGHIJKLMNOPQRSTUVWXYZ
abcdefghijklmnopqrstuvwxyz
12345 fbffffifflfhfk 67890

Romulus sans-serif faces: light, normal, semi-bold, bold.

ABCDEFGHIJK
LMNOPQRS
TUVWXYZ

Romulus Open.

Not long before his retirement in 1956 Raedisch engraved a white line in the large sizes of Romulus roman capitals, under Van Krimpen's direction. In the Lutetia Open the white line had been cut through the edges of the letters. In the Romulus Open the profiles are intact. Van Krimpen said the effect pleased him more.

About his Haarlemmer type of 1938, which was to be a private type for the printing of a Bible for an association of bibliophiles in Holland, Van Krimpen's book has nothing to say. I think the design had more promise than John Dreyfus's account of it suggests. Apart from an awkward W, due to an existing machine layout, there were no disturbing letter shapes. Certainly the narrow h, n, u and rather wide o and c were out of proportion and needed revision; and if the italic lowercase could have been made a little narrower it would have seemed to gain weight and would have harmonised better with the roman. The design would then have become an effective book type. But circum-

Gutenberg equipped the scholar with the accuracy of type. Prejudiced connoisseurs in the fifteenth century deplored the new mass-production of books, but men of letters eagerly hailed the *The invention of Printing from* THE INVENTION OF PRINT

Haarlemmer, Series 531.
By courtesy of the Monotype Corporation Ltd.

stances were against it. With the threat of war in Europe the bible project was abandoned, and the Haarlemmer type with it. The distinct contrast between its thick and thin strokes and the markedly oblique stress in its curves were to be fully realised in the later Spectrum face.

The war and the occupation of Holland by an enemy did not stop all creative endeavour. Like Haarlemmer, Spectrum was intended to be a private type for the publishing house of that name, to be used first for the composition of a Bible and later for other publications, as soon as Monotype were able to produce a series of sizes. The type was designed in the period 1941–43, and trial alphabets were cut and cast in 14 point in the Enschedé foundry. In the event, the Spectrum company relinquished its rights in the design to Enschedé who, in 1950, arranged with Monotype that a range of sizes should be developed jointly for general distribution.

The differences between the roman of Spectrum and Van Krimpen's earlier romans are plain to see: the x-height is larger and there is greater contrast between the main and thin strokes. The tops of the arches in m and n are sharply defined, and the upper serifs in those and other letters are wedge-shaped. The effect is crisp and positive, like that of seventeenth-century book types; indeed, the face seems to have some of the characteristics of the old style type cut by Hendrik Claesz which is in the Enschedé collection.

The italic is a distinguished design in itself, but it does not quite harmonise with the roman, being too narrow and a little too heavy compared with the broad-countered roman. A foreign phrase or a longish book title in a page of Spectrum becomes over-emphatic and the texture of the page becomes patchy.

Spectrum is the most practical of Van Krimpen's book types because it has proved itself suitable for a fair range of work in

In August 1861 I wrote another novel for the *Cornhill Magazine*. It was a short story, about one volume in length, and was called *The Struggles of Brown, Jones, and Robinson*. In this I attempted a style for which I certainly was not qualified, and to which I never had again recourse. It was meant to be funny, was full of slang, and was intended as a satire on the ways of trade. Still I think that there is some good fun in it, but I have heard no one else express such an opinion.

A B C D E F G H I J K L M N
O P Q R S T V W X Y Z
abcdefghijklmnopqrstuvwxyz
12345 ff fi fl ffi ffl 67890

*A B C D E F G H I J K L M N
O P Q R S T U V W X Y Z
abcdefghijklmnopqrstuvwxyz
12345 ff fi fl ffi ffl 67890*

Spectrum roman and italic.

general publishing. But it is not without faults. The f ligatures are too narrow (the fact that the letters are tied at the top is no reason for reducing the space between the uprights). That can be tolerated. So can the narrow cross-over W – though it is not so easy to accept it in the italic. It is the non-lining numerals which are hard to take – cramped and diminished, looking as though they belong to a type two sizes smaller. Van Krimpen gave no explanation for this curious departure from normal proportion. It was certainly not an accident: the numerals were included on his original drawing of the lowercase alphabet. An alternative set of numerals, in natural scale with the lowercase, is certainly desirable.

The Sheldon design was Van Krimpen's response to a commission from the University Press at Oxford in 1947 for a type to be made in 7 point and used for the composition of an octavo Bible, the text to be in two columns. He decided to make the lowercase unusually large and to centre it on the body, shortening the descenders and ascenders considerably. This, he thought,

CHAPTER 1

THE words of the Preacher, the son of David, king in Jerusalem.
2 Vanity of vanities, saith the Preacher, vanity of vanities; all is vanity.
3 What profit hath a man of all his labour which he taketh under the sun?
4 One generation passeth away, and another generation cometh: but the earth abideth for ever.
5 The sun also ariseth, and the sun goeth down, and hasteth to his place where he arose.
6 The wind goeth toward the south, and turneth about unto the north; it whirleth about continually, and the wind returneth again according to his circuits.
7 All the rivers run into the sea; yet the sea is not full; unto the place from whence the rivers come, thither they return again.
8 All things are full of labour; man cannot utter it: the eye is not satisfied with seeing, nor the ear filled with hearing.

have been before me in Jerusalem: yea, my heart had great experience of wisdom and knowledge.
17 And I gave my heart to know wisdom, and to know madness and folly: I perceived that this also is vexation of spirit.
18 For in much wisdom is much grief: and he that increaseth knowledge increaseth sorrow.

CHAPTER 2

I SAID in mine heart, Go to now, I will prove thee with mirth, therefore enjoy pleasure: and, behold, this also is vanity.
2 I said of laughter, It is mad: and of mirth, What doeth it?
3 I sought in mine heart to give myself unto wine, yet acquainting mine heart with wisdom; and to lay hold on folly, till I might see what was that good for the sons of men, which they should do under the heaven all the days of their life.
4 I made me great works; I builded me houses; I planted me vineyards:

Sheldon roman and italic.

By courtesy of the University Press, Oxford.

was better than reducing the descenders only. With some personal experience of designing types much smaller than 7 point I can assert with some confidence that Van Krimpen was wrong in his premise. The channel of white between lines of type is an indispensible aid to the reader's eye in its traverse across the page or column. The channel is composed of the space below the letter m in line 1 and above the m in line 2. If the lowercase letters are enlarged too much the reduction of the channel width will be detrimental to the reading process; and in a fairly narrow column the space between the lines may even be less than the average space between the words, still further disturbing the texture of the setting. Paradoxically, Sheldon would be easier to read if the lowercase letters were a little smaller.

The unnatural shortness of the ascenders is another reason why the Sheldon type is less effective than Van Krimpen intended. Ascenders are more important than descenders to the reader's comprehension of the text. The letters g, p and q may have their descenders shortened and yet not be confused with other letters; j and y with shortened descenders can be prevented from looking like i and v by careful designing; but the ascender parts of h and l are essential to their identity and cannot be reduced without seriously affecting their natural appearance and that of the words in which they occur.

The italic which Van Krimpen designed in 1949 as a companion See page 108. for the Romanée roman is not entirely satisfactory in that role. As he wrote himself: 'I am afraid that, despite the fact that the roman and italic are undeniably by the same hand, the distance of twenty years between the coming into existence of the one and the other in a way tells.' (His English is awkward but the meaning is clear enough.) Once again the contrast in colour and texture between the generous roman and the narrow italic is too great.

But in itself this italic is a notable design; it is so nearly upright (the angle is only 4 degrees) that it was thought possible to dispense with italic capitals, the roman being used instead. In fact, if the lowercase were not so narrow the roman capitals would work better than they do. As it is, the generous width of the capitals makes them too prominent in an italic text. And because the lowercase letters are so narrow the descender strokes seem excessively long; the f sometimes has the momentary effect of an opening bracket.

The Romanée italic was the last of Van Krimpen's types to be completed, though it was not his last essay in the designing of type. Shortly before his sudden death in 1958 he had started a design for use in a photo-typesetting machine. Since the design, when completed, would have been photographically transferred to the font disc, one wonders how Van Krimpen would have judged the outcome, in view of his stated belief that the punch-cutter Raedisch had always made an essential contribution to the appearance of his type faces. In a review of Raedisch's autobiography, Willem Ovink referred to the value to Morison, Mardersteig and Van Krimpen of the skills of the punch-cutters Plumet, Malin and Raedisch.

'Working with an interpreting reproductive craftsman suited Van Krimpen and his friends: it was easy, relaxing and stimulating. Easy because they did not have to keep making new sets of drawings; it was relaxing to be able to escape from the desk and drawing board to the restful company of the solitary craftsman and sit there for hours at a time, talking as creative artist to executant; it was stimulating because the type-cutter's technical questions forced the designer to become aware of and to formulate his motives, intentions and perceptions, so that perhaps ideas also came to him more easily than when he judged the results on his own'.

Precisely what, and how much, Raedisch contributed to the work is not clear. Van Krimpen's drawings were immaculate and unambiguous. It is unlikely that there were any deficiencies that Raedisch had to make good. It is more likely that Raedisch was so skilful in making a perfect copy on steel of the character on the drawing, without any deviation, that his contribution was to Van Krimpen's peace of mind rather than to the designs themselves. That is speculation, merely; Van Krimpen gives us no detail. Indeed, his writings in the last four years of his life are not very informative as to his ideas about type design in relation to what is actually printed and how it is read. He provides little evidence that he thought of himself as a contributor to the everyday realities of printing. About his 'motives, intentions and perceptions', to use Ovink's words, speculation seems necessary.

It was probably Stanley Morison who wrote the review of the

Lutetia italic in *The Fleuron* vi in 1928.* He began by referring to the roman, observing that it was 'in no recognisable way purloined from ancient times but instead rose freshly from the reasoned canons of type design'. The first part of that is acceptable; indeed, it can be applied to all of Van Krimpen's roman types. They certainly stand apart from the ranks of historical types from Aldus to Fournier (to say nothing of Firmin Didot), and they are visibly different from the faces designed by such contemporaries of Van Krimpen as Mardersteig, Dwiggins and Ruzicka, whose types are all in the mainstream of typographic letter forms. Only Gill's Perpetua, perhaps, prevents Van Krimpen's types from being *sui generis*.

The second part of Morison's statement is harder to accept. 'The reasoned canons of type design' implies that Van Krimpen had thought thoroughly about the requirements of particular kinds of printing and about the nature and purpose of type; had identified certain principles of design; and had then proceeded to the act of creation. It is no disrespect to Morison (after all, in 1928 his own venture in type designing was yet to come) to suggest that things were otherwise: that Van Krimpen's view of printing was a narrow one, that he had an incomplete understanding of the function of type, and that he worked not from a set of considered principles but from a single ideal. Most designers draw upon their knowledge of type designs of the past and present and approach the task of creating a new type face with an array of typographic referents in mind, and a consciousness of the circumstances in which the type will have to function. It is hard to believe that Van Krimpen worked like that. On the evidence of the types themselves it seems reasonable to suppose that, in spite of his presence in a great printing house, his considerable knowledge of historical type faces, and his experience as a book designer, Van Krimpen was not ruled by the designer's sense of 'fitness for purpose' when he was designing a type. Instead, his habit of thought was that of the classicist, the man with a vision of the perfect. His ideal letters were the Roman inscriptional capital with a lowercase designed to match; and his criteria were restraint, dignity and beauty of form. (It cannot be an accident that, referring to the capitals of Lutetia, he spoke of the 'classical Roman tradition'.) From this idealistic standpoint it would not have occurred to him that there is a difference between drawing the lettering for a monumental inscription and drawing an alphabet for a printing type; that is to say, he would not have perceived that one is an end in itself, the other a means to an end.

An overall view of his designs seems to support this hypothesis. To begin with, compared with other type designs his range was

*It does not actually say so in John Carter's *Handlist of the Writings of Stanley Morison* (Cambridge, 1950) or in his *Additions and Corrections* in *Motif* 3 (London, 1959).

unusually limited: his four roman text types, Lutetia, Romanée, Romulus and Spectrum, are remarkably similar in style. It is as though he carried in his mind an image of a single perfect alphabet, the quintessence of letters, and could do no other than produce a representation of it on each occasion – even when, as in Romanée, a particular model was in view and the task was specified. Only in the Spectrum roman, a late work, is there any sign that Van Krimpen had added to his vision an awareness of typographic characteristics; but the awareness is not very obvious.

The hypothesis holds good for his italic types, too. His ideal was evidently the written chancery hand of Arrighi and other masters of calligraphy of the early sixteenth century, to the exclusion of later typographic models. If this were not so, if he had shown equal willingness to take the italic types of, say, Granjon or Fournier as exemplars, he would have worked as they did, from a practical standpoint, fully aware of the need to make his italics true secondary faces, subservient to and thoroughly harmonious with his romans. But the italics for Lutetia, Romanée and Spectrum, and the Cancelleresca Bastarda that was intended to work with Romulus, show that, whatever he thought he was doing, he was actually concentrating single-mindedly on the design of a perfect alphabet in the chancery mode, and was probably oblivious to external considerations.

In short, Van Krimpen thought like an artist, not like a designer. He worked from an inner vision, not from a broad view of practical realities and requirements. That is not the best frame of mind (indeed, it is not the right one) in which to create something which is to function in a variety of texts to the full satisfaction of publisher and reader. In Van Krimpen's case the attitude produced, in my opinion, type faces that, though not wholly adequate in the functional sense, are, as letter designs *per se* (especially the capitals), unequalled as representations of classic letter forms in print. That is their significance in the history of type design. And it is also the reason why a close study of them is essential for anyone who aspires to a clear understanding of something that Van Krimpen seems not to have appreciated: the crucial difference between art, visual expression as an end in itself, and design, the creation of something to serve a practical function.

14: Some types by Frederic Goudy

'Van Krimpen's work as a book designer was more influential than his work as a type designer.' Thus the obituary in *The Times* of 21 October 1958, the day after Van Krimpen's death. True, no doubt; but it seems that one of his types had once had an influence on another worker in the field.

In Frederic Goudy's *A Half-Century of Type Design and Typography*, he says of his Deepdene type: 'This year (1927) was a prolific one for me. I find that I was working on six different designs. For one of them I began drawings of a type suggested by a Dutch type which had just been introduced into this country; but as with some of my previous designs, I soon got away from my exemplar to follow a line of my own.'

That passage was quoted in one of Paul Bennett's contributions to *Books and Printing*, with the phrase 'the Lutetia of Van Krimpen' interpolated after 'Dutch type'. No doubt Bennett had good reason to know that Goudy was indeed referring to Lutetia and not, say, to De Roos's Erasmus Medieval, which had been introduced in Holland three years before Lutetia, and may have been known in America.

There are a few similarities between the romans of Lutetia and Deepdene: for example, in the shapes of C, R, c, g, r, y, z. The dots of i and j are small and distanced from the stem of the letter in both faces. The E and F are quite similar; but Goudy had used the high middle bar in his Kennerley Old Style of 1911, and the broad form of those letters can be seen in his Goudy Modern and Italian Old Style, both earlier than Lutetia. However, the texture and colour of Deepdene are quite different from those of Lutetia, because the serifs and thin strokes in it are stronger than those in Van Krimpen's type, and the serifs are unbracketed. See overleaf and page 102.

Deepdene Italic, which was designed in the spring of 1928, bears no resemblance to the italic of Lutetia; in fact, Goudy wrote of it that he 'drew each character without reference to any other craftsman's work'. It is noticeably 'upright'; the angle can only be about four or five degrees. Curiously, the lowercase of the italic is remarkably similar to Van Krimpen's Romanée Italic, designed twenty years after Deepdene. See page 108.

Goudy explained his interest in the work of other designers in a speech at Syracuse University in 1936. 'Once in a while a type face by some other designer seems to present an interesting movement or quality that I like. I take an early opportunity to make it mine, frankly and openly, in the same way that a writer might use exactly the same words as another, but by a new arrangement of them present a new thought, a new idea, or a new subtlety of expression . . . By copying carefully a few characters of the type

ABCDEFGHIJKLMNOP
QRSTUVWXYZ& .,';:!?-
ABCDEFGHIJKLMNOPQRSTUVWXYZ&
abcdefghijklmnopqrstuv
wxyzfifffffflffl[ ] 1234567890
ABCDEFGHIJKLMNOPQRS
TUVWXYZ& abcdefghijklm
nopqrstuvwxyzfifffffifffflffl ct .,';:!?-
ABCDEGMPRI kzg gg gg gy

And now to the subject which has been assigned to me for this occasion—something about types of the past, type revivals, and a bit about type design, as I see it. I trust you will not find that my brief postprandial attempt bears out Gay's lines too literally:

So comes the reckoning when the banquet's o'er,
A dreadful reckoning, when men smile no more.

ONE hundred and twelve years ago type design was generally im-agined to be a matter that concerned only the letter cutter. J. John-son, author of *Typographia* (published in 1824), wrote of a type face that the printer needed only to "observe that its shape be perfectly

Deepdene roman and italic.

that appeals to me drawn by another hand, I try to secure in my own drawings some certain movement or rhythm his may pre-sent. I soon discard my model and proceed from there, as it were, under my own steam . . .'

The statement is interesting, because much has been said in recent years of the sanctity of the type designer's creations and the iniquity of plagiarism. Condemnation is certainly justified when a manufacturer flagrantly reproduces another's design without permission while the design is still within the period when copyright applies, or should apply, to that class of in-dustrial design. But it is unrealistic to disapprove of a designer who takes note of a feature or characteristic in another type and uses it as an element in a new design of his own. (Composers of music have frequently 'quoted' each other without criticism; indeed, Ravel said, 'It is by imitating that I innovate.'). Only if the borrowed feature has a dominant part in the character of the type may a charge of plagiarism be levelled at the designer.

Certainly that is not the case with Goudy. Whatever he bor-rowed from others was always thoroughly subsumed as soon as his own inventive powers, stimulated into action by the source of interest, took command of the work. The outcome was invariably and unmistakably a Goudy design.

In his own time Goudy was a hero figure in American printing: 'Glorifier of the Alphabet' was how a *New Yorker* profile described him in 1933. Though his reputation is no longer everywhere as high as it was, there are still many people in the United States who regard his achievements with warm-hearted, if uncritical, reverence. His life and work have been extensively recorded in his own lectures and writings and in the reminiscences of others. There can be few students of typography in the United States who are unfamiliar with the details of his career. On the other side of the ocean the case is different. The following short account of the main events of his professional life will, it is hoped, provide sufficient background to the appraisal of his type designs which is the chief purpose of this essay.

Goudy had a long life. He was born in 1865 in Illinois and died in 1947, in his eighty-second year. As a boy he had a keen interest in lettering, and when his father took up the real estate business in 1884 (he had been a schools' superintendent) Goudy worked for him and frequently designed the office advertisements, with hand-lettered headings to give them distinction.

For several years he worked as a cashier or clerk in various cities until he settled for a time in Chicago. In 1895 a chance meeting with a friend who offered to provide some cash enabled Goudy to start a small printing office, which he called the Booklet Press. He acquired the equipment – a Golding press, an imposition stone, a few cases of Caslon and an 'English' text – from Will Bradley, who had bought it for pleasure printing but was too busy to use it. No doubt Goudy added to this modest equipment, because the first substantial commercial job undertaken by the Press, soon renamed the Camelot Press, was the typesetting of the second year's issues of *The Chap-Book*, the influential literary journal published fortnightly by Stone & Kimball (the actual printing was done elsewhere). Bradley designed some covers and posters for it in skilful imitation of the style of Aubrey Beardsley. In Goudy's words: 'I began my work in that period of transition known as *le fin de siècle*; I belong to the Beardsley period, although actually never a part of it.'

Goudy was lucky to be in Chicago during the 1890s. Stone & Kimball and others made a significant mark on the American publishing scene, which attracted the interest of literary people in London and Paris. The high quality, literary and graphic, of the *Chap-Book* 'opened my eyes to a new world', said Goudy. He became aware that typography, properly executed, was itself a craft, and a source of visual satisfaction.

Whether he was much influenced by what he saw is difficult to say. There is no sign in his early work of any interest in the style and themes of the *art nouveau* then fashionable; but it is possible to think that the rough-edged weighty shapes of his Pabst and Powell types owe something to Will Bradley's other enthusiasm — the 'antique' style of printing practised by, amongst others, Field & Tuer of London, whose American distributors were Scribner & Welford. The style, which consisted of an absurd pseudo-Chaucerian 'englysshe' (*Olde Tayles Newelye Relayted and Enryched with all the Ancyente Embellyshments* is a typical title) composed in Caslon with deliberately crude woodcut decorations of figures in vaguely Jacobean costume, was popular in the United States. Perhaps the American at the bustling turn of the century admired what he took to be a reminder of the days of the founding fathers and the thirteen states. Bradley adapted the 'antique' style to his own purposes. The first six numbers of the *American Chap-Book* he wrote and designed for the American Type Founders Company in 1904 make much use of his 'quaint' cuts and old-style typography.

The running of a commercial printing plant was too uncertain an undertaking (it must have been very competitive: only a few years before there were over three hundred and sixty printers in Chicago), or else it was not to Goudy's taste, because after little more than a year he sold his interest in the plant (it failed a few months later) and looked around for work. For want of something to do he drew an alphabet of capitals and numerals, sent them to the Dickinson type foundry in Boston, and received ten dollars, twice as much as he had asked. The foundry added a lowercase and issued the type as Camelot. It was an undistinguished piece of 'art' lettering with nothing typographic in it; its only significance is that the acceptance of the design encouraged Goudy to go on. With advice from Clarence Marder, of the well-known Marder, Luce type foundry of Chicago, he sold two more designs (they were never actually made) before he decided that type designing was no way to earn a living, and took a job as cashier on a farming magazine in Detroit. One day he drew some lettering for one of the journal's customers, who criticised the lowercase. 'His remark put me on my mettle and I began seriously to study roman letter forms. This was about 1898.' Goudy was thirty-three.

In the following year he lost his job, returned to Chicago and decided to try his hand as a freelance designer of lettering and simple decorative work. He had a modest success, and was invited to teach lettering and design at the Holme School of Illustration. 'I had to study harder than any student . . . but I managed to keep at least one lesson ahead of the class.' W. A. Dwiggins, then about twenty, was studying illustration there. He visited Goudy's class one day and said it opened up a new concept of design to him.

Goudy developed an interest in books *as* books, and particularly those produced by the English private presses: Kelmscott, Doves, Vale and Eragny, which he was able to see as they arrived in the rare book department of the A. C. McClurg book store.

In 1903 he met Will Ransom, then twenty-five and recently come to Chicago to study at the Art Institute, having previously served an apprenticeship in a printing office and worked as a book-keeper. They established the Village Press at Park Ridge, Illinois, and dedicated it to the making of 'beautiful books of those things in literature which they enjoy'. Like the proprietors of the other private presses they admired they equipped themselves with a type of their own, the first Village type. The essay on 'Printing' by William Morris and Emery Walker, published by them in 1893, was the first title issued by the Village Press. For all the other books produced by the Press the type was set by Goudy's wife. (To be married to a wife who can set type is happiness indeed.)

In 1904 Goudy moved the press to Hingham, Massachusetts. He stayed there for two years but did not prosper. He then moved to New York, and made some new business connections 'that kept body and soul together'. But in January 1908 the office building in which the Village Press was located was partially destroyed by fire, and the stock of printed books, work in progress, drawings, type and equipment were lost. Goudy was obliged to return to his work as a lettering artist and decorative designer. By diligence and ability he succeeded well enough to afford his first visit to Europe in 1909.

His knowledge of good printing impressed Mitchell Kennerley the publisher, who commissioned Goudy to design an edition of H. G. Wells's story *The Door in the Wall*. The trial pages in 18 point Caslon Old Face were disappointing; the capitals looked too strong for the lowercase and the fitting was too loose. (Bruce Rogers was to make the same comment about the type in his report to the Cambridge University Press in 1917.) Goudy offered to design a new type for the work and have matrices engraved at his own charge, on the understanding that he could sell fonts of the type to the general trade to recoup the expense. Kennerley agreed. That was in 1911, the year when '. . . the typographic tide turns: I abandon my "amateur" standing and my life work as a professional type designer really begins'.

To give effect to this new enterprise Goudy started the Village Letter Foundry to cast and sell the Kennerley Old Style and his Forum Title. Two sizes of each of the types were described and displayed in the first number of *Typographica*, which Goudy published in September 1911. In the second number, issued in July in the following year, more sizes of Kennerley were shown, as well as a new type, called Goudy Old Style, which was later to be renamed Goudy Lanston. Four more numbers of *Typographica* were issued at long intervals: no. 3 in 1916, with a supplement in the same year; no. 4 ten years later; no. 5 in 1927; and no. 6 in 1934. They are fine examples of page design and typesetting, and desirable collectors' pieces.

Goudy seems to have enjoyed writing. *The Alphabet*, published in 1918, and *Elements of Lettering*, 1922 (they were later issued in one volume), are not great works of scholarship, and the latter, which was severely criticised by Stanley Morison in the first volume of *The Fleuron*, does place too much attention on Goudy's own type designs. But they are worth reading, so long as they are not regarded as the only necessary source of information. Goudy also edited the first four numbers of *Ars Typographica*, a 'quarterly' of high standing, and he contributed articles to many periodicals for most of his life.

By 1920 he had nearly forty type designs on record, and his reputation was high. In that year he was appointed 'art adviser' to the Lanston Monotype Company of Philadelphia. The first type he designed for them in that role (but not the first of his types they had produced) was the Garamont roman, which was, like most of the other versions of the *caractères de l'Université*, a notable commercial success – though, as Goudy wrote, it 'was not the result of inspiration or genius on my part . . .'

In 1925 he moved to Deepdene near Marlborough in New York state, and established the Village Press and letter foundry in an old mill, one of his recent acquisitions being the Albion hand press on which the Kelmscott Chaucer had been printed many years before (it had had several distinguished owners since Morris).

When the Pabst Italic was in production in 1903 Goudy had been interested to watch the matrices for it being engraved by Robert Wiebking in Chicago. They became firm friends, and Wiebking made the matrices for all Goudy's types, except those designed for Monotype, until 1925. Wiebking died two years later. Goudy decided to learn the craft himself: '. . . I attempted, with no previous type-founding experience or tutelage under any master, to learn every detail of type founding – making patterns, grinding cutting tools, engraving matrices – *after* I had passed my sixtieth birthday.' Most of the sixty-odd types he created from 1925 onward were in the fullest sense produced by his own hands. The loss of the sight in one eye did not deter him; in fact, the next twelve years were his most prolific period.

Disaster overtook him once again: '. . . suddenly, on the early morning of January 26, 1939, fire took from me the equipment so laboriously got together, the hundreds of drawings, master and work patterns, fifteen or twenty designs for types in process of production – all gone. It was a body blow.'

A fund was raised to help him start again. It enabled him to build a small studio in which he could write and draw in comfort; but he could not obtain machine tools for matrix engraving until

1941, when the University of Syracuse lent him some equipment, and he was able to resume his type designing in the thoroughgoing way he preferred. He continued work until 1944 – long after he had been described as 'veteran' by a reviewer in *The Fleuron* in 1930.

Admiration for his work was not limited to the printing trade. As early as 1904 he was awarded a medal for book printing at the Lousiana Purchase exposition in St Louis; in 1922 the American Institute of Architects awarded him their craftsmanship gold medal; and there were others. In 1920 he received the gold medal of the American Institute of Graphic Arts, and there were honorary degrees and other awards from several universities. He wrote, with some feeling, in the introduction to his *Half-Century*, '. . . I am constrained to acknowledge here that I have always deplored the fact that the first *real* recognition of my types came from an English writer [he was probably thinking of Stanley Morison's praise of Goudy Modern] and English printers [he may have meant Francis Meynell, who added Kennerley and Forum to the equipment of the Pelican Press, and possibly also George W. Jones, who commissioned a type from him], instead of from printers and writers in my own fatherland . . .' But he was being less than fair to his compatriots and overgenerous to the English, who have been indifferent to (or perhaps ignorant of) most of his work as a designer and as a beneficent influence on American printing for the larger part of the twentieth century.

Goudy's *A Half-Century of Type Design and Typography*, which will often be quoted here, was written for The Typophiles in 1943 and 1944. It is his personal account of the origins of his types and his opinion of them. It is certainly fascinating; but it must be said that it is not altogether satisfactory. He was approaching eighty when he wrote it, not in the best of health, and he may not have had total recall. Or he may simply have felt entitled to be reticent whenever he wished. Whatever the reason, there are places in the work where the information he gives is less than adequate, and I have supplemented it with a speculation of my own where it seems helpful to the understanding of a design.

Like other creative people designers are seldom good critics of their own work. Certainly some of Goudy's opinions of his designs are difficult to accept. For instance, about the Companion Old Style face intended for headings in the *Woman's Home Companion* magazine he wrote: 'I believe it is one of the most distinctive types I have ever made. It incorporates features which deliberately violate tradition as to stress of curves, but which are so handled that attention is not specifically drawn to the innovations introduced.' And of the Saks Goudy design: 'I believe it is as good a type as I have ever made, or can make . . .' But the plain fact is that those designs are distinctly clumsy; the curious disposition of the curves in both faces and the bent and tapered strokes in some letters in the Saks type suggest an uncritical striving for novelty and an unwarranted belief that originality, however achieved, is automatically commendable. That was a trait in Goudy's character, I think; but when he produced those faces he was particularly busy and may have had no time for reflection – which was too frequently the case. Writing about the types many years later in the *Half-Century* he may have set down, without re-appraisal, what he had thought about the designs at the time of their creation.

The aspect of Goudy's work most frequently remarked upon is the great number of types he designed: one hundred and twenty-three, by his own count. It is impossible to avoid the impression that he did not sufficiently distinguish between quantity and quality. Howard Coggeshall, who knew him well, wrote: 'About 1930 or 1931 Mr Goudy became distinctly quantity-conscious. He had made more than seventy designs – now the goal became a hundred . . . So he worked beaverishly. From the beginning of 1930 through 1935 he scored a total of thirty-five designs . . . a prodigious output.' But '. . . quite a few of them were not completed designs – work had been performed "sufficient to give them a work number".'

It is notoriously difficult to classify types precisely. The designs which are actually reproduced in the *Half-Century* (some are only mentioned, either because they were not manufactured or because the material was lost in the 1939 fire) may for con-venience be classed as: advertising text types, six; display types, thirty; black-letter (that is, those with something of the fraktur or uncial about them), fourteen; book types, fifty-one; various (typewriter, Greek, Hebrew, and other special types), nine. The personal selection that follows is of types that I think are interest-ing either for their merits as designs or for what Goudy said about them.

Of Goudy's types for advertising the first notable design is the Pabst roman of 1902. Although its origin was in lettering done for advertisements for the famous brewery after which it is named, the type was actually commissioned by a Chicago department store. The design owes more to the lettering mode of the time than to the conventions of type design. The uneven arches of m, the different widths of p and q, the 'artless' shapes of a and e, are quite similar to letters in Will Bradley's advertisements for Ault & Wiborg, the printing ink makers, and others. A particular characteristic of the Pabst type is the height of the lowercase, which is only about half the height of the capitals. This may have been the reason why Lucian Bernhard, whose own types had the same feature, regarded Pabst as one of the best of Goudy's de-

Easy Shoe Store

Many different styles in

Blucher Button or Ties

in

Men's Oxfords

Price

$2.50

All leathers

Main Street
Hilton, Vermont

Pabst roman and italic.
From the ATF *American Chap-Book* (June 1905).

signs. It is not a distinguished type, but it is a pleasant one. In *The American Chap-Book* for November 1904 Will Bradley, its editor and typographer, showed that as a text type in advertising the face made a good effect, so long as only a few capitals were present. It is not surprising that Pabst remained popular in the United States for many years. Some German foundries adopted the type in 1912, and called it Ohio. But its prominent capitals can hardly have made it a good choice for the printed German language, which requires an initial capital for every noun in the text. (The Pabst Extra Bold, still favoured in British newspapers, is not related to Goudy's type.)

The italic for Pabst was designed in 1903. So was Powell, a roman in the same style as Pabst but with a larger lowercase. For that reason the type is less interesting than Pabst.

A B C D E F G 1 2 3 4 5 6 7 8 9 0
H I J K L M N a b c d e f g h i j k
O P Q R S T U l m n o p q r s t u
V W X Y Z & $ v w x y z

EXPEDITION IS
Leaving this week
on a long trip into
the African Jungle

Powell, as made by Ludlow.

In that same year, Goudy designed the type which came to be called the Village type (the first of that name), in which he took particular pride. It began as a commission for an advertising type for a clothing firm. They liked the design but thought the cost of matrices and casting too high, so the drawings were returned to Goudy. Later that year the design was reworked and produced as a private type for the Village Press. Writing about it thirty years later Goudy said he took suggestions 'for my forms more or less from the types of Jenson, as exhibited in Morris's Golden type, the Doves, Montaigne, Merrymount, and types of that ilk'. That

PRINTED AT THE DOVES PRESS
No. 15 Upper Mall, Hammersmith, W.
from the Text of The Holy Bible newly
Translated out of the Originall Tongues
by speciall Commandement of his late
Majestie King James the First, 1611.

The Doves type.

seems unlikely. The design has almost nothing in common with the first three and only a little similarity to the last. In fact, it is much nearer to Goudy's Pabst design. The letters are less random in their proportions and their profiles are more regular; but the

&IT WAS THE TERRACE OF
God's house
That she was standing on,—
By God built over the sheer depth
In which Space is begun;
So high, that looking downward

The first Village type.

design shows the advertising lettering artist rather than the student of type revivals and is none the worse for that. No doubt the Village type is, by present taste in book types, too assertive in 'personality'; but it is much better than Ricketts's Vale Press type and Pisarro's Brook type, and at least as good as Goodhue's Merrymount design. (Bruce Roger's Montaigne type is in a different class, both of style and of merit.)

&In pinacothecam perveni, vario genere tabu-
larum mirabilem: nam et Zeuxidos manus vidi,
nondum vetustatis injuria victas; et Protogenis
rudimenta, cum ipsius naturæ veritate certantia,
non sine quodam horrore tractavi. Jam vero

On, still on, I wandered on,
And the sun above me shone;
And the birds around me winging
With their everlasting singing
Made me feel not quite alone.

The Vale type, 1896, and the Brook type, 1902.

The Copperplate Gothic which Goudy drew for the American Type Founders Company in 1905 became one of their most successful types, in the commercial sense, when it was developed into a family of several weights and widths. It was imitated by other makers under such names as Lining Gothic and (in Britain) Spartan, and is still in demand. But it can hardly have been an original design. Goudy had probably simply been asked to smarten up one of the existing monoline faces which possessed vestigial serifs. He undertook a number of humdrum tasks of that sort at this early stage in his career.

The Forum Title of 1911 and the Hadriano Title of 1918 are mentioned at this point because though not intended as advertising types they are essentially titling faces, for use on title pages and formal announcements. Both designs were adapted from

FOURSCORE &
SEVEN YEARS A

ABCDEFGHIJKLMN
OPQRSTUVWXYZ&
1 2 3 4 5 6 7 8 9 0
ABCDEFGHIJKLMN
OPQRSTUVWXYZ.·,
1 2 3 4 5 6 7 8 9 0 &

FOURSCORE AND

Forum Title and Hadriano Title.

rubbings of Roman carved inscriptions which Goudy made during his visit to Europe in 1910. Francis Meynell took pride in
offering Forum to the customers of the Pelican Press in 1923, and
Bruce Rogers employed both types in his typographic work. But
to my eyes they are too much of a good thing – especially the
Hadriano, which simulates the effect of weather-worn stone car-
ving to such an extent that the design is a piece of pseudo-random
lettering rather than a true type face.

Goudy Open, which was designed in 1918, was a display type
based on the caption to an eighteenth-century engraving. The
engraved letters looked too 'modern' to Goudy, so he strengthened the thin strokes, bracketed the serifs and increased the
curvature. The application of a white line to the surface of letters
almost always makes them attractive; but it is in every sense a
superficial charm, which may obscure defects in the basic letter

Fourscore & Seven Years
Ago our Fathers brought

Goudy Open.

structure. The chief significance of Goudy Open now is that it
was the foundation of one of Goudy's best-known types, his
Goudy Modern, which will be examined on a later page.

The last of the advertising types selected for notice here is one
of Goudy's best designs: the Goudy Heavy Face of 1925. The
Cooper Black which had been introduced by the Barnhart

Brothers foundry not long before was, I suppose, derived from a style of hand-drawn lettering which had been popular on posters and magazine covers for many years, and was usually in excellent harmony with the strong lines and masses of the illustration: for example, see the graphic work of William Nicholson in England

ABCDEFGHIJKLMN
OPQRSTUVWXYZ&
abcdefghijklmnopqrs
tuvwxyzfiffffffiflfflctst
.,';:!?-$1234567890
ABCÇDEFGHIJKL
MMNOPPQRSTU
VUWXYZ&.,';:!?-
abcdefgghijklmno
pqrstuvwxyzfiffffi
flffl$1234567890

Goudy Heavy Face.

in the late 1890s. Oswald Cooper's type had the convex terminals of his earlier Roman; in the Ludlow version of it they are concave, like those of the Keystone foundry's Ben Franklin type. These heavy faces became popular in publicity work, and Lanston Monotype, needing to compete with them, asked Goudy for a similar design. The letter forms of Cooper Black and Ludlow Black are obese and, to my mind, vulgar; and Linotype's Pabst Extra Bold is only a little better. Goudy's Heavy Face is superior to them; not so dark, but dark enough, and with cleaner profiles – the work of a designer familiar with, and respectful of, the letter forms of traditional printing types. The term 'fat face' is usually applied to types of the 'modern' class, such as the extra-bold versions of Bodoni. The Goudy Heavy Face might be called a 'fat old style'.

'Black-letter' types – those which show, more or less, the characteristics of early scriptorial work – were often in Goudy's mind from 1926 onward (though he had designed a set of Caxton initials as long ago as 1905), and he set a high value on them, possibly because he thought they demonstrated so well his ability with a pen and his skill as an engraver of matrices. But in most of his designs in this class the letter shapes are awkward and unharmonious; by comparison with Rudolf Koch's types in the

To give unity to a piece of Printed Matter the construc‑ tion and arrangement must be "kept going" as a whole, all the time, so & $1234567890

that the attention does not dwell too long on any one part; this is the very beginning of design, since it amounts to grasping the whole situation. To make anything serviceable the producer &

ABC DE E FF GG HI JKL M N
O P Q R S S T U V W X Y Z & . , ' ; : ! ? ‑
a b c d e f g h i j k l m n o p q r s t u v w x y z
fi ff ffi fl ffl ll ct æ œ $ 1 2 3 4 5 6 7 8 9 0

Medieval.

genre they are embarrassingly inferior. And yet he had success with them.

Describing his Medieval of 1930 he wrote: 'I come now to what I personally consider one of my most original designs, a letter based on a twelfth-century South German manuscript hand . . .' and later, rather confusingly, '. . . its lowercase borrows the freedom of the scribe's pen of the Renaissance'. He goes on to say that he had preserved the gothic spirit of the face while romanis‑ ing somewhat the individual characters. He gives the names of eminent people who had used the type; and he remarks that he began the design on 19 August, cut the patterns and engraved the matrices, and was casting type on 27 September – a brisk turn of speed for a man of sixty-five.

There is one design in this class which is wholly admirable: the Goudy Text of 1928, which was acquired by Lanston Monotype. Goudy described it as 'a freely rendered Gothic letter, composite in form from various sources'. The letters are very well matched to each other and produce a fine result when composed in text.

Goudy Text.
From *Portfolio Two*, Rampant Lions Press.

Fourscore and seven years ago our fathers brought this continent a new nation, conceived in liberty, and to the proposition that all men are created equal. No engaged in a great civil war, testing whether that nati

Book types make up the largest number of entries in Goudy's record of designs, and a fair number of them deserve comment.

The first Village type has been described on an earlier page, because of its origin as an advertising type. The next text face to note is the one correctly known as Monotype 38-E – though it has sometimes been called Goudy Old Style or Light. It was designed

ABCDEFGHIJKLM
NOPQRSTUVWXY
Z&ÆŒ:,';:!?-fi ff ffi fl ffl
abcdefghijklmnopqrstu
vwxyzæœ£$1234567890

Fourscore and seven years ago our fathers brought forth on this continent a new nation, conceived in liberty, and dedicated to the proposition that all men are created equal. Now we are engaged in a great civil war testing

Fourscore and seven years ago our fathers brought forth on this continent a new nation, conceived in liberty, and

*ABCDEFGHIJKLM
NOPQRSTUVWXY
Z&ÆŒ.,';:!?-fi ff ffi fl ffl
abcdefghijklmnopqrstu
vwxyzæœ£$1234567890*

Monotype 38-E.

in 1908, at the request of a magazine house which backed out of the project. It is an undistinguished design, but it does show that Goudy's studies of the work of the private presses and of text printing generally had had their effect. He now understood the essential difference between a piece of lettering drawn for a specific context and an alphabet whose twenty-six components would be used in an infinity of combinations.

In 1911 the roman of the celebrated Kennerley Old Style made its appearance (the italic was not designed until seven years later). The event which brought the type into being has already been described. There are conflicting accounts of the source of the design. Writing to John Henry Nash in 1930, Henry L. Bullen

ABCDEFGHIJKLMNOP
QRSTUVWXYZ&ÆŒ([]
abcdefghijklmnopqrstuvwxyz
æœfiffffiflfflctst.,';:!?-$1234567890

Fourscore and seven years ago our fathers
brought forth on this continent a new nation, conceived in liberty, and dedicated to
the proposition that all men are created
equal. We are now engaged in a civil war
testing whether this nation, or any nation

*Fourscore and seven years ago our fathers
brought forth on this continent a new nation, conceived in liberty, and dedicated to*

ABCDEFGHIJKLMNO
PQRSTUVWXYZ&ÆŒ
*abcdefghijklmnopqrstuvwxyz
æœfiffffiflffl.,';:!?-$1234567890*

Kennerley Old Style roman and italic.
In this and some following specimens the 'Fourscore' text is reproduced from McMurtrie's
American Type Design, and the alphabets from Goudy's *Half-Century*, by courtesy of
The Typophiles.

BCDE
STU
abcde
pqrst
23456

Some characters from the
canon size (about 48 point)
of the Fell type.

Quare multarum quoq; gentium patrem diuina oracula futurū:ac in
ipſo benedicēdas oés gentes hoc uidelic& ipſum quod iam nos uideūs
aperte prædictum eſt:cuius ille iuſtitiæ perfectioém non moſaica lege
ſed fide cōſecutus eſt:qui poſt multas dei uiſiones legittimum genuit
filium:quem primum omnium diuino pſuaſus oraculo circūcidit:&

Jenson's roman.
From *De Preparatione Evangelica* by Eusebius, 1470.

of the American Type Founders Company said: 'When he
[Goudy] designed Kennerley he worked from our copy of
Jenson's Eusebius of 1470 . . .'* Goudy's account was quite different. He said that the source was the canon size of the Fell types
held at Oxford, which Goudy was able to study in a copy of
Horace Hart's *Notes on a Century of Typography at the University Press, Oxford* (1900), given to him by Mitchell Kennerley. 'I
had drawn maybe a dozen letters when I noticed a movement in
my own type drawings not shown by the specimen types . . . I
went back over the letters already drawn and brought them into

*Quoted by Robert D. Harban in his *Chapter Nine*, The Typophiles (New
York, 1982).

harmony as to details with those that followed more completely my own conception of a new face.' It is not clear what he meant by 'movement'; but it is clear that the only characters in the Kennerley face which show any resemblance to the Fell type are C, S, W and 5. Not only are many other letters noticeably different from those in the Fell type; the contrast between the thick and thin strokes, which is considerable in Fell, is much less in Kennerley, and the edges are softened (this may partly be due to the design being realised in the form of engraved matrices rather than punches). There is so little of the character of the Fell type in Kennerley that one cannot help thinking that Bullen's reference to the Jenson model has some truth in it, and that Goudy had confused two of the many potential sources he had studied in his lifetime. Not that there is much of a resemblance to the Jenson type in Kennerley, apart from the e with the sloping bar (which he had already used in the Monotype 38-E). Bullen's remark to Nash that 'Kennerley is a spoilt Jenson' is unjust. There is so much of Goudy's own mind and eye in the face that it can certainly be called an original design. It is not one of Goudy's greatest; but it was a remarkable achievement for its time. In 1913 the Caslon foundry acquired the English and European rights to it, and in 1920 Lanston Monotype bought from Goudy the reproduction rights for the United States – though some other manufacturers had already produced the face under another name. Kennerley became very popular in the 1920s and 30s, and at the present time is in frequent use in film-set advertising.

The creation of Kennerley Old Style was an important event in Goudy's life, not only for its beneficial effect on his reputation but because it was the cause of his setting up as a type founder, first as a supplier and later as a designer-producer – and that had a facilitating effect on the amount of work he was able to do.

In 1912 Goudy received a commission to design a type for a book on Abraham Lincoln. The type was cast and the pages composed; and then the sponsor died. Goudy put the type on the market and named it Goudy Old Style. He changed the name to Goudy Antique when the other and ultimately famous Old Style was designed for the American Type Founders Company, and it was renamed again as Goudy Lanston when Monotype, years later, acquired the American rights in it.

The design is not perfect: the capitals are a little too tall, the hyphen is eccentric, and there are a few other idiosyncrasies. But it is a strong and expressive old style face, the letters well proportioned and balanced. Its vitality is largely due to the vertical strokes having baseline terminals which are slightly angled – a device which would come more readily to the mind of a lettering artist than to one concerned only with the characteristics of traditional printing types. In my opinion the face makes a better effect than Kennerley or the Goudy Old Style that followed

ABCDEFGHIJKLMNOP
QRSTUVWXYZ&.,';:!?˓
abcdefghijklmnopqrstuvwx
yzfifffﬃﬂﬄctæœ$1234567890

Fourscore and seven years ago our fathers
brought forth on this continent a new nation, conceived in liberty, and dedicated to
the proposition that all men are created
equal. We are now engaged in a civil war
testing whether this nation, or any nation

Goudy Lanston.

ABCDEFGHIJKLMN
OPQRSTUVWXYZ&
ABCDEFGHIJKLMNOPQRS
TUVWXYZ&fifffﬃﬂﬄ.,';:!?˓
abcdefghijklmnopqrst
uvwxyz$1234567890

Fourscore and seven years ago our fathers brought forth on this continent a
new nation, conceived in liberty, and
dedicated to the proposition that all
men are created equal. Now we are engaged in a great civil war testing whether

Goudy Old Style.

it — and, indeed, any of the later book types which gained so much
esteem.

In England the design was ill-treated; the descenders were
shortened and the face was issued under the inappropriate and
unattractive name of Ratdolt.

The Goudy Old Style design, commissioned by the American
Type Founders Company in 1915, is visibly related to the Kennerley face, but it is far superior to it. In the roman the bar in A, E,
F, H is lower, R, S, W, Z are better shapes, and h, m, n have
rounder arches. The bias in the curves of b, c, d, p, q is quite
marked, which may be the reason why the design makes a rather
bland appearance, though that is chiefly due to the general light-
ness of the face. Goudy's protest at the shortening of the
descenders, with an unfortunate effect on the g, was justified but
unavailing.

ABCDEFGGHIJJKL
MNOPQRSTTUVW
XYYZ& fi ff ffi fl ffl ct Qu
*abcdefghijklmnopqrstu
vwxyz.,';:!?-$1234567890*

*Fourscore and seven years ago our fathers
brought forth on this continent a new nation, conceived in liberty, and dedicated to the*

Goudy Old Style italic.

The italic is more interesting than the roman. At that date
Goudy had designed only two italics, those for Pabst and 38-E (he
had drawn an italic for the existing Cushing roman in 1904, but it
hardly counts as an original design). He therefore studied the
Aldine and other early sixteenth-century italics, and he seems to
have recognised two important facts: that the angle of an italic
need be only a few degrees from the vertical, and that the
lowercase letters should be narrower than the roman (the latter
was a precept he forgot in later italics, to their disadvantage). The
result of his studies was one of his finest designs – an excellent
secondary type when used with the roman, yet with a grace and
rhythm which made it very suitable as a text type in books of
verse (the lyric sort rather than the epic) and for advertising of
elegance. I am referring to the original version; there is a version
in present-day photo-composition which is wider, and the worse
for it.

The Goudy Old Style roman and italic are positive evidence of
Goudy's ability as a type designer. They were better than the
types being produced in Europe at that time (compare De Roos's
Zilver type of the same year) though the Imprint face, an adaptation of Caslon distinctive enough to be judged original, is an
exception; and they are better than Morris Benton's dull Cloister
Old Style of the year before.

The faces were promoted vigorously and a number of variations were developed – Bold, Extra Bold, Catalogue, Hand-
tooled, and so on – none of them by Goudy himself.

The next type selected for attention here is Goudytype,
designed for the American Type Founders Company in 1916. It is
interesting not as a design but for what Goudy said about his
frame of mind at the time. Thirty years after the event he wrote in
his *Half-Century*: '. . . I felt it presented a liveliness of handling
not hitherto expressed in type . . . but that in itself was not
enough to make it a good type. At that time I was beginning to
find myself; but as yet neither my studies nor my conclusions had

ABCDEFGHIJKL
MNOPQRSTUVW
XYZabcdefghijklm
nopqrstuvwxyz$&
.:;,-!?''1234567890

Goudytype.

given me the sureness and authoritative grasp of type problems that I hope I command today . . .' It is difficult to accept that, considering the confidence he had already exhibited in the Old Style roman and italic. He went on: '. . . I fear I allowed matters of mere technique to influence me – often mistaking excellence in the handling of details for excellence of design'. It is plain that in Goudytype there is a conflict of styles. The capitals and the lowercase v, w, y, z are calligraphic; the rest of the lowercase is typographic – the two graphic modes being essentially antipathetic. This is evidence, I think, not of an uncertain grasp of the nature of type but of that search for novelty by which Goudy allowed himself to be driven, not always wisely.

In 1918 Goudy produced a type which many people regard as one of his greatest achievements. When the Goudy Open was finished he took a proof, filled in the white lines in the letters, and decided the result would make a good text type. He called it Goudy Modern – though he later said the name was not really accurate because the face contained some old-style tendencies.

See page 131.

Stanley Morison drew attention to the design in his article 'Towards an Ideal Type' in the second volume of *The Fleuron*, which was published in 1924. He commended Goudy Modern as 'an admirable letter', and amplified his approval in a review of the type in *The Fleuron* vii (1930) and again in *A Tally of Types* (1953). Morison's enthusiasm may have influenced Francis Meynell; he used the face for three of the Nonesuch Press books, including the complete Shakespeare of 1953.

In 'Towards an Ideal Type' Morison named his two requirements for a satisfactory type face: that the essential form should correspond with that handed down (that is, that the shapes and proportions of the letters should be familiar), and that the letters should compose agreeably into words. With due respect, I do not think Goudy Modern meets the second of Morison's requirements, and I think he would have perceived that if he had not been so interested in what he imagined was the unusual source of the design. The fact is that a number of the lowercase letters are decidedly out of proportion with the rest. The m is so narrow and

ABCDEFGHIJKLM
NOPQRSTUVWXY
Z & . , ' ; : ! ? - fi ff fl ffi ffl
abcdefghijklmnopqrs
tuvwxyz1234567890

Fourscore and seven years ago our fathers brought forth on this continent a new nation, conceived in liberty, and dedicated to the proposition that all men are created equal. We are now engaged in a great civil war testing whether this nation, or any na-

ABCDEFGHIJKLMN
OPQRSTUVWXYZ&
abcdefghijklmnopqrstuvwxyz
fiffffifffl 1234567890.,';:!?-

Goudy Modern and italic.

the w and z so wide that they seem to belong to different type faces. When they occur in text, especially when they are doubled in words like 'common' and 'dazzle' or they are adjacent to letters of normal width, the disproportion is obvious and the effect disagreeable. The nose in a and s is close to the belly, which produces a clotted effect. The fitting of the type is strangely irregular; the letters collide or separate in a most erratic way. Taken together, these defects produce a noticeably uneven texture that makes the reading of even a short text an uncomfortable experience. It is allowed that perfect regularity in all respects in a type design is not an absolute requirement; indeed, it may produce a sterilised effect, a lack of vitality. Irregularities in a design are acceptable if they are an ingredient in its charm, do not affect its texture, and are unobtrusive. In Goudy Modern the irregularities of proportion and fitting, however caused, have gone too far.

As already said, the Modern is simply Goudy Open made solid: hence its weight. Goudy wrote that the starting point for the Open was the eighteenth-century French engraving reproduced as the frontispiece in A. F. Pollard's *Fine Books*, which was published in London in 1912. That tells us how Goudy began the design, but not why. In 1912 the Deberny & Peignot foundry in Paris issued a type called Cochin. It had considerable success. In

1916 it was reproduced by Lanston Monotype in the United States where, according to McMurtrie, it was deservedly popular (he rightly deplored Monotype's diminution of the vivacity of the original italic). Goudy must have been aware of the Cochin face and the fact that it was derived from lettering in engravings produced in France in the eighteenth century. As we know, Goudy was an opportunist, alert to the advantage to be gained from the circumstance of the moment. (This is said to define, not to decry – to use a phrase of Holbrook Jackson's.) It seems possible that the popularity of the Cochin type directed his mind and hand to the nearest example of a French engraving, the frontispiece in his copy of Pollard's book.

The engraving is from a painting by Hubert Gravelot illustrating a scene in an edition of Ovid's *Metamorphoses*, published in Paris in 1767. The legend below the picture reads, '*Deucalion et Pyrrha repeuplant la Terre, suivant l'Oracle de Themis*'. Since there are only four different capitals and seventeen lowercase letters in that wording, Goudy must have looked to other sources for the remainder of the letters – or else he invented them. The lettering in the caption is neat and regular. The a and s are normal, and the inner spaces of m are only slightly narrower than those in n (and the same is true of the Cochin type). So the eccentric letter widths in Goudy Modern seem to be Goudy's own. A particular feature of the lettering in the engraving is the unusual proportion of the heights of the capitals and lowercase – tall ascenders, long descenders and short capitals, characteristics which Goudy retained in his own design.

The italic of Goudy Modern is quite different from the Cochin italic; Goudy said it was entirely original. The C, G and S are awkwardly shaped. The lowercase has a more obviously 'modern' look than the roman. It is a little too wide, and rather dull.

Goudy Modern has been much praised in high places; too much so, to my mind. I prefer the lighter version of it which Goudy designed in 1932. He called it Goethe, because he produced it specially for a piece of printing which he contributed to the Goethe centenary exhibition held in Leipzig in 1932. The face was also used for the Limited Editions Club edition of Mary Shelley's *Frankenstein* (for which Bertha Goudy set the type – all three hundred pages of it).

See overleaf.

The peculiarities of letter width in Goudy Modern are also present in Goethe; but because of the reduction in weight they are less noticeable. Its vertical shading and its sober appearance, which set it apart from Goudy's other book types, are reminiscent of the face made by Binny & Ronaldson in Philadelphia at the end of the eighteenth century, issued as 'Oxford' by the American Type Founders Company, and used by Updike for the text of his great two-volume work on *Printing Types: their History, Form and Use*.

A B C D E F G H I J K L M N O
P Q R S T U V W X Y Z & . , ' : ; ! ? -
a b c d e f g h i j k l m n o p q r s t u v w x
y z fi ff fl ffi ffl æ 1 2 3 4 5 6 7 8 9 0

*A B C D E F G H I J K L M N O P
Q R S T U V W X Y Z & . , ' ; : ! ? -
a b c d e f g h i j k l m n o p q r s t u v w
x y z fi fl ff ffi Th ä ô 1 2 3 4 5 6 7 8 9 0*

Goethe roman and italic.

A B C D E F G H I J K L M N O
P Q R S T U V W X Y Z a b c d
e f g h i j k l m n o p q r s t u v w
x y z & $, ; : . - ' ! ? 1 2 3 4 5 6 7 8 9 0

Fourscore and seven years ago our fathers
brought forth on this continent a new nation, conceived in liberty, and dedicated
to the proposition that all men are created
equal. Now we are engaged in a great civil
war testing whether that nation, or any na-

Collier Old Style.

After the Open and the Modern (Goudy's only venture in the
direction of the 'modern' style) he returned to the ground he had
already worked in the Kennerley, Goudy Lanston and Old Style
types. This was to satisfy a commission from a Cincinnati advertising agency to create a type for their exclusive use. Collier Old
Style, as it was called, was a text type, not an advertising type as
such, and if it had been furnished with an italic it would have
worked very well in book printing. It is not without its quirks: the
figure 2 is exaggeratedly 'antique', and the 5 looks broken. The e
would have been better with a bar at less of an angle; and the S
and s are (as so often in Goudy's types) not as graceful as they
might be. But Collier Old Style was a good roman in a by now
familiar vein.

In the same style, but with stronger colour, was the Goudy
Antique, which was begun in 1919, the same year as Collier,
though it was not actually made as matrices and type until 1926.

more by turning the leaves of the book of experience in their chosen trade than they would gain in the formal institutions established for that end. This is particularly true of the art of printing, as the elements of good expression and the thoughts of the best intellects are forced upon the minds of those who work at the composing-case. 1 2 3 4 5 6 7 8 9 0

ABCDEFGHIJKLMNOPQURSTVWXYZ&
abcdefghijklmnopqrstuvwxyzſtȼtfifflflffffi.,':;?!

Goudy Antique.

It was, in fact, the first type in which Goudy attempted the whole process of type making – drawing the design, cutting the patterns, engraving the matrices, casting the type – a remarkable enterprise for a man in his sixty-first year.

In his *Half-Century* Goudy wrote that in 1920, when he had become 'art adviser' to Lanston Monotype, he said to the company, 'Why should not the Monotype present its products first instead of following the others?'; and that he then submitted his Garamont drawings to them. This may not be quite accurate.

The revival of the so-called Garamond types by the Imprimerie Nationale in 1898 had made them known and admired by type founders on both sides of the Atlantic. The American Type Founders Company issued a version in 1918, 'designed' by Morris Benton and T. M. Cleland in collaboration. It was not the first of its kind: a true Garamont had been made by the Ollière foundry in Paris five years before, but the world war prevented its full development. The ATF version was warmly welcomed in the United States. It seems probable that Lanston Monotype thought it imperative that they too should produce a Garamond, and asked Goudy to supply the drawings, which he did by closely copying the characters in the text of Anatole Claudin's *Histoire de l'Imprimerie en France au 15e et au 16e siècle*, printed in Paris, 1900–4. Naturally, there is little of Goudy in the result, though Beatrice Warde rightly called his lowercase w 'distressing'.

There is not much difference between the ATF version and Goudy's; both are good types. The English Monotype version is similar. The Stempel Garamond is a slightly darker letter which is rightly popular. (The fact that those faces are not authentic Garamond designs is of more interest to the historian than the typographer.) None of the many Garamonds now available has surpassed the roman of the Granjon face (a true Garamond) revived and supervised for the English Linotype company by George W. Jones in 1925. Bruce Rogers, the most discriminating of typographers, used it for some of his finest books.

The next design in Goudy's list, the roman he called Newstyle, which is dated 1921, is another example of his taking up an idea presented by someone else and developing it in his own way. In the early years of this century Robert Bridges, the English poet, advocated the use of augmented alphabets containing a number of phonetic characters, for the better representation of English pronunciation. This scheme of 'phonotypes', the basis of which was the Elstob Saxon type cut in 1715 and later acquired by the university press at Oxford, was described by Bridges in his *Tract on the present state of English pronunciation* (1913). That was probably the 'little book' that Goudy said he acquired in 1920 and that inspired him to create an alphabet less comprehensive and less radical than Bridges' 'that could be read by anyone but which at the same time would make pronunciation more easy'. He drew the capitals and lowercase, and added twenty or so extra characters to differentiate between long and short vowels, hard and soft g, and so on. (Readers may think of the Pitman Initial Teaching Alphabet which has been used recently in some British and American junior schools.) In his designing Goudy may have borrowed a few characteristics from the Elstob Saxon type – the bent top of the stem of m, n, and p, and the calligraphic x – but most of the letter forms are Goudy's own, including the archaic S, the strange Q, the fancy Z. The E and F are wide, and the middle bar is higher than is customary – a frequent characteristic in Goudy's book types. He wrote that he 'never got around to making any general use of the added quaint characters'. It was the regular alphabet characters in the design that achieved a reputation. The Grabhorn Press used the face for their folio edition of Whitman's *Leaves of Grass*, and other books. Bruce Rogers thought well of the type; in 1929 he actually considered it for his famous Oxford lectern Bible, until he decided that 'even with occasional modifications this type, much as I admire it, was too striking in effect and had too strong an appeal as "typography" to suit my purpose . . .' (That reference to modifications will become significant.)

In 1942 Goudy sold the design to Lanston Monotype, who evidently held it in abeyance until November 1945, when they learnt that the World Publishing Company had engaged Rogers to design a folio Bible for them; that Rogers wanted to use the Newstyle face, with certain modifications, and that Goudy had given Rogers a free hand to make any alterations he thought necessary. Monotype willingly agreed to put the face into production, and in December of that year they supplied Rogers with enlarged drawings of Goudy's characters. Two kinds of alteration were put in hand: the reduction in the width of certain letters (Rogers knew from experience that there are 4,631,056 letters in the Bible with the Apocrypha, so making the type fairly compact could have a useful effect on the economy of the work); and the alteration of the shape of some characters, presumably because of Rogers's earlier opinion that the type as designed was 'too striking' – by which I suppose he meant that the type would assert its personality to the detriment of the text. Six or seven capitals and about the same number of lowercase letters were

A B C D E F G H I J K L M N
O P Q R S T U V W X Y Z &
a b c d e f g h i j k l m n o p q r s t
u v w x y z ff fl ffl &t . , ' ; : ! ? -
1 2 3 4 5 6 7 8 9 0

Fourscore & seven years ago our
fathers brought forth on this continent a new nation, conceived in
liberty, and dedicated to the prop-

Newstyle,
The original design, and below, the face as it appeared
in the World Bible. The ampersand was omitted
in the revised font, so a Plantin ampersand has been used
in the first line of text.

A B C D E F G H I J K L M N
O P Q R S T U V W X Y Z
a b c d e f g h i j k l m n o p q r s t
u v w x y z ff fl ffi ʄr . , ' ; : ! ? -
1 2 3 4 5 6 7 8 9 0

Fourscore & seven years ago our
fathers brought forth on this continent a new nation, conceived in
liberty, and dedicated to the prop-

modified. The S, W, g, q and y were distinctly improved, and the R, r, s and t slightly; but the b suffered in the change. The numerals were replaced by a new set, smaller than the originals, and closely based on the Monotype Plantin face. The modifications eliminated most of the really idiosyncratic characters in the original design, but did not radically alter the texture of the type on the page.

As well as Bruce Rogers, other eminent people have expressed admiration of the Newstyle design. Abe Lerner has spoken of 'the full-bodied vigour of the World Bible page'. And Herbert Johnson, the authority on the work of Goudy and of Rogers, has given his opinion that Newstyle is one of the six great type faces designed by Americans. An outsider hesitates to disagree with such distinguished voices. But I am bound to say that I find the design, even after the Rogers revisions, restless and rough in texture, due to the over-large capitals and the dolphin-like e; in short, not at all easy on the eye.

In 1924 Lanston Monotype found themselves in need of a type to compete with Cloister Old Style, a face which had been popular ever since Morris Fuller Benton had supervised its creation at the American Type Founders Company in 1913. Goudy accepted the task of designing a suitable face. He chose not to work directly from the late fifteenth-century Jenson type that had been the source for Cloister, but simply to make a few references to the types of that period. They do not amount to more than a bar at the top of A, the two-way serifs on M, the convex leg on R, and the Jenson style of e. Goudy named his type Italian Old Style. In the roman the s is ungraceful and the dropped ear on r makes the letter look oddly small. The type does not compare well with other faces derived from the Jenson model – the Doves type, Bruce Rogers's Montaigne, and especially his Centaur. It is surpassed, too, by another type of the kind, the Venezia roman, the punches of which were cut by Edward Prince, last of the English punch-cutters, for George W. Jones. In 1925 Jones commissioned Goudy to design an italic to accompany the Venezia roman. It turned out to be much better than his italic for Italian Old Style – so much so that one wonders if Jones privately improved Goudy's design when it was put into manufacture by the English Linotype company.

It must be said that the opinion of Italian Old Style just expressed is a personal one. In the United States the face is well regarded. It was used for the text of Goudy's *Half-Century*. It sometimes appears in advertisements in the British press, including a recent series for Jack Daniel's Tennessee sipping whiskey.

The Marlborough face was designed in 1925 for a particular book – a large one, evidently, because the type size was 16 point. By Goudy's account the printer-publisher went ahead and composed the book in another type without waiting for the Marlborough; but it may be that the type was actually ready in time but both Goudy and the printer realised that it needed revision, the serifs and other details being too delicate, as Goudy admitted in his account of the face. He revised the drawings but never re-cut the patterns. The drawings perished in the 1939 fire. All this is sad, because to judge from the roman alphabets and numerals shown in the *Half-Century* the face would have been a

ABCDEFGHIJKLM
NOPQRSTUVWXY
Z & . , ' ; : ! ? - fi ff ffi fl ffl ct st ℂ
a b c d e f g h i j k l m n o p q r s
t u v w x y z $ 1 2 3 4 5 6 7 8 9 0

Fourscore and seven years ago
our fathers brought forth on this
continent a new nation, conceived in liberty, and dedicated
to the proposition that all men

*ABCCDEEFGHIJKLLM
NOPQQRSTCUVUWX
YZ& . , ' ; : ! ? - fi ff ffi fl ffl ct st
a b c d e f g h i j k l m n o p q r s
t u v w x y z $ 1 2 3 4 5 6 7 8 9 0*

*Fourscore and seven years ago
our fathers brought forth on this
continent a new nation, conceived*

Italian Old Style and italic.

ABCDEFGHIJKLMNOPQRSTUVWXYZ &
abcdefghijklmnopqrstuvwxyz 1234567890
ABCDEFGHIJKLMNOPQRSTUVWXYZ &
abcdefghijklmnopqrstuvwxyz

Venezia roman, George W. Jones's version of the Jenson type,
and Goudy's italic for it.

A B C D E F G H I J K L M N O P
Q R S T U V W X Y Z & . , ' ; : ! ? -
a b c d e f g h i j k l m n o p q r s t u v w x
y z æ œ fi ff ffi fl ffl ct $ 1 2 3 4 5 6 7 8 9 0

Marlborough.

good one, an old style without quirks, the x-height small, the ascenders and capitals unusually tall, the whole looking remarkably similar to the Estienne type, based on an early sixteenth-century French old style, made a few years later by the English Linotype company under the direction of George W. Jones. The absence of Goudy's usual hall-marks – the curly-tailed Q, the Jenson e, the awkward S, the fanciful Z – and the general reticence of the design, make Marlborough a puzzling item in Goudy's corpus of work. It would be interesting to know if he had a model for the design.

See page 122.

As described at the beginning of this essay, Goudy certainly had a model for the Deepdene roman, at least to start with. Perhaps that provided the discipline which ensured that the design ended up as an orthodox face with no idiosyncracies – though one wishes he had thought again about the S and s, and the disparate proportions of m and w. The uneven fitting in the Lanston Monotype version was not Goudy's fault. In the italic the lowercase letters are as good as those in the Old Style italic; but the capital G and U have not enough vitality for such a graceful type.

ABCDEFGHIJKLMNO
PQRSTUVWXYZ& ABCD
EFGHIJKLMNOPQRSTUVWXYZ&
abcdefghijklmnopqrst
uvwxyz ﬅ ﬁ ﬀ ﬃ ﬂ ﬄ .,';:!?-
1234567890

It is in the early printed books that the printer may find the sort of help he needs; there all the elements of type, ink, paper and 1234567890

Kaatskill.

In the Kaatskill design of 1929 it was again the capitals which needed more attention. The squareness of C and G is acceptable, but their serifs are weak. The R is below Goudy's usual standard; so is W. If those letters had been improved it would have been worth while for the English Monotype company, which acquired the design, to produce a range of normal book sizes, because the lowercase is a good plain design, better than Deepdene, I think, and one of the few romans in which Goudy gave the e a horizontal bar.

Goethe, number 80 in Goudy's list, has been described earlier, in the context of Goudy Modern. Its roman was designed in 1932.

ABCDEFGHIJKLMNOP

QRSTUVWXYZ&ABCDE

FGHIJKLMNOPQRSTUVWXYZ

abcdefghijklmnopqrstuv

wxyz fi ff ffi fl ffl 1234567890

In choice of types, those should be sought that
are sturdy, legible and easily discerned; but sturdiness need not necessarily mean & 1234567890

In choice of types, those should be sought that are sturdy,
legible and easily discerned; but sturdiness in type does
not necessarily mean faces over-bold or rough. Utility &

ABCDEFGHIJKLMNOP

QRSTUVWXYZ& abcdefg

hijklmnopqrstuvwxyz ct st ff ffl

Village No. 2 and italic.

In the same year Goudy designed the second Village type, for
use in his own Press. He later sold the reproduction rights to
Lanston Monotype. The lowercase is fairly broad; the z is a
repetition of the spurred z in Goudy Lanston. In the capitals the
unusual bias of the curves is tolerable in C, G and O but less so in
B, P and R. The Z is too exuberant a companion for the other
capitals. Goudy said, 'To my mind Village No. 2 is an excellent
type.' The roman is certainly good; but that cannot quite be said
of the italic, which has a fine lowercase, but four capitals, K, U, V
and W, which are deplorable. (In practice composition in italic
which did not contain those letters would look pleasant enough.)

Bertham, named in memory of Goudy's wife, was his hun-
dredth type face. It was designed in 1936, when he was in his
seventy-first year. Like Deepdene it began with Goudy's interest
in a design by another hand: in this case, the type used in a book
he had recently purchased, said to be based on the hybrid roman-
gothic face in a Latin edition of Ptolemy's guide to geography,
printed by Leonard Holle at Ulm in 1482. Goudy must have been
referring to one of the Ashendene Press books composed in the
Ptolemy type which had been drawn for that Press in Emery
Walker's office and which made its first appearance in the *Don
Quixote* of 1927.

Apart from the two-way serifs on M and N and a vague suggestion of fraktur in c and s, Goudy's design had little in common

See overleaf.

LES AMOURS PASTORALES

grande douleur, celui qui étoit écorné se mit en bramant à fuir, et le victorieux à le poursuivre, sans le vouloir laisser en paix. Daphnis fut marri

The Ashendene Press Ptolemy type.

with the Ptolemy type. It has unusual characteristics of its own: the tail of Q, the calligraphic Z and z, and the angled top of 5. They do not enhance the design. Goudy wrote that he drew the eighty characters in the font, cut the patterns, engraved the matrices and cast the type, in sixteen working days. Energy and determination to be admired; but there cannot have been much time for the objective scrutiny which every design should undergo before it is allowed to emerge from the workshop.

ABCDEFGHIJKLMNOP
QRSTUVWXYZ & .,’;:!?-
a b c d e f g h i j k l m n o p q r s t u v
w x y z fi ff fl ct st 1 2 3 4 5 6 7 8 9 0

ABCDEGHLMNORSTUW

Everyone knows what printing is; the simple inking of types that have been carefully arranged, properly impressing them on paper, and the thing is done. Sim-

Bertham.

The type that is now known as Californian was at first called University of California Old Style. It was a commission from the university for a private type for the university's own press. Goudy worked on it in December 1938; but with only a week to go before he was due to submit a proof he decided he must start again. A new design was put through the engraving process and type cast and proofed in time for the visit by Goudy's university patron. The design is not particularly notable, but it is pleasant enough to read at 12 point and smaller. The 10 point captions in the 1952 edition of Goudy's *The Alphabet and Elements of Lettering* are more agreeable than the 18 point text. In the larger sizes some peculiarities show themselves: C, E, F and T look unfinished, s is too light, and in the italic the ball terminals in S are at odds with the other capitals, though they are acceptable in the lowercase s. The face has recently been re-drawn for filmsetting and named Berkeley Old Style.

A B C D E F G H I J K L M N O
P Q R S T U V W X Y Z & . , '- : ; ! ?

ABCDEFGHIJKLMNOPQRSTUVWXYZ

a b c d e f g h i j k l m n o p q r s t u
v w x y z fi ff ffi fl ffl ct st Æ Œ æ œ
1 2 3 4 5 6 7 8 9 0

A B C D E F G H I J K L M N O P Q R S
T U V W X Y Z & Æ Œ æ ct st . , '- ; : ! ?
a b c d e f g h i j k l m n o p q r s t u v w x y z
fi ff fl ffi ffl A B C D E G M R T g v w

"*The Story of St. Francis* (Frank Morris), *St. Gonsol* (Dr. Frank Gunsaulus) *and the Devil* (himself and no other) is a quaint and delightful bit of bookish foolery written years ago by Eugene Field; when and where it first appeared the present printers of it are not aware. It was printed in nineteen hundred and two by Frederick Thompson in New York City, and it is on

Californian roman and italic.

In his writings Goudy set down his views on the nature of letters and the duty of the type designer, and what he wrote contains no pretensions and argues no claim for the expression of the designer's personal fancies. Thus, in his introduction to McMurtrie's survey of *American Type Design* (1924): 'Letters . . . are not shapes made to display the skill of their designer; they are forms fashioned solely to help the reader' – a thoroughly orthodox view, and clearly implying that self-effacement is the designer's chief duty. Goudy the designer, though, seemed to think along different lines from Goudy the writer. Instead of consciously acknowledging the discipline of self-criticism he seemed willing to be driven by his ambition to add yet one more design to the record; willing, too, to believe that quantity is not the enemy of quality. And yet there are areas of design into which he hardly ventured. For instance, he had nô liking for hard-edge faces. In *The Alphabet and Elements of Lettering* he wrote disparagingly of the sans-serif form. His only efforts in that style were his Lining Gothic of 1921 and the Sans-serif Heavy and Light of 1929 and 1930. In the Lining Gothic he thought he could make the form interesting by adding a suggestion of serif 'to take away the hard and precise ending of the stems'. The result is much inferior to Berthold Wolpe's fine Albertus type, which observes the same principle. The Sans-serif Heavy and Light were designed at the request of Lanston Monotype, to compete with the new sans-serif types then appearing from Germany. 'I attempted to give my type a definite expression of freedom and a personal quality not always found in this kind of letter.' He seems not to have realised that, on the contrary, it was the strict geometry and the impersonal quality of Futura and Erbar which were gaining the favour of the typographer and printer of the time.

Goudy never attempted a slab-serif type. Nor did he look with interest at the modern face, with its severely vertical stress, strong contrast in stroke thickness and unbracketed serifs. The Goethe design was the one approach he made to that style, and that face was only as 'modern' as is Bulmer or Bell.

Goudy's types, except for those he designed directly for Monotype, were cast from his own engraved matrices, in which the action of the rotary cutting tool makes it impossible to obtain the precise angles and corners needed in hard-edge faces. It is therefore tempting to think that he turned a practical limitation into a prejudice of taste. There may be something in that; but it seems more likely that he simply was not interested in those classes of type design where plainness and impassivity are of the essence. He wanted each new design to be clear evidence of his individuality, so he preferred the old style model because it gave him the latitude to express himself as often as he wished. But the fact is that although in the old style form the subtle variations of letter shape, stroke thickness, serif form and x-height are apparently inexhaustible, the designer himself has natural limits to his versatility; he can create only so many designs in a particular style which possess both individuality and consistently high quality. To force himself to produce several dozen variations on the theme, as Goudy did, was to over-stretch his talent. I think many would agree with that comment, though not everyone will agree with the criticisms of particular types that have been made in this essay.

If I do not think that all the thirty or so designs selected here from Goudy's considerable tally of types would stand every test of critical judgement, I do believe that Goudy Old Style, Goudy Text and the Heavy Face are very fine designs of permanent value; and that if Goethe, Marlborough and Goudy Lanston were to be reworked by a sensitive hand and eye they would be gratefully received by discriminating book designers. Even if those few types had been the sum total of his work in the field he would have earned his high place in the ranks of twentieth-century type designers.

15: Three types by Rudolf Koch

In his description of the typographic creations of the Klingspor type foundry Julius Rodenberg remarked: '. . . among the many examples of modern types there are some . . . which may be regarded as truly artistic because in them the personality of the artist is paramount. Whenever the creative power of the artist is so strong that the impress of his personality is still clearly discernible in the finished type, even after it has passed through the long and complicated manufacturing process . . . we may speak of a truly artistic type.' If Rodenberg was including in that observation the kind of type intended for continuous text, as in a book, many of us would want to modify, even reject, his statement. Long familiarity with the classic book types – the well-tried Baskerville, Janson, Garamond, Bembo and the few other staples of American and British book printing – has imbued us with such a deep-seated preference for plain and unobtrusive faces that some of us find it difficult to accept even such an excellent artistic type as Palatino in that role, however willing we are to use it in other sorts of printing. But Rodenberg's dictum is entirely acceptable when the subject is a type meant for persuasion, as in printed advertising, or for pleasure, as on an invitation card. I find convincing evidence for that view in the type designs of Rudolf Koch, the most important of the distinguished designers who worked for Klingspor.

Rudolf Koch was born in Nuremberg in 1876, the son of a sculptor of very modest means who died when Koch was ten years old. At sixteen a family friend in Hanau took him in as an apprentice metal worker. Koch later wrote: 'With eleven hours work every day and evening classes of two hours several times a week [he studied drawing] the apprentice lived a strictly ruled life.' After nearly four years he grew dissatisfied with metal-chasing and was allowed to return to Nuremberg, where he enrolled in the school of arts and crafts. He thought he should try to make a career as a drawing master; was thwarted in that, and found himself a job in a lithographic firm in Leipzig as a draughtsman and painter, but soon gave it up because he thought he was incompetent. For a time he tried to sell his drawings privately, but without success. Someone suggested he try his hand at designing book covers. He did so ('water-lilies in the *Jugend* manner'), and after what had been a long period of hardship he gained a post in a bookbinding firm. The salary was modest but the job gave him security, congenial work and the means of becoming a good draughtsman. In 1902, after three years in the firm, he left it to work on his own, this time with the advantage of practical experience. For four years he did well enough as a freelance illustrator and designer for the book trade. 'May God forgive me for the things I produced in those years,' he wrote in 1922. But he was not a hack. He was probably keenly aware of what was being said and shown in such stimulating journals as *Jugend*, *Die Insel* and

GIULIANO
MANTEGNA · LIVORNO!
S LORENZO DEI MEDICIS
RAPHAEL
FRANCESCO DEI RIMINI·73

An early lettering exercise by Koch, before he became a master of
the pen and graver.

Pan, in which the work of William Morris was described. It was an item in *Jugend* in 1903 which prompted him to take an interest in calligraphy.

In 1906 he was accepted for a post in the Rudhard type foundry in Offenbach – possibly on the strength of his gothic lettering shown in the third volume of Von Larisch's *Beispiele Kunstlerische Schrift* (Vienna, 1906); the lettering is very similar to the heavy weight of the Deutsche-Schrift, Koch's first type for Klingspor. The foundry, re-named in that year for the Klingspor brothers – its owners since 1892 – was achieving a reputation for adventurous typographic development of notable quality. With his new-found awareness of printing types as a field of design it is easy to understand why Koch later wrote, with feeling, 'The ambitions of my life were coming to fulfilment.'

In 1908 he was asked to teach lettering in the art school at Offenbach. The First World War, in which he served as an infantryman, interrupted his career; but in 1918, after some months in an army hospital, he returned home and resumed his work at Klingspor and the school. His classes were over-crowded and, believing in the need for a close relationship between teacher and student, he asked for a change in his role. He got what he wanted: his own room, with just a few students to whom he could be 'helper and guide', to use his own words. In later years some of the most distinguished designers of this century were to recall with gratitude the time they spent as Koch's students or associates in the Offenbacher Werkstatt, as it was called: Berthold

Wolpe, the eminent designer of types, books and much else; the illustrator Fritz Kredel; the typographers Henry Friedlander, Gotthard de Beauclair, Warren Chappell, to name a few. Calligraphy and lettering were their main interests; but they did not limit themselves to graphic work. Carved inscriptions, tapestries, coins, metal work, even church bells – wherever lettering had a place Koch and his helpers would eagerly devote their minds and hands to it. Rodenberg says it was from the work done in Koch's lettering classes that his types were developed.

Koch died in 1934, at the age of fifty-eight. Although the nature and character of the work produced in the workshop, and its 'Renaissance-like atmosphere' (to quote Warren Chappell), might have enabled it to escape the harsh attentions of political authority with greater success than did the Bauhaus, some of its members were vulnerable, or found the prospect before them inimical to the tranquillity they needed. So they sought a new life elsewhere.

In the period of remarkable activity in German creative life which began about 1900 and extended until 1934 there were a number of developments which must have interested Koch and helped to form his ideas and attitudes as a designer.

To begin with, there was the gothic-or-roman argument that engaged the attention of those publishers and printers who, at the turn of the century, had become dissatisfied with the lifeless gothic types which had prevailed for so long. There was a growing desire for types of a simpler style, with something of the openness of the roman. Curiously (as it seems to us now) it was the printed work of William Morris, and in particular Morris's Troy type of 1892, which played a part in strengthening that attitude. The type was copied by the American Type Founders Company and sold under the name Satanick. A number of German founders imported the type from America and issued it

This Troy type was the model of the type on this page, which is made in the United States by the American Type Founders Co. on many bodies from 6-point to 72-point. It is a composite letter—so made by adding gothic mannerisms to a fat-faced and angled roman.

The Satanick type.

Reproduced from De Vinne, *The Practice of Typography: Plain Printing Types*, 1900.

The g in the Satanick type and the bold version of Koch-Antiqua.

under names of their own choosing: Morris-Gotisch, Archiv, and Uncial. They even made light, heavy and open versions of it – clear evidence of its popularity. (Incidentally, it may have been the lowercase g in that type that took Koch's fancy so much that he adopted its form for his Antiqua, Wallau and Kabel faces.) German designers pursued the idea of a type combining the characteristics of the gothic and the roman. The government printing office in Berlin produced an unusual calligraphic roman by Georg Schiller, and Otto Hupp designed an interesting simplified gothic for the Genzsch & Heyse foundry. In 1900 the Rudhard foundry

Nature Poems of henry Scott

Illustrated by John Richard Brough

The Neudeutsch type by Otto Hupp.

EVERY few months, during recent years, some literary or typographical Knight Adventurous has started on the quest of the New Type, — the type which is to be perfectly original, or, at the least, altogether unhackneyed, and yet which is to be so normal that no one will be able to object to the form of any of the letters as fantastic or unfamiliar. The quest is no new one, though an unusual number of people are interested in it just now. It has

The Eckmann face.

Catalogue Exhibition of the German Empire

The Behrens type.

issued Otto Eckmann's type, an extraordinary design owing more to *art nouveau* than to gothic or roman. Rodenberg said it was a great success. About the same time the foundry issued a design by the architect Peter Behrens, similar to but rather more gothic than Schiller's type.

These innovations caused considerable interest and discussion amongst German printers, and a certain amount of punditry. In 1905 Klingspor published an essay by Gustav Kuhl (now more interesting to look at than to read) called, in the English-language edition, *On the Psychology of Writing*. It put the argument for the gothic as being the proper letter form in which to express German culture, and for the roman as being easier to read, and settled for an amalgam of the two, such as the Behrens design. But though the Eckmann and Behrens types made the Klingspor foundry's reputation, they did not last long in favour. A conservative element continued to regard roman as appropriate only for 'foreign' work; but the majority of publishers and printers came to see the advantage of allowing gothic and roman equal status for the expression of the German language and, as time went on, to recognise that only in the roman was it going to be possible to create the variety of type faces needed to satisfy the demands of publicity printing.

The gothic, then, continued in favour; but there was a general desire to see it revitalised, a task in which Koch took a dominant role. He became the foremost designer of gothic faces. His first, the Deutsche-Schrift (often called Koch-Schrift) became immensely popular. Of the forty-five types, including variations, credited to Koch in the *Handbuch der Schriftarten* − many of them, no doubt, drawn by others under his direction − twenty-four are gothics, and it is on them that Koch's high reputation in Germany is based.

'Lettering gives me the purest and greatest pleasure,' Koch wrote. He owned a copy of Edward Johnston's *Writing and Illuminating and Lettering*, and, as previously noted, he contributed to the *Beispiele Kunstlerischer Schrift*, the books of examples of lettering that Rudolf von Larisch began to edit in 1902 (C. R. Mackintosh, Georges Auriol, Alphons Mucha and Emil Weiss were amongst those whose work was shown). Koch probably found Von Larisch far more stimulating than Johnston. As Alexander Nesbitt has pointed out, Johnston's efforts in reviving historic writing styles and his teaching of the use of the broad pen were, and are, valuable in the early training of the student of lettering, but they were limited in their scope and purpose and had little relevance to practical applications. By contrast, Von Larisch encouraged inventiveness. His chief interest was in developing the creative abilities of students by the use of all sorts of writing tools − brushes, ball-pointed pens and blunt sticks as well as the traditional broad pen − and by a flexible and unfettered attitude of mind. In regard to that it may be said that in Koch's time the designers of lettering and type faces in Germany had a potential advantage over designers in other parts of the world. They had two species of alphabet to explore and cultivate, the gothic as well as the roman. Their creative powers must have been vitalised by the richness of the one and the comparative simplicity of the other. And because the roman was a fairly new field of interest for them, designers were not constrained by a sense of tradition, and one might expect that they would have produced some fresh and attractive designs in the genre. It must be said, though, that the roman types designed in Germany up to 1940 were respectable rather than notable, and the italics were hardly more than serviceable – Wolpe's Hyperion being a distinguished exception. Koch's only 'normal' roman design, the Marathon, had so many inconsistent features as to make one think he was not really interested in it.

The remarkable activity in the visual arts in Germany during the first two decades of this century must have had a stimulating effect on Koch. No doubt he was aware in 1905 that the desire of young painters to free themselves from academic realism, Impressionism and *Jugendstil* had resulted in the formation in Dresden of 'Die Brucke', one of the most active groups in the movement that came to be called Expressionism, whose purpose was to externalise the inner world of the spirit, and whose means were the exploitation of a 'primitive' style, unbroken colour and the dissolution of perspective. Koch must have been particularly interested in the work of those artists who used the woodcut as a medium for highly charged effects on the covers of Expressionist writings. When Koch began to produce illustrative woodcuts in 1919 he employed the same vivid manner of expression – the violent-seeming tool cuts, the powerful contrast of white and solid black – as had Heckel, Schmidt-Rottluf and others, though in the examples I have seen his subjects are the simplicities of his religious faith and his love of nature, not the manifestations of emotional intensity so often characteristic of the Expressionists. As to the harshly vibrant lettering that was sometimes to be seen in Expressionist woodcuts, I think Koch's Neuland type is evidence of his awareness of it and also of the value of working directly into the material, though the type is much more disciplined than was, say, the Mendelssohn type, of which more later. It is in Koch's calligraphic work rather than his drawn lettering or his type designs that the full effect of his own kind of expressiveness is to be seen.

Another source of creative activity in Germany which must have interested Koch, though it does not seem to have influenced him much, was the Bauhaus. It was directed by Walter Gropius, who had worked in Peter Behrens's architectural office, and included Kandinsky, Klee and Moholy-Nagy on its staff. Its troubled progress was brought to an abrupt end in 1933 by political power, just as its activities and ideals were beginning to make an effect. Koch may have had more sympathy for Gropius's statement that 'the sensibility of the artist must be combined with the knowledge of the technician to create new forms in architecture and design' than for Moholy-Nagy's belief that 'mathematically harmonious shapes . . . represent the perfect balance between feeling and intellect'; but in Koch's workshop in Offenbach he and his friends took a simpler view: that the craftsman, with the sensibility of an artist, should create forms which, whether new or old, expressed the heart and mind of the individual.

Koch's first type was the heavy weight of the Deutsche-Schrift. It was issued by Klingspor in 1910, and light, bold and condensed versions followed during the next three years. His other gothic types include the Maximilian, the Frühling, the Wilhelm-Klingspor, the Jessen and the round gothic Wallau, which Rodenberg called Koch's most beautiful type face. And there was the Claudius face, issued after his death. The variety, vigour and richness of the letter forms in those types are easy to appreciate, and the texture they present is a visual pleasure of a special kind, making a page of roman seem, in comparison, noticeably pallid and formal. A thorough study of the gothics, though, is a task for more competent hands than mine. In any case, it is better here to concentrate on three of Koch's roman types which not only gained international favour when they were introduced but are available now in at least one electronic typesetting system.

Rudolf Koch's gothic types.

Amtlicher Fremdenführer durch Allenstein

Deutsche-Schrift bold.

Richard Wagner: Der fliegende Holländer

Maximilian.

Die schönsten deutschen Märchen für unsere Kinder

Frühling.

Die Kulturgeschichte der europäischen Völker

Wilhelm-Klingspor.

Die Grundzüge der gotischen Malerei

Jessen.

Ouvertüren und Arien von G. Puccini

Wallau.

Erzählungen aus dem Sachsenwald

Claudius.

abcdefghijklmnop

qrstuvwxyz

ABCDEFGHIJ

KLMN

OPQ

RSTUVWXYZ

1234567890

The annual picnic this year will
be held at the new reservation at
NANTASKET BEACH

Koch-Antiqua roman.

Koch's first roman type, apart from the set of decorative capitals called Maximilian Antiqua, was the type known as Locarno in Europe and as Eve in America. In Germany it was called Koch-Antiqua; and because it appears in a current catalogue in that name it seems the best one to use here. The roman was issued in 1922, the italic in the following year and the bold in 1924. The origin of the design can be seen in a lettering exercise done by Koch at the Offenbach school in 1921, and then reproduced in his *Das Schreiben als Kunstfertigkeit*, published in Leipzig in 1924. As Rodenberg pointed out, this was one of several cases where Karl Klingspor, on seeing a piece of Koch's lettering, encouraged him to develop it into a type face. The Klingspor private press introduced the type in a special printing of Alfred Lichtwark's *Der Sammler*; a sample page of it was included in *The Fleuron* v. The type was chosen for the text of the Limited Editions Club's *Grimm's Fairy Tales* (1931), where it must have been the perfect companion to Fritz Kredel's woodcuts. The Curwen Press in London used the italic for several books. But Koch-Antiqua is not a book type; it is too mannered for that purpose. I know of no type more elegant; but it must be said at once that the elegance is deliberate, not artless; lively, not restrained. The impress of the designer's personality, to recall Rodenberg's phrase, is clearly visible. Koch-Antiqua is a highly individual design. It reveals the working of a fastidious mind and a skilful hand.

Anyone fortunate enough to have access to the type specimens issued by the Klingspor foundry (the quality of their typography and printing has never been equalled) should take time to study this fascinating type letter by letter. The unusual characteristics of the face are numerous. There is its weight, which is notably light; the considerable height of the capitals and ascenders compared with the lowercase; the great difference in width between B, P, R, S, T and A, C, N, O. There is the tapering of the vertical strokes in the tall letters, a feature derived from the use of a flexible pen. And there is Koch's distinctive lowercase g, making its first appearance. Every letter shows something of interest, often of an unorthodox kind. Note, for example, that h has two-way serifs at the top of the stem but a single serif on its right leg; that i has one serif at its foot but r has two; that the top half of s is larger than the lower half; that the y is oddly out of character. (A similar y was included in Koch's Jessen gothic type when it was supplied to printers outside Germany. With its two oblique strokes it was out of harmony with the strong verticals of the rest of the alphabet. The letter y occurs rarely in the German language. Perhaps German designers of the time had the same sort of uncertainty about the correct form of the letter as there sometimes is when a non-German designer has to draw the German double-s character.)

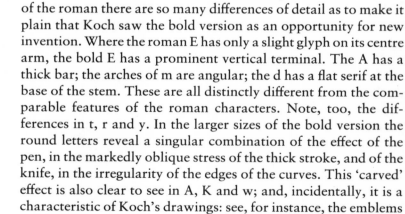

Song of Home
GRINDER
Rode through the natural
HAIL COLUMBIA
BARGE

Koch-Antiqua Bold.

The sign for brother,
from *The Book of Signs*,
the English version
of Koch's *Das Zeichenbuch*.

Although the bold version of Koch-Antiqua is a close relation of the roman there are so many differences of detail as to make it plain that Koch saw the bold version as an opportunity for new invention. Where the roman E has only a slight glyph on its centre arm, the bold E has a prominent vertical terminal. The A has a thick bar; the arches of m are angular; the d has a flat serif at the base of the stem. These are all distinctly different from the comparable features of the roman characters. Note, too, the differences in t, r and y. In the larger sizes of the bold version the round letters reveal a singular combination of the effect of the pen, in the markedly oblique stress of the thick stroke, and of the knife, in the irregularity of the edges of the curves. This 'carved' effect is also clear to see in A, K and w; and, incidentally, it is a characteristic of Koch's drawings: see, for instance, the emblems in his *Das Zeichenbuch*. There was a heavy version of Koch-Antiqua, with so much weight added to the thick strokes as to cause the loss of everything that made the other weights attractive. It was not exported.

The italic of the light face is less admirable than the roman; pretty and affected rather than elegant, the angle rather too acute, though e is almost upright, and the d is a positively ugly letter. In the 12 point and smaller sizes the capitals are single stroke; but from 14 point upwards the main strokes in the letters have a thin line added – an idea which only a designer thoroughly familiar with the elaborate capitals of some of the older German gothic

*When, in the course of human events it be=
comes necessary for one people to dissolve
the bands which have connected them with
another, and to assume, among the powers
of the earth, the separate and equal station
to which the laws of nature and of nature's
God entitle them, a decent respect to the*

OPINIONS OF MANKIND

*Men in all conditions of
life, the lowest as well as*

THE HIGHEST

Koch-Antiqua italic.

**Object is photographed twice
the size the plate is to be when**

COMBINING THESE

Koch-Antiqua Bold italic.

lettering, and uninhibited by the traditions of roman and italic,
would apply to an italic face. The bold italic is a different case.
The lowercase is a sloped roman and therefore comparatively
plain, though it is not very comfortable to read because the round
letters are too upright. The capitals from 18 point upwards have
the double-line main strokes, and because the capitals are less
fanciful than those in the light italic they make a pleasant effect
when used with each other in titles – better, in fact, than when
they are the initials in lowercase words.

The Koch-Antiqua types, especially the light versions, were
obviously well suited to such ephemeral printing as invitation
stationery and fashion advertising, so swash versions of the
capitals were produced as alternatives. This was gilding an
already decorative lily. And in response to an American fashion
of the 1930s, the founders even offered special tall capitals and
ascenders letters, four times the height of the ordinary lowercase.
It is difficult to believe that any printer would accept such an
unrealistic notion.

The Koch-Antiqua design became very popular in the 1920s;
the American Type Founders Company even engaged Willard

Sniffen to design a close imitation of it, called Rivoli. Koch's design was perfectly suited to express in print the idea of 'elegance' in social and business affairs. The type probably has no place in the 1980s; the notion of elegance is under-valued now, even when it is understood. But for the student of type design Koch-Antiqua is interesting not only as an unusual type in itself but for the contrast it makes with the next type to be considered – a type from the same hand, and one of the most remarkable designs of the twentieth century.

Koch's Neuland type appeared in 1923. It has two obvious characteristics: it is a sans-serif, and the letter forms seem to be unpremeditated and 'accidental'. In both respects it is not the first of its kind. Sans-serif lettering of the same blockish style had been used to powerful effect on posters designed by Oskar Kokoschka in Vienna before the First World War, the lettering looking as though it had been rapidly cut from paper; and, as previously

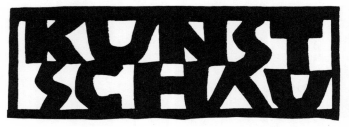

From a poster by Oskar Kokoschka, Vienna 1908.

noted, a primitive unregulated effect was the chief characteristic of the titles in the woodcuts on the covers of Expressionist publications. The Neuland type is, though, entirely Koch's own in its handling and realisation. And there is no doubt that it was his own idea to create the type, not Karl Klingspor's. Klingspor disliked the face, but he respected Koch so much that he allowed it to be produced (though he omitted it from his book on type design, *Über Schönheit von Schrift und Druck*, published in 1949 shortly before his death).

Neuland was much admired in its time. Francis Meynell used it in 1924 for the Nonesuch Press edition of *Genesis*, where the type accompanied a set of white-line woodcuts by Paul Nash. Stanley Morison referred to the type as 'very fine'. The normal and the inline version of the face were popular with advertisers in Britain. And Monotype produced an imitation of it called Othello (its name was the best thing about it). At the present time the face is included in a catalogue issued by a manufacturer of filmsetting equipment; but it seems unlikely that the type will regain much of its former popularity, because of its distinctive and powerful personality and the absence of a lowercase. Yet the design is well worth examining, for reasons that will emerge.

In the first specimen of the type issued by Klingspor there is an introduction signed by Koch himself. He begins by telling us that, as was once the custom, the creator of this design and the maker of the punches is one and the same person. There was no previous design on paper, he says; the type emerged directly from the action of the tool on the metal. The file alone produced the letter forms – first in the shaping of the counter-punches, which were struck into the face of the punches to make the interior spaces, and then to fashion the outer edges of the letters. So far, so good. He then says: 'Since the invention of printing until well into the nineteenth century punch-cutting was done in exactly that way.' That is true enough as to the physical operation, at least in some quarters; but Koch's statement might lead the reader to think that the punch-cutters of the past produced their punches without any sort of reference in front of them. No doubt they did not work from drawings of the modern kind; but the evolution of type designs during the four centuries since Gutenberg makes it plain that punch-cutters must have had some sort of model or pattern at hand – a professionally written manuscript, a printed page, a font of type, or a previous set of punches; and their shaping of the letters on the metal, with whatever subtle divergence from the model was intended, was premeditated and deliberate, and as accomplished as time and skill allowed.

The final words in Koch's note are interesting. 'This method allows a measure of freedom in the formation of characters which could not have been achieved by any other means, and therein lies the justification for the undertaking.' This is a strong clue to his motive. I suspect that he wanted to see in type form the kind of vigorous and untrammelled lettering he had often included in woodcut prints and block books; that he could get the effect he wanted only by cutting the punches himself; and that by so doing he was demonstrating his belief that the craftsman and the artist should be one – a view he held strongly and sincerely, as Rodenberg records.

Spontaneity and the fortuitous effect were to be the chief characteristics of the type; and that, it was thought, would be the

ABCDEFGHIJKL
MNOPQRSTUV
WXYZÄÖÜ 123
4567890.,:·'!¡
-()/»«-&✶✚

Neuland.

STUDIUM LITTERARUM

DER KUNSTKRITIKER

WISSENSGEBIETE

BUCHDRUCK

BREISGAU

ARBEIT

RHEIN

Neuland: note the changes in letter shape from one size to another.

natural result when the letters were cut directly on the metal by the designer. But was the design as artless and 'natural' as it seemed?

Some, but not all, of the letters vary in shape from one size to another. Consider the E, for example: the treatment of the ends of the horizontal strokes is so different from size to size as to make one think the difference is contrived, not accidental. By contrast, the shape of the S hardly changes; if it had done so, it could only have become ugly or absurd. The thought occurs that some of the variations are the result of intention, not chance; as if, having cut the first size, Koch realised that an apparently random result in the other sizes could only be achieved by deliberately shearing the strokes in another way, so that the E, for instance, would be noticeably different in one size from the next. A much greater illusion of spontaneity would have been gained if several variations of each letter had been made in each size, to be used by the printer at random, as was done much later in Freeman Craw's Adlib type. That may indeed have been the intention, because there are variant forms of C, R and U to be seen in the 28 point (possibly the pilot size), but not in any other.

When in *Dossier A–Z 73*, Charles Peignot said, 'A clear distinction must be made between lettering and type design. In lettering, fantasy is of the essence; in type design, discipline is the first requisite', he was stating a truth (though I would prefer 'freedom' to 'fantasy' and 'regularity' to 'discipline'). In the Neuland type Koch seems to have been trying for the unattainable, the perfect fusion of lettering and type; to put a free style of lettering into a system – the ordered accumulation of letters in a text for printing – in which the individual characters are essentially repetitive, the second and third A in a line being exactly the same as the first. The more frequent the occurrence of a letter the more it diminishes the illusion of spontaneity – at least for the typographically trained eye. For the layman the casual effect may seem quite convincing – until a line of Neuland is associated with another type, when the contrast of the 'free' and the formal may produce in the subconscious a vague sense that something is not what it purports to be.

Erhebe die Hände,
Angesicht,
urnamenlos
über mein Haupt,
das feucht ist von Wein und Lachen!
Ich stürze in blitzende Stunden,
reisse mein Blut hoch in blühende Frauen,
und wiege dahin in singende Geigen ⁓
siehe ⁓

The Mendelssohn type.

The point is made clear by the Mendelssohn type, which was introduced by the Schriftguss foundry of Dresden in 1921 (two years before Neuland) and used by the publisher Jakob Hegner in books with woodcut illustrations. The 'unpremeditated' appearance of the letters, particularly the e, is negated by the frequency of their occurrence, especially when there are two of them in a word. The same is true of the Houtsneeletter cut for the Enschedé foundry in 1927, a similar exercise in the 'primitive'. And the point applies equally to those informal script types, simulating the effect of brush or pen, which appear on the typo-

ORDE OP DE 🐌 MOUW, EN
had onder den arm een ver
sleten 🌿 portefeuilletje, 🍃
waarin de boeken van een
🍃 of ander leesgezelschap
werden rondgebracht. 🐌

André van der Vossen's Houtsneeletter, for Enschedé.

graphic scene from time to time. Even Mistral, perhaps the most thorough attempt to achieve the illusion of rapid handwriting, ceases to be convincing after one's first sight of it, in spite of its numerous alternative characters. (As to alternative forms: they are a practical possibility in a system of manual composition, such as 'rub-down' lettering; but in a keyboard-directed film-setting system a special computer program is needed to call the alternatives into position – a process which is necessary and advantageous in the composition of Arabic but hardly justifiable for a display roman used only occasionally).

The Neuland type, then, demonstrates that free lettering is incompatible with the inevitable regularity of type in print. The intention that brought the design into being was unrealisable. In the strict sense, the type is a failure. But failure is often more interesting than success. And after all, it is a matter of degree. The strength of the illusion of spontaneity varies according to the number of the 'free' letter forms, and the context. A one or two-word title in Neuland, in which the letters do not repeat themselves too often, in association with one of Koch's gothic types – the bold Koch-Schrift, the Jessen or the Wallau – makes a fine and homogenous effect. But when Neuland is used with a roman text face it seems to be over-acting – which leads to the thought that there is a place for a roman with something of the angularity of the gothic; the quality, in fact, of which we catch a glimpse in Berthold Wolpe's Pegasus roman and in Warren Chappell's Trajanus type.

'The task of creating a type with a pair of compasses and a straight-edge has always attracted me . . .' A curious statement from Koch who, according to Siegfried Guggenheim, a friend of many years, was proud of his title 'der Schreiber' and to whom, as Fritz Kredel said, a handwritten book seemed the pinnacle of achievement. Yet the words were quoted by Julius Rodenberg in an article he wrote soon after Koch's death – and Rodenberg was a careful writer. My guess (it is just that) is that Koch was rationalising what was for him an uncharacteristic piece of work; not out of conceit – he was reputedly the most modest of men – but to help make it clear that he alone was responsible for it and any defects it might have. He went on: 'People are always saying that I try to express my own personality in type design, but that is not at all true; on the contrary, I do my best to avoid such expressionism. Only I am not always successful. Even in this case I have not succeeded.' (Whether or not that was a bad thing remains to be seen.) It is my impression that the Kabel sans-serif type – for it was that that Koch was referring to – was not the outcome of a long-held personal desire to add ruler and compass to his familiar lettering pens and woodcutting knives (how could such an artist, or anyone else, for that matter, develop affection for a ruler or a compass?). I suspect it was simply his response to an exterior demand, perhaps from Karl Klingspor himself. And having accepted the task he applied himself to it with enthusiasm, soon forgot the commercial origin of the task and remembered only the new experience it provided.

Klingspor must certainly have been aware of the lively interest that was being shown in the idea of a modernised Grotesk, and he may well have seen trial proofs of the faces that Jakob Erbar and Paul Renner were creating for rival foundries. If so, he would have told Koch that the new style that they had contrived for the sans-serif derived from the use of geometric forms. Koch may have learnt that independently. In any case, he responded to the idea in his own way. In the designing of Kabel his attitude was rather different from that of other designers; the geometry was there, but so was art – the 'personal' features to which Koch alluded in the statement quoted earlier.

The light version was the first to appear, in 1927. In the following year a thirty-two page booklet (the most handsome type founder's specimen I know) showed all the sizes of Kabel Light from 6 to 84 point. It included a set of diagrams which are as interesting for what they do not show as for what they do. They are reminiscent of the instructions for designing roman letters published by Fugger of Nuremberg in 1538 and by Dürer before him. The diagrams show the proportions of capitals to a square,

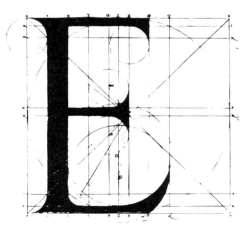

A letter from a manuscript instruction book by Johann Neudorffer (1497–*c.*1560).

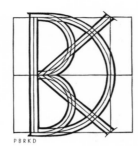

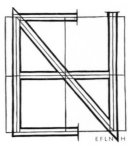

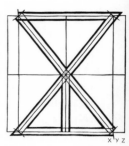

OCGQS PBRKD EFLNTH X'YZ

'Construction' grid letters from the Kabel specimen.
Both Neudorffer (see preceding page) and Koch probably drew
their letters without constraint, and 'rationalised' them afterwards.

and to each other. The explanatory text speaks of the great
variety of letter widths which can be made from a straight line at
various angles, circles large and small, and sections of them. This
variety of widths, says the text, is stimulating to the reader; it was
always understood in the past, but recently the designers of 'grotesques' have regulated the widths of capitals and produced a
monotonous effect unsuited to today's needs. It all looks as
though there is a module, the square divided into a certain number of vertical parts, and that the width of the capitals is determined by it. But it does not take long to discern that the square is
not really the controlling element in the diagrams: that the widths
of B, D and U have been decided visually, not geometrically, and
that the diagrams are simply an attractive piece of window dressing to influence people into accepting Kabel as a rational design.
But Koch was evidently not a man to be bound by arbitrary rules.
In Kabel Light the arms of E are actually of three different
lengths; the bowl of R is deeper than that of B, and in P it is deeper
still; the U has a full-length vertical at the right; and Y does not
have the vertical stem shown in the diagram. In short, Koch's
sense of style is in command, rather than any geometric formula.
The result is an alphabet of capitals that relate perfectly without
need of the 'mathematical harmony' that Moholy-Nagy spoke
of. They are, for my taste, the most attractive of all sans-serif
capitals.

The lowercase is not quite so pleasing. The x-height is little

Kabel light.   more than half the height of the ascenders, which certainly makes

The firm, the enduring, the simple
and the modest are near to virtue
THAT IS THE QUESTION

for a pleasant effect in text sizes. But there are some unfortunate letter shapes. The narrowness of m is very noticeable against round letters. The w is too wide for h, and looks awkward in the 'wh' association which is frequent in English words. There are wayward details in some letters: the shortened bar in f (t is better looking), the inadequate ear on r, the cropped head of a – though in later specimens an a with a wider top made an unannounced appearance in some sizes of some of the faces of the family. Most particularly, there is the excessive angle of the bar in the e.

The medium weight of Kabel also shows those obtrusive characteristics; but the bold version (actually hardly more than semi-bold) has some interesting differences. There are changes in proportion: for instance, the D – see the specimen below on this page – is wider, and the r and some other lowercase letters are in better relationship. Only the e is a disturbing character, too 'active' for this class of design. The sheared terminals of the straight strokes, clearly visible on the H in the specimen overleaf – a feature which owes nothing to geometry – ingeniously increase the liveliness of the design. (As noted earlier, Eric Gill wanted to do something like it in the descender characters of his sans-serif type, but was dissuaded. Dwiggins had the same idea, and got away with it.)

Della stessa famiglia del primo premio, i due lavori
IL RISORGIMENTO GRAFICO   12345678

Della stessa famiglia del primo premio, i due lavori
IL RISORGIMENTO GRAFICO   12345678

Das Wanderbuch

Das Wanderbuch

Am Rosenhag

Am Rosenhag

Kabel medium, bold and heavy, showing the alternative characters.

The heavy version is different again. Because of the considerable increase in weight (the strokes are about 75 per cent thicker than those of the bold version) the lowercase x-height is necessarily larger. Several letters have a new shape: A, M, R, S, W and a are notable. The E, F, L and T retain the distinctive

GOETHE

Kabel Bold: from a Klingspor specimen book.
Later specimens show G with an internal bar.

chamfered horizontals, but all other strokes have squared-off terminals. No doubt the designer realised without hesitation that to shear such heavy strokes at an angle, however slightly, would produce an undesirable restlessness in the face. (The types under scrutiny here are, of course, the ones created by Koch and issued by Klingspor in 1929, not the modern American travesty of them, which should in decency have been given another name.)

In its early days Kabel was much admired. Harry Carter spoke of it as 'almost as good as Johnston's sans, and is thought by many to be better'. However, Futura must have been a formidable rival for the printer's favour, and Klingspor evidently decided that some of the idiosyncracies of Kabel were an obstacle to its commercial success. So an alternative version of the letters W, a, e and g, and an uncrossed 7 for the light and medium, were See previous page. offered under the name 'Neu-Kabel'. I do not see much value in them. In a type as stylish as Kabel the cross-over W should have been acceptable, though the alternative plain version would have been advisable in the sizes below 10 point. The original a (but with the long top) is more legible than the round form. Koch's original g is more expressive than the alternative, though it would have been better with a larger upper section, as in the italic. As for the e: though normally averse to the Jenson form, especially in a sans-serif, because it disturbs the stability of a word, I think that in Kabel the form contributed to the vitality of the design. However, if the bar of e had been angled at about 15 degrees instead of 32 the vivacity of the type would not have suffered and the rhythm of the letters would have been improved.

The condensed versions of Kabel were not outstanding; and the shaded, called Zeppelin in Germany, was an awkward

GRAND EMPIRE

INSTRUCTOR

Prisma, 30 and 36 point.

mixture of effects. The really interesting and attractive decorative version of Kabel is Prisma. It is not, as might be thought,
merely the capitals of the heavy face with their strokes engraved,
but a revised and regulated version (note the E, R and M) with an
ingenious system of corrugation. The large sizes had five black
lines to the stroke; but the smaller sizes had four lines, to maintain the 'colour' and to prevent filling-in – a practical refinement
not likely to be offered in modern filmsetting versions of the face.

The three types that have been studied here are the most personal, the most independent from previous models, of any discussed
in this book. In all three the letter shapes are distinctive and
distinguished, the work of a refined and inventive mind; and in
two of them, the Koch-Antiqua, especially the bold version, and
the Neuland type, the hand-cut edges of the letters create a keen-
featured appearance which is in refreshing contrast to the regular
and impassive profiles of the majority of type faces. And that sets
up a train of thought.

Suppose an accomplished and sensitive designer, dispirited by
the deadening effect of the total accuracy of present-day photographic methods of type manufacture, recognises the spirit which
animated Koch and decides to adapt to modern materials and
tools the method he used in the creation of Neuland. He sketches
a set of characters on paper, directly and freely but with enough
care to establish a coherent style and a decent balance in the
proportions of the letters one with another. He does not then
make a highly finished drawing of each letter, as is commonly
done, but cuts the characters directly in a laminate masking film –
these 'friskets' to be used for the making of the master font.
Without straining to make all the strokes exactly equal in weight
and the serifs identical in shape, he allows the hand and blade to
make their natural effects on the contours of the letters, while
firmly resisting the temptation to produce a 'hand-carved' effect.
If in the final printed result the letter shapes are natural, the type
is thoroughly readable, and the method of creation is unobtrusive, we might applaud the designer for restoring to type
something of the human quality that Updike and Van Krimpen
thought had been mechanised out of existence. It might be
objected, though, that the notion is only feasible in a system
employing simple characters-on-film fonts and through-the-lens
output, where the designer's work would be quite unaffected by
the manufacturing process, whereas in the modern method of
producing type faces by digitising and editing, the free-hand
characteristics of the design would be so tampered with as to
nullify the hoped-for effect. Not only that. It might be regarded as
an aesthetic solecism to create a set of letters by such a craft-like
method only to have them re-constituted as vectorised outlines –
a criticism that, if valid, would preclude the designing of any type

that owes its characteristics to a tool, such as pen or brush scripts. Indeed, some may say that the only logical design tool today is the light pen or the cursor spot on a display screen. Perhaps we must wait for the day when vectorising is an automatic process, editing is unnecessary, and the result is a true facsimile. When the designer's work can be reproduced directly and with complete fidelity, without any sort of doctoring, we may hope to see, just occasionally, type faces with something of the originality and craftsmanlike quality that were Koch's particular contribution to twentieth-century type design.

16: The types of W. A. Dwiggins

Of the five designers whose work is discussed in these pages W. A. Dwiggins is the one who most closely engaged himself with the manufacturing processes of type faces for mechanical composition, accepted their limitations and made use of their possibilities. He is the only American designer to create a sans-serif type of any merit; he created one of the best book romans of the twentieth century, and also one of the most popular; and he produced a number of designs which, though they were not put on the market, are of considerable interest, and some would have been a positive asset to the printer.

Dwiggins's career is as well known to the American typographer as is Goudy's. In Britain his work is not so well known, though his Metro type has been a constant favourite in British newspaper printing for over forty years, and his Caledonia is frequently seen in the text of modern publicity matter.

William Addison Dwiggins was born in Martinsville, Ohio, in 1880, the son of a doctor. At the age of nineteen he moved to Chicago to study art at the Frank Holme School of Illustration. He met Goudy there, became interested in lettering, and did some miscellaneous work for advertisers. In 1903 he removed to Cambridge, Ohio, and started a small printing office, but it proved inadequate as a means of making a living. When Goudy announced his intention to move east to Hingham, Massachusetts, in 1904, and invited Dwiggins and his wife to join in the venture, Dwiggins agreed, and lived there until his death in 1956. For his first twenty years or so there he had a successful career as a designer and illustrator in advertising. Amongst much else he did some work for a music publisher in close imitation of the elaborate cartouches to be seen in French and Italian engravings of the second half of the seventeenth century. It has been said that he had a liking for the chinoiserie fantasies of Jean Pillement, a predilection which sometimes shows itself in the head and tail pieces he used in his book work.

By 1928 he had become dissatisfied with the ephemeral nature of publicity work, and he decided to concentrate on the designing and illustrating of books. He had already met Alfred Knopf, the eminent publisher of the Borzoi titles, for whom Dwiggins eventually designed nearly three hundred books. In 1932 he designed and illustrated Daudet's *Tartarin of Tarascon* for the ·Limited Editions Club, and he was responsible for a further seven books for that distinguished imprint before his death. He worked for Random House, the Lakeside Press and other publishers of note, and gained a considerable reputation in that field.

In regard to the illustrating of books Joseph Blumenthal, the eminent American printer, has expressed an interesting view. 'As a general rule I do not believe in book illustration . . . Illustration in the literal sense can only portray, at best, the artist's personal view of the text.' But suppose the artist's mind is in perfect accord with the author's, as, for example, George Cruikshank's was with Dickens's: is not the reader's enjoyment of the writer's work immensely increased? I think so. Applying that criterion to the limited amount of Dwiggins's book work I have seen, I do wonder if his reputation was wholly justified. To me his drawings lack vitality, and his line is not expressive. Added to that, his amiable cast of mind, which by all accounts made him a very agreeable man to know, may have prevented him from responding fully to some of the literature he was asked to illustrate. For instance, in his treatment of *Gulliver's Travels* for the Peter Pauper Press he loaded the book with devices and images quite alien to the spirit of Swift's satire, and not at all interesting in themselves. His double-page title for the Random House edition of *The Time Machine* (1931) has been much admired; but it seems to me to be entirely out of touch with Wells's bleak fable of the end of all life, and to be no more than a self-indulgent display of ill-arranged and disparate elements. Some of them are the decorative units which he assembled from home-made celluloid stencils. Beatrice Warde, writing as 'Paul Beaujon' in 1928, made much of these, and quoted Dwiggins about them: 'The thing is not to draw the working machine, but the curve that is in the mind of the engineer before he designs the thing.' That is just fancy talk, and would have brought an emphatic comment from the engineers I used to know. Some of the stencil units are arcs of various sizes and thicknesses, drawn with a compass; others are simplified leaf shapes; some are geometric forms. With these, and with lines and shapes added for the occasion, he would produce two-dimensional constructions suggestive of plants or buildings, or abstractions like the work we now call *art deco*. Their novelty is undeniable, and they evidently charmed the publishers of the time. Later on he used the stencil technique to create an attractive range of decorative borders for Linotype. And he made use of stencils – or rather, templets – in his type designing, as we shall see.

The wording on the title opening of *The Time Machine* was not typeset but hand drawn; not really calligraphic, though part of it is in a light script. The title and the name of the author, designer and publisher are in a careful representation of typographic letter forms. Beatrice Warde was perceptive when she wrote, 'Mr W. A. Dwiggins has not yet published a type design; yet his talent is above all typographic . . .' Although the quality of his work as illustrator, book designer and decorator is a matter for argument there need be no doubt about the standing of his type designs.

Curiously, his first commission was not a book type, but something quite different. In his *Layout in Advertising*, published in 1928, he had expressed a need for a better sans-serif type. 'Gothic capitals are indispensible, but there are no good Gothic capitals. The type founders will do a service to advertising if they will provide a Gothic of good design.' A member of Linotype's staff in New York read this and invited Dwiggins to design such a type. (No doubt the Linotype people had already become aware of the Erbar, Futura and Kabel types imported from Germany, had recognised their own need for a modern sans-serif, and were looking around for a designer.)

When Dwiggins's attention was drawn to some of the new European sans-serif faces he conceded that the capitals were good but thought the lowercase could be better. It was into the lowercase of his own design that he put particular effort and introduced some unusual features. It looks as though he and the manufacturers were thinking of the new type as a display face, or for use in short paragraphs of advertising copy, and not as a text type for general use, because the face which Dwiggins actually drew himself was the bold type, known as Metroblack. It was issued to the public in 1929.

The capitals are a plain well-balanced set of letters, nearer to the style of the Gill sans-serif than to the German faces. The lowercase too, like Gill's design, is suggestive of traditional letter forms rather than the 'new' geometric ones. The ascenders and descenders, except y, are sheared at an angle – a good device, I think, for 'humanising' the overall effect (see the chapter on Rudolf Koch for his use of the same device.) The a, e and g have a distinct variation in stroke thickness; it is more acceptable in the a than in the other two letters, where the thin parts have an unsettling effect on words. The most unnatural letters are f, t and j, which are cropped at head or foot, so that they look as though they have suffered damage in casting. Those defects in the bold lowercase are not nearly so obvious in the light version, called Metrolite, which was designed by Linotype but supervised by

ABCDEFG abcdefghijk
HIJKLM nopqrstuv
NOPQR wxyzab

AGJMNVWagvw,;''
AGJMNVWagvw,;''

Metroblack and its alternative characters.

Dwiggins. That applies to Metromedium, too. Taking the three weights together, the widths of the characters are noticeably at variance. In the bold, the foundation design, the width is normal. The light face is wide, because its characters had to fit to the widths of the bold characters with which they were duplexed. The sprawling appearance of the light face probably troubled the Linotype design people, because in the medium weight they reduced the width – and rather over-did it. There was a fourth version, Metrothin, available in the United States but not in Britain.

Not long after the Metro faces were introduced it was evidently decided that they would gain extra favour if they could be given some of the distinctive characteristics of the German sans-serif types which were taking the eye of American printers and their customers. Alternative versions of seven capitals were designed (the W in two forms), five lowercase letters (the Jenson e was later discarded), and three punctuations. These 'No. 2' forms are the ones that are supplied in the photo-composition fonts of the Metro faces.

In the United States Metro lost much of its popularity when Futura became available for slug composition by Intertype and, under the name Spartan, by Linotype. For over forty years Metroblack and Metrolite have been used by British newspapers for intros and crossheads, and have continued in use even though other sans-serif types are available. There are certainly better sans-serif types than Metroblack and its companions (and some much worse); but though the design can hardly stand with other types of its time – the work of Erbar, Renner and Koch in Germany and Gill in England – it does have a degree of originality which, from a first-time designer, deserves respect.

Linotype were sufficiently impressed with the type, and with Dwiggins himself, to offer him a contract: on their side, to pay him a regular retaining fee, payment for the designs he supplied, and a guarantee to make punches and matrices of any trial design he sent in; and on his part, to create for the company type faces of commercial application and promise (that they would be of high quality could be taken for granted). Thus began an association which lasted twenty-seven years and resulted in twelve type designs (not eleven, as Paul Bennett has said), though only five were actually made available to the trade. Dwiggins's associate in the work ('partner' would be more appropriate) was C. H. Griffith, who had started in Linotype in 1906 as a salesman, graduated to assistant to the president and, about the time under discussion, became responsible for the company's typographic development. Dwiggins now had to use his experience in lettering for advertising to formulate ideas about letters for printing. Griffith had to learn to understand the characteristics of the designs which Dwiggins put forward; to supervise their manufacture, in which he was able to rely on the experienced eye of Nils Larsen, head of Linotype's type drawing office; and to evaluate the faces in discussion with Dwiggins. The two men educated each other. Their correspondence, with many drawings and type proofs, is preserved at the University of Kentucky. If this were a full biographical study of Dwiggins it would be necessary to make a thorough examination of the Kentucky archive; but the chief purpose here is simply to make a personal appraisal of his type designs, and fortunately proof sheets and other specimens are at hand.

In the early 1930s the Linotype drawing office and matrix-making plant in New York were occupied with the Granjon and Janson book types, the Textype and Excelsior newspaper faces, and the Poster Bodoni type for display purposes. Dwiggins himself was busy with his book designing. So it is not surprising that their working arrangement took time to reveal itself. Two years passed before there was any sign of Dwiggins's second type, in the form of trial characters; and it was 1935 when it was introduced to the printing trade. Electra, as it was called, was a book type. Rudolph Ruzicka, writing in 1948, described it as 'the crystallization of his [Dwiggins's] own calligraphic hand. Though highly disciplined, the pen hand is still revealed in the flick of the weighted horizontal serif, in the finial of the lowercase c and other subtle accents, and in the sweep of the curves generally.' It is not easy to accept that as a description of the Electra roman, where the discipline is much more evident than the calligraphy. But it must be said that Ruzicka was echoing what Dwiggins himself had written in the specimen booklet which introduced Electra to the public: 'The weighted top serifs of the straight letters of the lowercase: that is a thing that occurs when you are making formal letters with a pen, writing quickly. And the flat way the curves get away from the straight stems: that is a speed

CHAPTER I
THE AUTHOR GIVETH SOME ACCOUNT OF HIM-
SELF AND FAMILY; HIS FIRST INDUCEMENTS TO
TRAVEL. HE IS SHIPWRECKED, AND SWIMS FOR
HIS LIFE; GETS SAFE ON SHOAR IN THE COUN-
TRY OF LILLIPUT; IS MADE A PRISONER, AND
CARRIED UP THE COUNTRY.

MY FATHER had a small Estate in Not-
tinghamshire; I was the Third of five
Sons. He sent me to Emanuel-College
in Cambridge, at Fourteen Years old,
where I resided three Years, and applied my self close to my Studies: But
the Charge of maintaining me (although I had a very scanty Allowance)
being too great for a narrow Fortune, I was bound Apprentice
to Mr. James Bates, an eminent Surgeon in London, with

——Nec si miserum Fortuna Sinonem
Finxit, vanum etiam, mendacemque improba finget.

Electra roman and italic.

product.' In such a context Ruzicka and Dwiggins were not very
precise in using the terms 'calligraphy' and 'writing', which
strictly mean the forming of letters by the flowing action of a pen,
held at an unchanging angle. A better word would have been
'lettering', meaning the drawing of letters, the pen or brush being
lifted and angled at each stroke so as to achieve a particular
modelling and style. Here and there in Electra it is possible to see
a resemblance to the lettering in the simulated advertisements
with which Dwiggins illustrated his *Layout in Advertising*. But
the fact is, to describe the Electra roman in terms of calligraphy or
drawn lettering is more misleading than helpful. It is hard to
think of any twentieth-century book type plainer and less expressive than Electra. But it is not faceless: it has character and
distinction, the result of unobtrusive features like the unbracketed serifs, the flat arches of m and n, the refinement of R, the
modelling of a and g. In American book production it ranks as a
modern classic. In Britain four sizes of the roman with italic had
been made when the outbreak of the Second World War brought
the work to a halt; it was not resumed when the war ceased. The
absence of some necessary sizes, and of the cursive, prevented
Electra gaining favour in Britain. Some typographers were un-
aware of its existence until it appeared in filmsetting catalogues.
   Dwiggins and Griffith were familiar with the writings of Stanley Morison, and a study of their personal papers might support
the belief that, like Jan van Krimpen, they were impressed by

Morison's theory, propounded in *The Fleuron* v, that the proper form for the secondary companion to a roman was a sloped roman. That is what the first 'italic' for Electra was – a sloped version of the roman, without any concession to the letter forms of traditional italics, the flowing f, the round a, the looped e, and so on. Linotype did nothing to inform the printing trade that the italic of Electra was designed according to a new doctrine. Even if they had done so it is most unlikely that the face would have gained total acceptance. It did not; and Griffith and Dwiggins evidently felt it necessary to produce an alternative italic in

Electra with Electra Cursive, 12 Point. Electra Cursive has sufficient stress to use with texts *for emphasis,* as may be noted here. So clever is its design that *only the lower-case letters* and the usual 'f' ligatures need be added to convert outstanding fonts in use. The new Cursive is shown here in five sizes: 8 to 12 point, inclusive. *Linotype's Electra Family* comprises

Electra Bold with 'italic' and Cursive.

traditional style. Electra Cursive, as it was called, appeared early in 1940. It consisted of lowercase and the f ligatures. It was Dwiggins's first attempt at a normal italic; he was to do better later. The a looks small; d and u are flat-bottomed; the face lacks the 'action' that Dwiggins was so keen on. It is this Cursive which is supplied in the current digital fonts; the original sloped roman is no longer made. Electra was also given an attractive bold companion for display setting.

The third type from Dwiggins's hand, his Caledonia, was also a book face. It appeared in 1938. He wrote that the design of the roman grew out of a liking for the sturdy version of the modern face which was developed by some Scottish type foundries in the early years of the nineteenth century (hence the name Caledonia), together with his liking for a type cut by William Martin about 1790 and used by Bulmer. Those were severely impassive faces;

GRMD hst

TWELVE POINT ON FOURTEEN POINT BODY. The *fine* printer begins where the careful printer has left off. For 'fine' printing something is required in addition to care—certain vital gifts of the mind and understanding. Only when these are added to a knowledge of the technical processes will there result a piece of design, i.e. a work expressing logic, consistency, and personality. *Fine printing may be described as the product of a lively and seasoned intelligence working with carefully*

Caledonia roman and italic.

Dwiggins's design is decidedly more vital and expressive. Much of its character is due to the slight curve in the terminal of the stems, easily seen in the display sizes. Even in text sizes that feature does a great deal to ensure that the face avoids the dourness of Scotch Roman. To my eye Caledonia roman is not so refined and unassuming as the roman of Electra, which I regard as one of the best text types designed in this century, but the italic of Caledonia is better than Electra Cursive. Electra and Caledonia have a permanent place in the American book designer's list of text types; and Caledonia, which has a good bold companion,

Here is a new type of vigor and distinction – sharp, clean-cut, crisply modern in feeling, with fine letterforms and the necessary degree of emphasis to arrest the reader's eye.

Caledonia Bold.

is also frequently used in publicity work on both sides of the Atlantic.

In 1937, when Caledonia was off the drawing board and in course of manufacture, Griffith may have asked Dwiggins to turn his mind to areas of American printing in which the line-casting machine had an important role. The next two items in the list of Dwiggins's designs are certainly very different from his previous work. Charter, a kind of script type, hardly seems the sort of design that Dwiggins would have thought of without prompting. It is an interesting effort, though not an important one. In *Postscripts on Dwiggins* Paul Bennett referred to it as a 'special purpose' face, but did not specify the purpose. It may be the type referred to in Dwiggins's letter to Griffith of January 1937: 'I send a start on the Eve/Cochin/Egmont project. A brochure type somewhere between Eve and Nicolas Cochin.' (Eve was the

The Council have thought meet to appoint & set apart the 29th. day of this instant June, as a day of solemn Thanksgiving & praise to God for such his goodness and favour, many particulars of which mercy might be instanced, but we doubt not those who are sensible of God's afflictions, have been as diligent to espy his returning to us; and that the Lord may behold us as a people offering praise & thereby glorifying him; the Council doth commend it to the respective Ministers, Elders and people of this Jurisdiction; solemnly and seriously to keep the same.

The Charter experimental face. The capitals are Electra.

American name for Koch's Locarno.) That suggests a type intended for the text of advertising material for, say, a fashion house
or a hotel chain. But the type seems too decorative for anything
more than a line or two. There is another possibility. Griffith may
have told Dwiggins that Linotype did a steady trade with the
printers of wedding and other social stationery, and an alternative to the well-known Card Italic and Lino Script would be
useful. Charter was an informal letter (except for e), upright but
suggestive of script, though the letters did not join. Only the
lowercase was made; trials of an ornamental 'Tuscan' T and V
and a script M were not taken further. In 1946 the type was given
a selective public showing in (surprisingly) book form – a limited
edition of Andrew Lang's *Aucassin and Nicolete*, produced by
the Golden Eagle Press at Mount Vernon, New York. In place of
the non-existent font capitals the small capitals of Electra were
used. The general effect is charming at first sight, affected at a
second view, and not very useful as a specimen of what was
obviously not a book type. Charter was never completed for sale
to the trade.

Soon after Dwiggins began his association with Linotype he
evidently felt that he should contribute to their activity in newspaper type designing. Griffith, who was much involved in the
development of variations of the Ionic type and anxious about
their commercial success, firmly asked him to stay away from
the subject. It was not until 1936, when the 'legibility group' of
newspaper text faces – Ionic, Textype, Excelsior, Opticon and
Paragon – were clearly on the way to dominating newspaper
typography in America (and, indeed, in most of the world), that
Griffith felt able to attend to Dwiggins's ideas and experiments.
But on this subject it appears that Dwiggins was able to say more
than he was able to perform. In a letter to Griffith in 1937 he
referred to Ionic and the derivatives as 'the first intelligent effort
in the line ever made . . . You have taken the style of letter established by custom as "the" newspaper face, and have modified
it step by step until it will print under modern conditions, and can
be read when printed . . . This style was taken over for historical
reasons. It was the style of type-letter in fashion when newspapers began their expansion after the Civil War, and when
Linotype began its career. There wasn't any other kind of letter to
work on, so far as body matter went. So, naturally, Linotype's
experiment fastened upon this style, and by so doing fixed it as
the only kind of type face proper for newspapers to use. The style
was (and is) a much-modified bastard descendent of an original
"Scotch modern". In its post-bellum form it was not what one
could call a highly legible face.' That was sound enough, and
Stanley Morison would have applauded it – having expressed
similar ideas (though not so well) when his Times Roman was
introduced five years before. Unfortunately, the implication in it

The captain was still prowling about the deck. Hubbard heard him lift up his voice in a hail, "Masthead, there! Keep your wits about you!"

"Aye, aye, sir."

The poor devil of a lookout up there was the most uncomfortable man in the whole ship, Hubbard supposed, without sympathy for him. It was interesting to note that the captain was apparently a little uneasy still about the possible appearance of British ships. Peabody had brilliantly brought the Delaware out to sea—the first United States ship to run the blockade was a touch of elaboration about his gesture which conveyed exactly enough contempt both for the ceremony and for the first lieutenant to annoy the latter intensely, and yet too little to make the captain's clerk liable to punishment under the naval regulations issued by command of the President of the United States of America—not even under that all-embracing regulation which decided that "all other faults, disorders and misdemeanors not herein mentioned shall be punished according to the laws and customs in such cases at sea." The young cub

The Hingham experimental newspaper type, with Ionic capitals.

– that any alternative news face would have to arrive from an entirely new direction – was not borne out by the result. In spite of much experimental work, recently described in detail by Gerard Unger, it looks as though Dwiggins was unable to put the Ionic out of his mind, and could only think of altering its details. In the event, the Hingham design was so much like the Ionic it was meant to surpass that it is now chiefly interesting as evidence that he was being allowed by Griffith (rather reluctantly, in this case) to free-range over a wide area of typographic possibilities. (As it happened, it was Griffith himself who carried the design of newspaper text types to a new level, with the Corona face of 1941.)

A design not mentioned in Bennett's *Postscripts* and never named – it was known only by its factory number Experimental 267D – is a type of particular interest, for several reasons. In February 1942 Griffith sent Dwiggins a number of working drawings for study purposes, including a projection of a letter of 9 point Times Roman; and in a covering note he said, 'On the whole I think we have made a sound approach to the original problem of finding a face with the reading qualities of Bookman and a style somewhere in the region of Caledonia and Times Roman.' Plantin must also have been in their minds, because later in that year Griffith thanked Dwiggins for his analysis of the type and himself remarked on its 'dry and "engineery" effect'. But it seems to have been Times Roman that concerned them most. (Griffith was occupied in supervising the production of Times Roman for the Crowell-Collier company which adopted the face for the text of its magazines at the end of 1942 in a considerable flutter of publicity.) Dwiggins referred to 267D in a letter in December 1943: 'I was always sorry that it had to be laid aside to make way for the Times Roman cutting, because I think it is a better reading letter than T R and more useful. As a matter of fact it is one of the most successful designs in our list, right through the alphabet . . .'

I think he was right; 267D was potentially a much more attractive and effective type than Times Roman – plain enough to

Proof NO. 1 (3-16-'42)— hi
Proof NO. 2 (5-18-'42)— CEFHIMNSTabcdefjlmnoprstuvy
Proof NO. 3 (6-3-'42)— hi
Proof NO. 3 (6-25-'42)— gkqwxz
Proof NO. 4 (11-17-'42)— ABDGJKLOPQRUVWXYZ
Proof NO. 4 (11-17-'42)— *a*
Proof NO. 4 (12 point) (11-17-'42)— an
Proof No. 5 (6-28-'45)— E
Proof No. 5 (6-28-'45)— *efjmnop*
Proof No. 5 (Redesigned) (6-28-'45)— *ahi*
Proof No. 5 (Redesigned) (6-28-'45)— a
Proof No. 6 (Redsigned) (2-26-'46)— DGOQ
Proof No. 6 (Redsigned) (2-26-'46)— E
Proof No. 6 (2-26-'46)— O
Proof No. 6 (2-26-'46)— *bcdgklqrstuvwxyz*

8-25-'47

Props

This comes to us from a fine woman in Chicago. It seems that the junior boys of the settlement house in Chicago—you know the one—were rehearsing "Treasure Island" and found themselves without enough guns for the defense-of-the-stockade scene. Next night one of the youths showed up with a bulky newspaper package. It contained seven .32-calibre automatics. "We c'n use 'em for the rehearsals," he said, "but not

Taxidermist

Three bright little boys entered the Metropolitan Museum one day, and made for the Egyptian exhibits, where they told an attendant they had come to see "the dead men." He showed them where the mummies were, and they stood in front of the cases for about 15 minutes, just looking. As they were going out, one of the innocents approached the attendant and asked, "You kill them and stuff them yourself?"

Experimental 267D.

be unassertive but with just enough character to avoid dullness. (The fact that Times Roman was created as a newspaper type and 267D was intended as a text face for magazines and paperbacks does not affect the comparison. Times Roman achieved its popularity chiefly in general printing, not in newspaper work.) At first sight the roman lowercase of 267D has some similarity to Times Roman, due to its narrowness and its modified old style appearance; but it only needs a few moments study to recognise that it is in no sense an imitation of it. Indeed, in its details the face shows more affinity (unintentional, no doubt) with Dwiggins's own Eldorado, a type we shall meet shortly. The capitals (except for the Q) are superior to those of Times Roman – narrow and of the right weight to harmonise with the lowercase. The italic needed some revision; the a was out of proportion with d, the closed top of w muddled the identity of the letter, the tail of y, which should be the distinguishing feature of the letter, was insufficient. Compared with most types the roman of 267D was distinctly weighty, and since the face was also narrow it would have been difficult to design a bold companion for duplexing with the roman with enough weight for adequate contrast yet with interior spaces open enough for clarity in printing; a problem which did not actually arise, because although work on the project was resumed for a spell in 1947 the type was never completed. There would be no such difficulty in designing a bold version should the type be brought out of obscurity and made available for filmsetting. The thought has much to recommend it. Considering how emaciated some text faces become in modern offset printing the strength of the 267D face would be very welcome.

Spaces and areas seen together in a group do something to the eye, much in the same way that musical tones heard together do something to the ear. You can hear harmonies and discords, and you can *see* harmonies and discords. *Why* harmonies please and discords disturb is still a moot question— the fact is that they do. In music, if your sense of "pitch" is good, you are aware of a harmony immediately and without question, and with a like certainty you mark down a discord.

Under the conditions that control the manufacture and sale of trade-edition books it is not possible to turn out a product that represents the highest possible achievement of the book-making art . . . With no limits set on time and money spent, a book can be made a work of art of the first rank. Paper: *a felt as pleasant to the touch and as beautiful to the eye as the finest woven fabric, firm, pliable, enduring.* Type: *the most legible and graceful letter-shapes that the type-founder can*

Eldorado roman and italic.

East is *n*ot best if it is an fact tactics ease Ei*n*stein

Trial letters for 36 point Eldorado.

Like Experimental 267D the Eldorado type began in 1942, and it is not surprising, as already said, that there are similarities in the two types, and not only because both of them are narrow by intention. According to a note written by Griffith in 1951 there were two motives for setting the work in motion. One was the need to supply printers with a type which would provide the maximum degree of spatial economy, in view of governmental restrictions in the world war period. The other was a desire expressed by South American publishers for a book type which would reflect in an authentic manner some of the flavour of Spanish typographic tradition. When these points were put to Dwiggins he turned to Updike's *Printing Types* and, according to Griffith (quoted in a specimen booklet issued by Mergenthaler Linotype in 1953) Dwiggins found a suitable model in a type cut by Geronimo Gil in Madrid about 1787. However, Dwiggins said in a footnote that though the Gil type was talked about it was not condensed enough for the purpose, so he concentrated his attention on a type used by Antonio de Sancha in 1774 (see Updike, vol ii, figure 236). Perhaps Dwiggins was able to borrow a copy of the original work mentioned by Updike, because the reproduction in *Printing Types* is neither clear nor comprehensive. Progress on the design, which came to be called Eldorado, proceeded a few characters at a time through the war years until 1953, when it was announced for sale. In a few letters, the a and g, for example, and in the strong colour of the face, there is some resemblance to the Spanish type; but the face is really Dwiggins's own. The roman made a pleasant effect on a smooth paper, but on ordinary book paper the soft edges of the letters – due, perhaps, to an incautious liking for the effect of type printed on dampened hand-made paper – may have caused some publishers to mutter darkly about low-grade stereotyping or press work. The italic was wholly Dwiggins's, and he indulged himself in some fancies: not only the curly-topped T as in Baskerville's italic, but a crossed X and Z and a Greek style Y – which was also present in the roman. There was also a tailed G and a mannered Q. Pretty as all these were, they may have had a limiting effect on the popularity of the type for book work.

Except for Metroblack all of Dwiggins's designs were a long time in development, and for most of the years of his association with Griffith there were several experiments on hand, in the form of proofs of trial characters which Dwiggins liked to brood over at leisure. Falcon was one of a number of designs that took their time. It began as an experimental cutting in 1939; but evidently it disappointed the two men. In 1942 a fresh start was made, and the face was eventually carried through to the completion of seven sizes of roman with italic. It was an attractive old style book type, the roman lowercase narrower than that of Electra and Caledonia and its x-height moderate, which emphasised the fact that the capitals were in fact a little too tall and obtrusive. The italic lowercase was mildly calligraphic, much better than Electra Cursive, except for the v, w and y, which had an inward-turning flourish that probably looked charming on the drawing but, to my eye, is irritating in print. For a short time in the 1950s Falcon was available, on special order only; but it was withdrawn when attention had to be concentrated on type face production for photo-composition. Griffith would have been sad; he had written to Dwiggins in 1942, 'I am determined to carry this through to a successful conclusion, even if I have to re-cut it a dozen times!'

Although Eldorado was the last of Dwiggins's types to be made fully available to the Linotype user, it was by no means his last design. Early in 1943 Linotype cut the first trial characters of

Paper . . Paper has more to do with making a *comfortable* book than any other single thing. If a book is printed on a satisfying paper it will be tolerable even though the type-face and press-work are shockingly inferior. On the other hand you may use the finest type available, arrange it with taste, print it to perfection—and still your book will be spoiled as a reading implement if the one point of paper has been mishandled. Appreciation of books begins with the appreciation of paper.

Arrived from China by caravan across remote frontiers, bales of a strange fabric consigned to merchants in Arabia and eagerly awaited there—fibers of cellulose shredded in water, shaken into a felt, and dried flat and smooth so you could write on it. A remarkable fabric, valuable to savants seeking to set down in script

ABCDEFGHIJKLMNOPQRSTUVWXYZ&ÆŒ
abcdefghijklmnopqrstuvwxyzæœfiflffflffiffl

*ABCDEFGHIJKLMNOPQRSTUVWXYZ&ÆŒ
abcdefghijklmnopqrstuvwxyzæœfiflffflffiffl*

Falcon roman and italic.
From a trial proof (the text
by Dwiggins himself).

meet a dwarf waving a fiery dart which burns up everything around it within twenty paces of the apple-tree from which I must pluck an Apple. If I escape the flames and get the Apple, I shall have to go in search of the Laughing Flower, but to pluck this I must beguile a lion whose mane is of living snakes. I shall wait till the lion sleeps (the snakes are for lake, *and on reaching the thither side* a fight will begin between me and the Black Man, whose weapon is an iron ball that returns of itself to the master after every throw. After that I shall enter the Valley of Delights to

Stuyvesant roman and italic.
Note the revision of
italic v and w.

ABCDEFGHIJKLMNOPQRSTUVWXYZ
abcdefghijklmnopqrstuvwxyz

*ABCDEFGHIJKLMNOPQRSTUVWXYZ
abcdefghijklmnopqrstuvwxyz*

Proof No. 5 (11-15-'43)—	*ghijklmpqrstuvwxyz*
Proof No. 5 (11-15-'43)—	E
Proof No. 5 (11-15-'43)—	5
Proof No. 6 (4-25-'44)—	ABCDGIJKLNPQSUVXYZ
Proof No. 6 (4-25-'44)—	*ABCDFGIJKLNPQSUVXYZ*
Proof No. 6 (4-25-'44)—	5
Proof No. 7 (redesigned) (4-4-'45)—	*fvwz*

another book type. Once again Updike's *Printing Types* had provided Dwiggins with a line of thought: the few lines of roman
shown at the foot of a page in the specimen book issued by J.F.
Rosart in Brussels soon after 1760 (Updike, figure 214). It is a
clumsy piece of punch-cutting, but Dwiggins liked the 'metallic'
look of the face and the 'fat terminal bulks − these come out as
little black accents . . .' After a long period of trial and revision
the type that emerged, named Stuyvesant by Dwiggins, had little
evidence of 'metallic' quality in its roman; but the emphatic blobs
are there, in the terminals of a, f and r, and the dots of i and j.
Apart from those the roman, a narrow old style, has no distinctive characteristics; it is a pleasant enough face, but it has none of
the 'well-fed robustness' that Dwiggins said he saw in the Rosart
type. The italic is less attractive − noticeably 'modern' in style and
therefore at odds with the roman. The C, G and O are awkwardly
angled. *Postscripts* says Stuyvesant was used in *The Shirley
Letters* published by Knopf in 1949, but the design was never
developed beyond the 12 point pilot size.

As already said, Stuyvesant was an old style. It appears to be a
contradiction, then, to read in *Postscripts* that, commenting on
the early trial letters of the Arcadia design which were proofed in
June 1943, only a few weeks after the trial characters of Stuyvesant, Dwiggins wrote, 'I am convinced that a narrow, soft, old
style treatment doesn't belong. The letter needs to be round and
crisp . . .' But what he probably meant and Griffith understood
was that if Arcadia was continued in the style of its first trial
letters the type would turn out too much like Stuyvesant; so it had
better be revised. A surviving proof shows a distinct reduction in
stroke weight and contrast in the redesigned version of the trials.
The finished type face, when the 12 point roman and italic were
completed in 1947, was a design that could only have come from
the hand that created Electra, lacking the subtle modelling of that
type but with an agreeable italic. Its most serious fault was in its
numerals: the 2, 3, 5 and 9 are surprisingly inept. Arcadia was
used for the text of Alfred Knopf's *Some Random Recollections*,
issued by The Typophiles in 1949; but the face was never made
for general sale.

On the title page of Knopf's book the readers had a glimpse of
another experimental face, called Tippecanoe. It was an essay in
'the Bodoni-Didot theme', as *Postscripts* puts it − though there is
little sign of any of the Didots in it. Dwiggins was right to assert
that all the available versions of Bodoni seemed 'stodgy', making
a book page look stiff and lifeless. That opinion should surely
have sent him back to the originals, to Bodoni's own designs and
to those of Firmin Didot in particular, and his followers Léger,
Molé and Walbaum. A study of the 'classique' types created by
them might have stimulated Dwiggins into producing something
original and interesting, as Imre Reiner did in his Corvinus type −

In 1923 we were laying plans with Mencken and Nathan for *The American Mercury* and it was only natural to turn over the complete design of the magazine to Elmer, who also did the initial prospectus and much other printed matter that we got out in connection with it. We had planned to have the magazine printed by the Rumford Press and, indeed, they had set a good deal of the matter bought for the first couple of issues.

ABCDEFGHIJKLMNOPQRSTUVWXYZ&
abcdefghijklmnopqrstuvwxyz
1234567890

ABCDEFGHIJKLMNOPQRSTUVWXYZ&
abcdefghijklmnopqrstuvwxyz

The Arcadia face.
From Alfred Knopf's *Some Random Recollections.*

ABCDEFGHIJKLMNOPQRSTUVWXYZ
abcdefghijklmnopqrstuvwxyz

ABCDEFGHIJKLMNOPQRSTUVWXYZ
abcdefghijklmnopqrstuvwxyz

separation from Beacon Street and the Province Club? There is a tendency among non-New Englanders, we believe, to associate Bostonese—at least Bostonese of the Apley brand—with an English accent of broad "a's," slow syllables and shortened vowels. But a writer in a current bulletin of "The Atlantic Monthly" warns New

Tippecanoe, compared with Bodoni, below.

from Beacon Street and the Province Club? There is a tendency among non-New Englanders, we believe, to associate Bostonese—at least Bostonese of the Apley brand—with an English accent of broad "a's," slow syllables and shortened vowels. But a writer in a current bulletin of "The Atlantic Monthly" warns New though Dwiggins might have felt inhibited by his own Caledonia, which was, after all, an exercise in the 'modern' manner. What Dwiggins seems to have done was to take the familiar so-called Bodoni face of Morris Fuller Benton and rework it by a combination of plastic surgery and cosmetic treatment. The stems were given entasis; the interior of round letters was abrupt in one quarter, smooth in another; the italic O had sides of unequal thickness, while N had an obtrusive blob attached to one corner; and there were other features that force one to the conclusion that Dwiggins's view of the task was too superficial to have any likelihood of success. It is a measure of Griffith's willingness to allow Dwiggins a free hand that he did not demur at the project.

Dwiggins's last venture in type design is interesting on two counts: it was potentially a very distinguished book type, but its purpose and development were confused by an ill-conceived linguistic theory which Griffith should have dismissed, politely but firmly, at the beginning of the work.

In short, Dwiggins's theory was that the roman letter was satisfactory for the visual representation of Latin, for which it was created, but not for the English language, which had once had its own style of letter, the 'English-Irish book hand'. He pointed out that eleven of the normal roman lowercase letters have ascending or descending strokes: b, d, f, g, h, j, k, l, p, q and y; and he thought that their frequent occurrence in printed English means that the language looks less graceful on the page than Latin, where they are less frequent and k and y never occur. Some years before he had written, 'It is surprising how little descenders and ascenders have to do with legibility as such. Their function seems to be largely aesthetic: to compel a good-looking amount of paper between lines . . .' – a curious notion. In fact, legibility derives from the differences in letter forms, and the ascenders and descenders (particularly the former) are important aids in the recognition of words. Dwiggins's proposal was to replace the common form of some of those letters by an uncial form, similar to their capital counterparts, so as to achieve a more pleasing texture on the page. In the text of a trial proof he refers to the King's Fount designed by Charles Ricketts for his Vale Press in 1903. All through 1945 punches and matrices were made, proofed and revised, for a new type face in roman and italic, called Winchester, which would embody these ideas. The letters b, d, f, g and h were made in conventional form and also in uncial form; at one stage there were uncial versions of k and t, too. (Goudy had experimented with similar letters in his Newstyle type in 1921, though for a different theory.) In March 1946 a specimen was printed. It included Dwiggins's explanation of the idea, pages in English and Latin for comparison, and two pages in English, one of them including the uncial sorts and the other the familiar lowercase letters. (With my copy there is a

ABCDEFGHIJKLMNOPQRSTUVWXYZ

abcdefghijklmnopqrstuvwxyz
abcdefghijklmnopqrstuvwxyz

aʙcᴅeꜰ𝗴ʜijklmnopqrstuvwxyz
aʙcᴅeꜰ𝗴ʜijklmnopqrstuvwxyz

Winchester: the regular characters
and the uncial alternatives.

Tʜere is no reason to ꜰear tʜat tʜe printinɡ traᴅe will
trample out valuaʙle lives in its stampeᴅe to aᴅopt tʜis
(or any otʜer) revision oꜰ Enɡlisʜ. No traᴅe is more conservative tʜan tʜe printinɡ traᴅe. . . Anᴅ yet . . a time
oꜰ ꜰlux . . letter ꜰorms (anᴅ otʜer ꜰorms) alreaᴅy ʜave
underɡone consiᴅeraʙle moᴅiꜰication . . It miɡʜt pos-
siʙly ʙe tʜat we are movinɡ into some Anɡlo-American
reɡion wʜere a new kinᴅ oꜰ Enɡlish script woulᴅn't ʙe
so unreasonaʙle. . .

Winchester with its uncials.

There is indeed one set of men our inveterate enemies;
they are those whom the madness of P. Clodius has trained
up, and supported by plunder, firing of houses, and every
species of public mischief; who were spirited up by the
speeches of yesterday, to dictate to you what sentence you
should pass. If these should chance to raise any clamour,
it will only make you cautious how you part with a citizen
who always despised that crew, and their loudest threat-
enings, where your safety was concerned. Act with spirit

Winchester in traditional form.

pencilled note by Griffith: 'The uncial d is not successful and
should not have been used.') Visually, the uncial characters in the
'English' page, as it was called, make the page look lighter than
the 'Roman' page, because there are fewer ascending strokes; but
that hardly makes it more 'graceful'. In economic terms, the
'English' page loses eleven words (a full line) because the uncial
letters are wider than the roman. The two versions were used in
the setting of a limited edition of Matthew Arnold's *Tristram and
Iseult*, issued by the Golden Eagle Press in 1946.

Such mild interest as there may now be in all this, as showing
something about the effect of ascenders and descenders on the
texture of type in mass, cannot really be justified by the amount
of effort that was put into what can only be called a futile project:
feeble in its execution by comparison with Victor Hammer's
American Uncial type, which was at least a thorough-going
scheme of letter forms; and as a reform, an unrealistic one on

several grounds, including the undesirable one of separating printed English from the printed forms of other major languages which use the roman letter. And English itself is now such a rich mixture of pickings from other tongues, Mediterranean, Teutonic and much else, that to propose to represent it by the use of characters created by scribes working in religious communities in Ireland and northern England over a thousand years ago makes no sense at all. Time and space have only been spent on the subject here because it was described in *Postscripts* without comment. But ignoring the uncial letters, there is real value to be had from a study of the Winchester roman and italic in their orthodox forms.

The roman was an old style somewhat reminiscent of Granjon. Apart from a slightly awkward d, the design is not only faultless but as good as anything Dwiggins ever did; indeed, I think it is superior even to Electra and Caledonia. Other things being equal, it would have been one of the finest text types of the twentieth century. The thing that is not quite equal in quality is the italic, of which only the lowercase was produced. The f suffered more than was necessary from its inability to kern, and the v, w and y have the obtrusive ingrowing stroke which had made its first appearance in the Charter face.

Winchester made a limited public appearance in Dorothy Abbe's *Stencilled Ornament and Illustration* (Hingham, 1979), the text being set by hand from types cast in a single-type casting machine from a surviving set of matrices (too few, perhaps, to be used in the normal way in a Linotype machine). Unfortunately, the fitting of the characters is much looser than in the original version of 1946.

Dwiggins was thoroughly professional. For him, the drawing of the alphabets of a new type was only the beginning of the work, not the end of it. In 1937, when Linotype commissioned Rudolph Ruzicka to design a book face (it was the admirable Fairfield), Ruzicka asked Dwiggins how *he* set about the task of designing a type. Dwiggins replied in a letter which he subsequently rewrote for publication by the Harvard College Library in 1940. 'The way I work at present [he was presumably referring to his work on Caledonia] is to draw an alphabet 10 times 12 point size, with a pen or brush, the letters carefully finished. I start with the lowercase, and let its characters settle the style of the capitals. Ten times 12 point is a convenient size to work; and I have a diminishing glass that reduces the letters to something like 12 point size when I put the drawing on the floor and squint at it through the glass held belt high. This gives a rough idea of what the reduction does to curves and things. Having got a start on what I want by this means I turn the drawing over to G. [Griffith] and he puts a few of the characters through – possibly lowercase h and p. He makes his large pattern drawings (64 times 12 point), cuts, casts and proves the trial characters; and sends me his large drawings, my 10 times drawings, & proofs on smooth and rough paper. By looking at all these for two or three days I get an idea of how to go forward – or, if the result is a dud, how to start over again. From the large pattern sheets I can see just how details behave when they get down to size, and can change the weights of serifs, thin lines, etc. etc. accordingly. Curves do all kinds of queer things when reduced; and the way lines running together make spots is a thing that will surprise you; but one or two tries on these points give you the information you need. I am beginning to get the drift of it and to foresee from the large drawings what will happen in the type. I can *modify* in the large outline drawings, but so far I can't *originate* in that medium.'

Dwiggins then described another method for establishing the character of a design. For the Falcon type he made stencils for parts of letters, at 24 point size, and constructed letters from them. Those letters were enlarged to the ten-inch size by Linotype; the enlargements were sent to Dwiggins, and he then cut templets, at that size, of common elements such as stems, arches, loops and so on, with which he built up a further range of characters (a similar method is used by some computer-aided designers). Examples of Dwiggins's templets can be seen in Dorothy Abbe's book. His letter to Ruzicka describes the next stage. 'When G. and I have settled dimensions, etc., to our liking, I go ahead with the alphabet on thin bond paper in pencil outline, in the working drawing size . . . My drawing is free-hand (except in such cases as the Falcon templets). I haven't any complaint to make about the staff's French curves – they do a surprisingly faithful job . . . so far as I can observe from the final proof they keep the original touch here too.'

Writing about Dwiggins's ability to design at the ten-inch scale Jackson Burke, Griffith's successor, said, 'This technique is not for the ordinary designer. It involves an ability to think in terms of effects . . .'; and Ruzicka called it an 'unexampled *tour de force* in type design'. That is putting it a little too high. Personal experience has shown that given the opportunity to compare the large letter drawings with proofs of the characters at actual type size it is possible, after a time, to develop fairly reliable judgement as to what will be the final effect of a letter that is drawn many times larger than life.

What Dwiggins did not explain was the amount of thought he put into his type design work at its several stages. It must have been considerable, because it can only have been from much creative thought and experimental drawing that the quality of his designs was derived. Naturally he had his limitations (as we all have), though he may not have recognised them. The Hingham newspaper type could not have succeeded. The Tippecanoe experiment was not well conceived, I think, and a few characters in some of the other types required a second thought. But those are not important in a total view of his achievement. It is unfortunate for us as well as for him that external events – restrictions imposed by the Second World War, the onset of photo-composition and its effect on Linotype's development plans – halted the progress of the Falcon and Stuyvesant faces, which would certainly have been attractive additions to the book printer's repertoire, and prevented the Winchester design from joining Electra and Caledonia in the ranks of modern classics. They would have reinforced my belief, though it is firm enough, that Dwiggins was one of the most distinguished type designers of the twentieth century.

17: Stanley Morison's Times Roman

Times Roman is by now the most remarkable typographic phenomenon of the twentieth century, a basic type in every printer's stock for most of the past fifty years, in spite of the fact that its creator thought at first that the type had only limited application: 'It is a newspaper type – and hardly a book type – for it is strictly appointed for use in short lines . . .'

Times Roman was Stanley Morison's only venture in the field of type design. He had been typographical adviser to the Monotype Corporation and to the Cambridge University Press for several years when in August 1929 he was asked by *The Times* to supply proposals for the improvement of the appearance of the paper. After producing a report on the types in use in the paper he formally proposed, in October 1930, 'that the type faces used in the editorial and advertising columns be redesigned and brought up to the standard obtaining in the average book . . .' (The reference to book typography should be noted.) To propose that the paper needed a better text type than the 'modern' it had been using for over a century was not in itself an original thought. Four years earlier Linotype of New York had introduced the Ionic text type, and it had been enthusiastically adopted by many American newspapers as a welcome solution to the problems caused by the destructive effect of stereotyping and high-speed rotary letterpress printing on the very lean text types then in use. Ionic made its first appearance in Britain in March 1930, in the redesigned *Daily Herald*, where it aroused a great deal of interest. Other newspapers rapidly adopted the type (it is still the preferred text type in the English national 'popular' press), and no doubt the production people at *The Times* took note of its practical effect-

Ebn R

iveness. It seems certain that they would have had to make some
sort of change in their own text face, even if Morison had not
been on the scene. Morison was critical of the Ionic face; but his
printed remarks about it show a curious ignorance of Linotype's
achievement. The Ionic as finally issued was actually their fifth
redesigning of the type, not a straight recutting of the nineteenth-
century original, as Morison appeared to think. However, he
was certainly right to dismiss Ionic as unsuited to the particular
character of *The Times*.

In November 1930 he submitted a memorandum in which the
argument for the revision of the typography of *The Times* was set
out against a background of the history and nature of type designs and recent studies in legibility. It referred to, but did not
describe, an experimental type then in preparation. This was
evidently the 11 point size of Perpetua, equipped with shortened
ascenders and descenders, to cast on 9 point body. Although
Morison was disappointed with its effect – it 'stared at the
reader', he wrote later – it was included amongst the several trial
settings presented to a meeting of *The Times* people at the end of
January 1931, the outcome of which was an instruction to
Morison to prepare two things: a 'modernised Plantin' with
sharper serifs, and a thickened Perpetua (which seems to have
been soon forgotten). What happened then is not at all clear.
Morison's own statements about the creation of the design are
insufficient and unreliable. Insufficient, because he was quite un-
conceited about his work and never said more about his methods
than he thought necessary (not enough, alas, for those who study
his achievements); unreliable, because in two publications issued
within a short time of each other he gave accounts of the origin of
the type which are different, if not actually contradictory.

Over twenty years after the event, when he was preoccupied
with other matters and may have wanted to simplify a complicated piece of history, he wrote in *Printing The Times since
1785*, published in 1953, that when the various trial settings were
being studied it was recognised that there was much to be said for
the sturdiness of Plantin and its economical letter widths but it

was found to be not crisp enough after repeated stereotyping. I quote: 'It was decided therefore to modify the normal Plantin' by sharpening its serifs and reducing its thin strokes. This can only refer to Monotype Plantin 110, the type used for the trial setting. But in the first edition of *A Tally of Types*, also issued in 1953, he said: 'Finally it was decided to put in hand a new design to be excogitated by Morison . . . He pencilled the original set of drawings and handed them to Victor Lardent, a draughtsman in the publicity department of Printing House Square [*The Times*] whom he considered capable of producing an unusually firm and clean line. Lardent made a first-class set of finished drawings of the capitals and lowercase out of the pencilled patterns given him.' That seems to be saying that the design emerged from Morison's mind as a wholly original creation which he himself drew on paper in a manner sufficiently explicit for the draughtsman to follow without difficulty.

Victor Lardent's particular forte was the drawing of lettering for advertisers who did not employ an agency. In 1965, when he drew an experimental heading type for me on behalf of *The Times* (it was a failure; my fault, not his) he was unable to tell me anything of the creative process of the Times Roman types – perhaps because in 1931 it had seemed to him to be no more than a lettering job, not greatly different from others. James Moran had a similar experience in 1968; but he did elicit the information that Morison did not give Lardent any patterns, but did give him a photograph of a page of a book printed by Plantin 'to use as a basis'. This phrase of Moran's has been taken literally in eminent places to mean that the Times Roman type was developed directly from an ancient original – the Gros Cicero cut by Robert Granjon. A note to that effect was included in the new edition of *A Tally of Types* in 1973.

Morison may well have given Lardent a specimen of that type; but I think it more probable that it was a photograph of a page, or pages, from Dr Rooses's edition of the *Index Characterum* published by the Plantin-Moretus Museum in 1905. Rooses's introduction is set in the Gros Cicero type (including some wrong fonts). Morison certainly knew the book; the St Bride Library copy has a pencilled note in his hand on a page of ornamental borders. Whatever the source of the specimen I think it was intended only as a reference for particular details, not as the actual basis for the new type. To make drawings from a sixteenth-century book type – the letters inevitably rough-edged because printed on unsurfaced paper, the alphabets incomplete, the serifs not nearly so sharp as had been specified for the new type – would have been a difficult task, which anyway had already been done in the creating of Plantin 110, as no doubt Morison knew. And it would probably have taken a good deal longer than the nine weeks that elapsed from 28 January 1931, when Morison was

B C D E F G H I J K L M N O P Q R S T U V

W X Y Z a b c d e f g h i j k l n q r ſ s t v w x

y z Æ æ ﬅ & ﬀ ﬃ ﬄ ﬁ ﬂ œ ſb ſi ﬁ ﬅ ﬃ ﬅ ℞ ℣

á à â ā ç é è ê ë ē ę í ì î ï ī ñ ó ò ô ō p̄ p̧ ,p

q̄ q̧ ꝗ q̨ q́ ú ù û ü ū 1 2 3 4 5 6 7 8 9 0 , '

. ; : ! ? ([- * ☙ §   a i m o p u

i m m o p p r ſ u u u ﬁ

instructed to proceed, and 8 April, when Monotype put the 9 point in hand for punch-cutting. On the other hand, Plantin 110 and Times Roman show dimensional similarities that can hardly be coincidental. The first thing to compare is the character widths in each face. This can be done with precision by taking note of two features in the Monotype system: the 'set', which provides the basic factor for calculation, and the 'unit arrangement' table, which shows the number of units allocated to each letter. As to the set: in both types the 7 point size was $7\frac{3}{4}$ set and the 9 point was $9\frac{1}{4}$ set – at least at the beginning, though 9 point Times Roman was afterwards changed to 9 set to tighten the fitting. The basic unit of width measurement was therefore the same in each type. The unit arrangement of Plantin was No. 4 in Monotype's list and for Times Roman it was No. 325. The differences are slight. Only three lowercase letters vary: a is 8 units and k and o are 9 units in Plantin; in Times Roman they are one unit wider. The other twenty-three lowercase letters have the same values in each face, and since the set was the same it follows that the letters had the same actual width. In the capital alphabet, A, R, S and Y are one unit wider in Times Roman, but I and L are one unit and T is two units narrower than in Plantin. The remaining nineteen capitals have the same widths in each face.

For the vertical dimensions of the two types we should look at the alignment and the lowercase x-height. In 7 point Plantin the 'line' (the distance between the top of the matrix and the baseline of the face) was .1257 inch; in Times Roman it was .1268 inch, a difference of .0011 inch (.027 mm). In the 9 point faces the difference was .0013 inch (.032 mm). These differences of just over a thousandth of an inch are so small that they could have been unintentional (Monotype did not work to standard alignments). As for the x-heights it can be assumed that if there is a difference it

See overleaf.

ABCDEFGHIJKLMNOPQ
ABCDEFGHIJKLMNOPQ
RSTUVWXYZ
RSTUVWXYZ
abcdefghijklmnopqrstuvwxyz
abcdefghijklmnopqrstuvwxyz

Monotype Plantin 110 and Times Roman 327 compared.

will be less at 7 and 9 point than it is at 12 point. Monotype's published dimensions in the 12-point sizes of Plantin and Times Roman show a difference of only .0004 inch (.01 mm).

Those details may not be conclusive evidence in themselves; but the variations are so small and the similarities so many as to support my view that Lardent was instructed to work to the proportions of Plantin 110, especially the character widths, as closely as possible, to ensure that the 'economy' of Plantin (that is, its characters per line) was maintained in the new type; and that the best way for him to do that was to use specimens of the Plantin 110 – possibly photographic enlargements, and even copies of Monotype's working drawings – as the actual basis for his own drawings.

At this point it will be useful to recall the origins of Plantin 110. To do that we should look first at a type that preceded it: Imprint, a type of some importance in the history of English type design. Imprint came into being in 1912 because J. H. Mason could not find a suitable type for the journal which Gerard Meynell, Mason and others intended to publish. Mason was a former compositor at the Doves Press, a self-taught scholar and a man of taste. His part in the development of Imprint was to suggest a new type, modelled on Caslon Old Face, with a larger x-height and with an italic harmonising more closely with the roman than does the Caslon italic. He would scrutinise trial proofs and pass judgement on the development of the new face. It was probably Fritz Steltzer, head of the Monotype drawing office, who was responsible for the actual design work. Thus Monotype were the first of the composing-machine makers to produce an original type face 'in the house'; and it was a very good one. In her enlargement of Morison's introduction to *A Tally of Types* (second edition) P. M. Handover wrote that the example of Imprint encouraged Monotype to create another type in the following year, to be developed by the same method. There was probably more to it than that. James Moran suggested that Monotype had taken note of the commercial success of a type recently issued by the Shanks foundry, a kind of bold Caslon, called 'Plantin' Old Style ('in honour of', perhaps, rather than 'in imitation of'). Monotype may have thought it would be good for business if they too had a type of that name, and sensibly referred to the collection of the Plantin-Moretus Museum, and in particular the Granjon Gros Cicero. I think it possible that the text pages of the catalogue, the *Index Characterum* of 1905, served as the source of the new type, which was designated Plantin Series 110. There was certainly a copy of the book in the Monotype plant in 1923, when it was perused with a view to producing a 'true' version of the face. Note that Imprint and Plantin came into existence by the same process: the substantial remodelling of a type of exalted origin so as to satisfy the requirements of modern mechanical techniques of type making and printing.

No doubt Morison was well aware of Steltzer's central role in the successful realisation of the Imprint and Plantin types. In fact, in the previous five years or so he had been able to observe Steltzer's ability at first hand, in the development of several types which Morison had himself instigated. Why then did he not place the preparation of the new types for *The Times* directly into the hands of Steltzer, with such instructions as to the desired outcome as were necessary? There may have been several reasons. Perhaps he surmised that it was going to take much trial and effort to turn his general sense of what was wanted into a satisfactory reality, and therefore decided that the work had better be done close at hand, not in a drawing office twenty miles from London. And it is possible that because Morison was keen to achieve a prominent and lasting position on *The Times* and had a strong desire to impress the editor and manager with his creative ability, he saw that that ambition would be well served by arranging for the new types to take shape in the newspaper's own premises, with Lardent, their own man, involved in the creative process.

The reducing of the thin strokes of Plantin 110 and the sharpening of its serifs could not have been as simple a task as it sounds. How much to take off, and just where to start and finish the process in each letter, were matters for thought – assisted, it seems probable, by a study of existing examples. No doubt the incisive look of the recently-completed Perpetua was kept in view. Charles Bigelow has reported Mike Parker's suggestion that Morison may have taken note of two types cut by Hendrik van den Keere, in 1565 and 1573, both in the Plantin Museum collection and both notable for their large x-heights. Indeed, Morison may have cast his net quite widely for any type which would provide useful ideas about stroke and serif weight. For

They are shown overleaf.

abcde
fghijlm
ABCDEF
GHIKLMN
abcdefghijkl

Characters of Van den Keere's types of 1565 and 1573.

Senatus hoc intelligit, consul vidit:
hic tamen vivit.   Vivit! imo vero
etiam in senatum venit : fit publici

J. C. Bauer's Neue Kirchenschrift, 1862.

example, he may have had a specimen of the Neue Kirchenschrift made by the Bauer foundry in 1862; the type, a modernised old style unusual for its time, is very similar to the final form of Times Roman. It is hard, though, to take seriously James Eckman's assertion in *The Heritage of the Printer* (1965) that Times Roman was derived from the original De Vinne face, 'with a few changes and adaptations'.

The capitals in Lardent's drawing of the roman alphabets contain several features – the sixteenth-century C and S, the pointed centre of R – which appeared in the first proof of the 9 point roman of 22 April 1931; but they were soon discarded. If he had turned the drawing sideways (always a useful thing to do) he

On the facing page:
Victor Lardent's drawings
of the roman (reduced).

ABCDEF
abcdefghij
klmnopqr
stuvwxyz
GHIJKL
MNOPQ
RSTUV
WXYZ

would probably have noticed and corrected the dropped shoulder of capital B. On the drawing the serifs of the letters are elegant; but the drawing being about twenty-two times larger than the final type size, they are much too thin for reduction to 9 point, and the Monotype draughtsmen must have had to strengthen them considerably. In fact, the design process included a great deal of trial manufacture; many punches and matrices were scrapped and remade 'on account of errors in engraving [there cannot have been many of those – the Monotype workmen were very skilful] or second thoughts on the part of the designer'. This supports the view that Morison did not begin with a clear vision of the ultimate type, but felt his way along, so to speak. As to his second thoughts: although, as Allen Hutt remarked, Morison was no draughtsman, he was quite capable of expressing the revisions he needed in the form of sketches; and if he did so it was those, perhaps, that he was thinking of when he wrote his account of the gestation of the type in *A Tally of Types*.

The number of recut punches was 1,075, a figure often mentioned, presumably as evidence of the earnestness that went into the work, though it is also evidence of an inability to make effective decisions at the drawing stage. The figure is large; but a pos-

It may be claimed that *The Times*, with its new titling, its new device, and its new text types, possesses, from the headline on the front page to the tail imprint on the back, a visual unity. But this is no more than the beginning of typographical wisdom, for visual harmony, whatever its significance for the artist, has little value for the general reader unless and until it accompanies the basic factors of textual legibility. The reader needs a definite plainness and familiarity of type design;

It may be claimed that *The Times*, with its new titling, its new device, and its new text types, possesses, from the headline on the front page to the tail imprint on the back, a visual unity. But this is no more than the beginning of typographical wisdom, for visual harmony, whatever its significance for the artist, has little value for the general reader unless and until it accompanies the basic factors of textual legibility. The reader needs a definite plainness and familiarity of type design; the greatest possible size and clearness of impression; and that adjustment of the spacing, first, to the single letters, next to their combination in words, lines, paragraphs, columns, and pages which makes the whole "look right" to him. From this point of

It may be claimed that *The Times*, with its new titling, its new device, and its new text types, possesses, from the headline on the front page to the tail imprint on the back, a visual unity. But this is no more than the beginning of typographical wisdom, for visual harmony, whatever its significance for the artist, has little value for the general reader unless and until it accompanies the basic factors of textual legibility. The reader needs a definite plainness and familiarity of type design; the greatest possible size and clearness of impression; and that adjustment of the spacing, first, to the single letters, next to their combination in words, lines, paragraphs, columns, and pages which makes the whole "look right" to him. From this point of view what, if anything, was wrong with the founts which served until yesterday? Were the types wrongly designed, or were they wrongly used?

All the current newspaper types—the so-called "moderns"—are designed upon a century-old model ; the former type of *The Times* was no exception to this rule, although it was much the best of its kind. But English craftsmen have come to lead the world in all that belongs to the design and printing of books, by studying the art of

The design was created for three essential sizes:
9, 7 and 5½ point.

sible explanation is that several sizes of the faces were already in manufacture when proofs were being studied. For example: the 7 and 5½ point roman were actually put in hand for punch-cutting only five days after the 9 point was proofed. The revision of a letter in the 9 point would affect the other two sizes, and the number of rejected punches would multiply. The same process might have occurred in the making of the other faces in the family.

Early in June 1931 sample drawings and cast type of the roman were supplied to Linotype, who were to make the matrices for the linecasting machines which were used at that time to compose the bulk of the paper. By the end of the year the paper's composing room had been furnished with matrices of the text sizes, and it probably also had Monotype matrices of the heading types (it is curious that Linotype did not begin work on the heading faces until August 1932, only two months before the new types publicly replaced the old). For most of 1932 the date of the change-over was undecided, partly because of editorial preoccupation with the effects on the country of the economic depression and the formation of the coalition government, but chiefly because of internal disagreement about Morison's proposal that the paper's Gothic title piece should be changed to roman. But by 3 October 1932 all was resolved. On that day *The Times* appeared in its new typographic dress, to general admiration.

Something else was new on that momentous day. 'A make of paper, newly manufactured according to a formula for expressing the new fount to best advantage, has simultaneously been introduced to serve it.' Anyone who consults the files of *The Times* of the 1930s will immediately be aware of its high standard of printing, made possible by the journal's comparatively small circulation and the quality of the paper, heavier and far more opaque than present-day newsprint. That the quality of the paper was significant in the effectiveness of Times Roman as a newspaper type was shown in 1956 when, for reasons of economy, a lighter weight of paper was adopted, with a smoother surface (in aid of the famous half-page picture at the back). This made the text type look sadly feeble; so on Morison's advice the text size, which by then was 8 point, was changed to 8 point cast on 7½ point, the descenders being specially shortened. This deliberate reduction of the inter-line white space strengthened the overall colour of the text, but gave it a disagreeable clotted appearance. The practice was abandoned later. It is evidence of the fact that as a newspaper type Times Roman lacked the physique for production conditions less favourable than those enjoyed by *The Times* in the 1930s – a fact always more obvious to American than to British newspaper production managers.

For a year *The Times* retained the sole right to use the type, and then in October 1933 the makers were free to offer the face for general sale. Until about 1950 Monotype called the face '*The Times* New Roman'. Since then they have called it 'Times New Roman' – though after half a century the word 'New' has no significance. Linotype always named the face Times Roman, and that is how most people refer to it.

Times Roman has gained its universal popularity not in newspaper work but in the larger area of printing: book work, especially non-fiction (the *Encyclopaedia Britannica* is a notable example), and magazine and general printing in all its variety. There is no doubt that when printed to a decent standard on unsurfaced paper Times Roman and its italic are effective enough – at least, up to the 10 point size. The bold is less satisfactory. In display sizes, where the professional eye becomes aware of individual characters, some unfortunate features in both the roman and bold obtrude themselves. (It is the original types, those made by Monotype and Linotype for the introduction of the design in 1932, that will be considered here; not the many replications, which vary in details of design and proportion, particularly the versions of limited typographic quality offered by some word processors.)

In the roman the capitals are slightly too wide for the lowercase, though that is not too noticeable. They are also a little heavy. Proof of this is that because all nouns in the German language have to be set with an initial capital some German printers found the capitals of Times Roman objectionable, and Monotype were obliged to produce Series 727, a set of alternative lighter capitals for use with the standard lowercase. In the roman the u, v, w, x, y and z are too tall in comparison with i, j, m, n, p and r, which have a steeply inclined serif at the top of the stem. The same applies to the crossbar of f and t and the arm of k. The fault, which becomes obvious in words like 'divide' and 'jump' in 24 point and upward, may be due to the original draughtsman contenting himself with drawing the letters in alphabetical sequence and leaving it at that, instead of making tests of various letter combinations in word formation. The feet of v and w are sharply pointed and do not extend sufficiently far below the baseline; the two letters sometimes look oddly diminished, especially in electronic typesetting.

The italic looks well, in spite of some ill-proportioned capitals. The lowercase y is ungraceful. The z was originally designed in the curled form to be seen in Garamond, Baskerville and other book types. It is still present in the Linotype version; but Monotype changed the design to a severe straight-stroke form – though the curled style lived on in their later semi-bold and bold italics.

The bold companion face is a puzzle. The requirement of du-

omxiennx

omxiennx

Compare the heights of x and i; the difference in the serifs of
roman and bold; and note the very narrow counters in the bold.

ABCDEFGHIJKLMNOPQ
RSTUVWXYZ
abcdefghijklmnopqrstuvwxyz

ABCDEFGHIJKLMNOPQ
RSTUVWXYZ
abcdefghijklmnopqrstuvwxyz

plexing with the roman, which was probably a factor in the
designing of the italic, did not apply to the bold face. *The Times*
was going to use it for occasional lines, not for text matter, and
needed only the $5\frac{1}{2}$ and 7 point sizes for its line-casting machines;
they were supplied as single-letter matrices. In the designing of
the bold face, then, there was freedom to allow the letters to
become a little wider than those of the roman, as the balancing of
the interior spaces with the thicker vertical strokes demanded.
That would have been the natural course; but quite the reverse
occurred. The unit arrangement table No. 324 for Times Bold
shows that in the lowercase only the x is wider than the roman, by
one unit. Eleven other letters, b, d, h, m, n, o, p, q, u, v and w are
one unit narrower. (And remember, the roman lowercase was
itself an intentionally narrow type.) In the capitals, J is two units
wider than the roman and O, P, Q and Z are one unit wider, but
A, D, F, G, K, N, R, S, U, X and Y are one unit narrower. The
only explanation I can suggest for this unusual procedure is that
Morison was anxious to prevent critics within *The Times* from

picking on any of the new types as being uneconomical, instructed Lardent to keep the bold face narrow, and Lardent (if it was he) observed the requirement too faithfully.

The narrowness of the bold face, especially in the lowercase, should have set a limit to the amount of weight on the strokes. But Times Bold is too heavy, and the weight is not properly distributed. Too much weight was given to the main strokes and not enough to the thin strokes and serifs. This means that in h, m, n, u and b, d, p and q the interior white is tall and narrow, which emphasises the verticality of the main strokes. The result is a harsh 'picket fence' effect. A little less weight on the uprights and a little more on the horizontals would have achieved sufficient contrast in a less staccato manner. Against this cramped lowercase the capitals as we know them look noticeably wide. It is now forgotten that at the beginning Monotype announced two versions of the bold capitals. They were described as follows in the presentation pamphlet: '*The Times* New Bold-face No. 1 is used in three sizes of upper and lowercase, 5½, 6, 7. In these sizes the capitals are wide but the lowercase is condensed. It is designed for use with the New Roman.' '*The Times* New Bold-face No. 2 in 7, 9, 11 and 12 point consists of capitals which are condensed equally with the lowercase.' Actually eleven of them were unchanged. The condensed capitals in the No. 2 version were C, M, O and Q, three units less than the first version, G, N and S, two units less, and D, H, J, L, P, T, U and V, one unit. These condensed letters sorted better with the lowercase than the No. 1 version; but they would have made a poor effect in a line set entirely in capitals. They were, of course, a plain acknowledgement of the fact that something had gone wrong in the design process, and were a forlorn attempt to improve matters. They continued to appear in the Monotype catalogue as Series 345 for many years, but only in the original four text sizes. The over-wide No. 1 capitals have always been the ones in general use, and have been imitated by most other manufacturers.

The style of the Times Bold lowercase is another puzzling matter. In this age of type-on-film it is an accepted thing that any new type design, other than a script or fancy letter, will be made in a variety of weights (more than are really necessary, it often seems). But that was not the case in 1931 when the Times Roman types were being created. There were very few old style types with a properly related bold companion; but there were enough of them – the bold version of Monotype's Garamond, Horley, Plantin and Baskerville, for instance – to serve as a general guide as to how such a task should be handled. And the Bold Face Series 53, so familiar at that time as a working companion for various old style faces, would have been a good model for an effective partner to the new roman. So why was it decided to design the bold face with some of the characteristics of the modern style –

vertical stress, and flat head serifs in the lowercase? It may be that
when the whole project had advanced to the stage of designing
the bold version Morison lost a little of his confidence in 'old
style' as a suitable style for a newspaper text type, even for a
paper as distinguished as *The Times*, and turned to the modern
for plainness and lack of bookish characteristics. This disparity
in style between the roman and the bold was evidently something
the German Linotype company thought should be eliminated. In
the version of Times Roman they issued in 1935, first called Neue
Romanisch but then named Toscana, the bold lowercase was

> **Bierbaum, Otto Julius. Sonderbare**
> **Geschichten.** 3 Bde. München, Paul
> Müller 1908. 8°. Orig.-Halbpergbde.
> Dabei: **Derselbe. Irrgarten der Liebe.** Mit
> Buchschmuck von Hnr. Vogeler. Leipzig,
> Insel-Verlag 1902. Kl. 8°. Orig.-Lederbd.
> **Derselbe. Stilpe.** Roman aus der Frosch-
> perspektive. **Derselbe. Die Schlangen-**
> **dame.** Roman. 2 Bde. 8°. Berlin, Schuster
> & Loeffler 1906. 8°. Original-Leinenbde.

The Neue Romanisch bold face (1935).

redesigned in the 'old style' mode. The idea of harmonising the
bold with the roman was logical; the actual execution, especially
the character spacing, was not well done. The type soon disappeared. The designers of recent types in the Times Roman style,
such as Life and Concorde, have been more successful in achieving the desired compatibility. For that matter, the Jubilee newspaper type of 1953, for which I was responsible, was an earlier
attempt to obtain that result.

It is now appropriate to turn to the other types in the Times
Roman family.

The five titling faces, which had an important role in the redesigning of *The Times* in 1932, were of various weights and
widths to suit the degrees of emphasis to be given to news items.
The design of four of them was derived from the capitals of the
text roman. The 24 point size of the Heavy Titling Series 328 was
the first to be worked upon. A 1937 specimen sheet shows (by a
composing-room error, no doubt) in the 24 point only, the serifless G and S that can be seen in Lardent's original drawing of the

FARM GARDEN IS BATHED
IN SHADOWS AND BY THE
ABCDEFGHIJKLMNOPQRSTUVWXYZ

24 point Times Titling 328, showing the G and S as first made,
and as actually issued.

ABCDEGHIJ KLMNPQRS TUVWXYZ

Titling 339.

ABCDEFGHIJKLMNOPQRSTUVWXYZ

ABCDEFGHIJKLMNOPQRSTUVWXYZ

ABCDEFGHIJKLMNO PQRSTUVWXYZ

Titlings 329, 332, and 355 (Hever).

roman. The Extended Titling, always called simply '339' in the paper's composing room, was quite the finest set of capitals in the family. Allowing for the fact that the letters are by intention fairly broad, it is instructive to compare them in detail with the capitals of the familiar Times Bold, and to note how much better they are, particularly the C, E, F and G. The most original of the titlings was the Hever, Series 355, which was used in the paper's arts columns. Its design owes nothing to the basic roman, but something, no doubt, to Poliphilus, at least in the C, G, S and W.

Incidentally, all the titlings were unusual in not filling the body size. In fact, the capitals and numerals are smaller than those of the ordinary roman and bold faces. There was a good practical reason for making them carry a substantial amount of 'white' below the baseline; it eliminated the need to insert spacing 'leads' between the lines of a heading – and to be able to save say thirty seconds per heading amounted to a welcome benefit in page make-up in the hectic hour before press time.

There was another member of the family created at the outset, the Times Roman Wide, which was thought to be the version of the roman that would be preferred for book work. In the 10, 11 and 12 point the baseline is slightly lower than in Times Roman,

ABCDEFGHIJKLMNOPQR STUVWXYZ

abcdefghijklmnopqrstuvwxyz

ABCDEFGHIJKLMNOPQR STUVWXYZ

abcdefghijklmnopqrstuvwxyz

22 point Times Roman Wide 427.

ABCDEFGHIJKLMNOP QRSTUVWXYZ
abcdefghijklmnopqrstuvwxyz

24 point Times Semi-Bold 421.

ABCDEFGHIJKLMNOP QRSTUVWXYZ
abcdefghijklmnopqrstuvwxyz

Times Bold Italic.

so the face is a little taller; and the set is wider, to enable the characters to be expanded – a process that would have been better avoided in the case of the italic. The type has never become popular.

Times Semi-bold was created in 1936, in 7 point, for the composition of a hand-held Bible. The person in charge of the design must have been aware of the excessive height of v, w and other letters in the original Times Roman, as mentioned earlier. In the Semi-bold they are much improved. In the Monotype original version the Semi-bold is excellent up to 12 point. At 14 point the design becomes curiously narrow. Present-day film-set versions make a better effect in display sizes than did the metal version.

Times Bold Italic is not one of the original set of faces. It appeared in 1956, almost twenty-five years after the bold roman. The design follows the style of the italic companion to the roman, and therefore has sloping head serifs in the lowercase. If it had been modelled on, say, Bodoni Bold Italic it might have harmonised better with the bold roman.

To express a personal view, I think the task that Morison instigated and directed in 1931 was the remodelling of an existing type, the Plantin 110, to an extent that fully justified him in calling the outcome 'new'. In a letter to Updike in 1937 he wrote, 'It has the merit of not looking as if it had been designed by somebody in particular . . .' This was not only a dig at Goudy but an expression of his dislike of any sign of egoism – and no one will disagree with him in that. But in saying that the type showed no evidence of being designed by someone Morison indicated what I regard as the cause of its chief defect. After all, a type of its kind is not just an artefact; it is a design, the result of a sustained creative act. It ought to have enough of a persona to make it more than merely recognisable. It should have a character. To be sure, it should not be a demonstration of a designer's conceit; but neither should it be faceless. To my eye Times Roman lacks the insignia of true creation; it is too much the reworking of something else, the Plantin type – which was itself, as we know, a regulated version of an earlier design. Its letter forms are well-bred but dull, without subtlety of shape or engaging characteristic. (Francis Meynell devised a way of providing its precursor with an attract-

See page 50.

ive persona, in the type called 'Nonesuch Plantin'; perhaps Times Roman would respond to similar treatment.) This absence of character is obvious, and a little depressing, in display sizes; it is less so in text sizes. Paradoxically, this dullness, which for me denies the type a place in the first rank of distinction, becomes a sort of virtue in that broad variety of work we might call 'plain printing' – reference books, official printing and much else – but not, to my mind, web-offset printing, where the serifs often dematerialise so that the roman looks lifeless and the bold disagreeably strident.

To make that criticism is not to diminish the magnitude of Morison's efforts in the typographic transformation of *The Times*; it was a remarkable achievement. After all, his one and only venture in type designing was not the outcome of leisurely contemplation and experiment, but of expediency; a set of types designed to serve in a particular area of printing (indeed, in a very particular newspaper), an area which he had lately studied from the historian's viewpoint but in which he had had no practical experience. In such circumstances uncertainties of judgement are more than likely, as I know to my cost. The creating of the type faces must have taught him a great deal. If the course of his life had been different and he had produced a second type it might well have been a masterpiece.

Prospects

The paperless office is a reality. Many people have put away the blotter and the stapler, and spend their working hours in front of a desk-top screen, contemplating letters of the alphabet made of dots of light – an absorbing and valuable experience, no doubt, but not one to induce an admiration for letter forms *per se*. The paperless society is talked about; but, thankfully, it is still only a gleam in the eyes of the matchmakers for the marriage of telecommunications and the computer. Printed matter, and all that goes with it – the news stand, the public library, the junk mail through the door – will be with us for some time yet, and typographic letter forms will continue to be a source of interest and pleasure for many and of revenue for some.

'Printed matter' is a very general term, taking in things as different in kind as a birth certificate, the *New Yorker*, an airline ticket, the Yellow Pages, *War and Peace*, and everything else one can think of. It might be thought that, as in other fields of industrial design, a type designer would have a particular sort of work in mind when he or she begins a new type face. Types for newspaper text or a telephone directory are certainly treated as designs for a specific purpose. Serious attention is given to the constraints in production and usage which test the designer's willingness to give precedence to the functional over the aesthetic aspects of the design. But many of the type faces that have been introduced in recent years seem to have been designed not for a specific task but for the favour of a class of people, the typographers, who, for the past sixty years or so, have made a profession of dealing with the verbal part of printed matter. The type design studios and the suppliers of type fonts think of typographers as being free to use any type face they fancy, and as having the power, through the advertising agency or design office that employs them, to influence typesetters to install a new type series, however short-lived the typographers' favours are known to be. Before the advent of filmsetting the typographers' power in that respect was limited by the high cost to the typesetter of matrices and the storage of them. It meant that typographers had to be quite sure about the merits of a new type design before they felt entitled to twist the arm of the typesetter. Filmsetting has changed that. Digital fonts are not expensive and are becoming cheaper. Storing them is not a problem. Typesetting houses, whose numbers increase, take the capital expenditure on new fonts as a matter of course, and some of them make a play for the typographers' favour with the blandishment of the latest type before being asked for it.

The abundance of types now available, and the rate at which new designs are introduced, ought to be wholly beneficial; but they seem to have had a soporific effect on taste and judgement. There can be no other explanation for the low quality of some designs now current. A number of faces introduced in recent years, text types as well as display, can only have been designed by the incompetent and produced by the cynical. The fact that they have found any approval at all induces the impression that there are typographers whose appetite for anything new is stronger than their discrimination. That comment hardly applies to book typographers, most of whom are not much moved by fancy. They are generally in that field of work because they like books and want people to read them and, except when they tackle a coffee table book too enthusiastically and allow the layout to overwhelm the text, they are usually content to design a plain readable page and to choose for it one of the tried and tested text faces. Publicity typographers work under a different compulsion. Their need to make print attractive and persuasive seems to lead some of them to think that the reader will respond more readily to a new type than to a familiar one. 'New' and 'familiar' have meaning for the typographer but little or none for the ordinary reader, who, understandably, can only just identify a 'block' letter from a 'small' one. What the reader actually responds to are the simple attributes of clarity in the message and harmony and polish in its presentation – qualities which, in Britain at the time of writing, are more evident in television titles and captions than in printed publicity work.

However, typographers are by definition knowledgeable about type designs and most of them have some taste in the matter, latent though it may sometimes be. It is to be hoped that before long some means will be created – an independent journal, perhaps – which will be more than just a source of information about new designs derived from suppliers' handouts, but will act as a forum in which critical judgement on typographic matters can be expressed and debated, so that typographers will be moved to examine their own preferences and prejudices, and type designers will know that their latest offerings must undergo the appraisal of people who not only enjoy type but have a critical eye for its aesthetic and functional merits.

No doubt trashy type faces will continue to be designed so long as their makers can see a profit in them. We must hope there will be fewer of them, and more of the kind that can be admired for something other than mere novelty. Typography may be no more than 'a minor technicality of civilised life', as Stanley Morison remarked, but it deserves the best we can give it.

List of works consulted

For the history and development of type designs the following titles have frequently been consulted in the course of this work:

De Vinne, T.L., *The Practice of Typography: a treatise on the processes of type-making, the point system, the names, sizes, styles and prices of plain printing types* (New York, 1900)
Johnson, A.F., *Type Designs, their History and Development*, 2nd edn. (London, 1959)
Nesbitt, Alexander, *The History and Technique of Lettering*, 2nd edn. (New York, 1957)
Updike, D.B., *Printing Types: their history, form and use*, 2nd edn. (Cambridge, Mass., 1937)

The following is a work of particular interest. It is composed in twenty-one different book faces:

Books and Printing: a treasury for typophiles, ed. Paul A. Bennett (New York, 1951)

Some of the following works have been useful on several occasions, but they are listed only under the title of the chapter for which they were chiefly consulted.

1: THE VOCABULARY OF TYPE

British Standards Institution, *Typeface Nomenclature and Classification, BS 2961:1967* (London, 1967)
Dreyfus, John, *Typorum Conspectus* (Cambridge, 1957)
Southward, John, *Practical Printing: a handbook of the art of typography* 2nd edn. (London, 1884)
Tracy, Walter, 'Type Design Classification', *Visible Language*, v, 1 (Cleveland, 1971)
'The Vox Classification', *Linotype Matrix*, 28 (London, 1958)

2: TYPE MEASURE

Tracy, Walter, 'The Point', *Penrose Annual*, 55 (London, 1961)

3: TYPES FOR STUDY

Morison, Stanley, *A Tally of Types: with additions by several hands* (Cambridge, 1973)

5: THE MAKING OF TYPE

Bigelow, Charles, 'Technology and the Aesthetics of Type', *The Seybold Report* (24 August 1981); 'The Principles of Digital Type', *The Seybold Report* (8 and 22 February 1982)
Bullen, H.L., 'Linn Boyd Benton, the Man and his Work', *The Inland Printer* (Chicago, October 1922)
Carter, Harry, 'Optical Scale in Typefounding', *Typography*, 4 (London, 1937)
Flowers, Jim, 'Digital Type Manufacture: an interactive approach', *Computer* (Los Amitos, May 1984)
Fournier on Typefounding: the text of the Manuel Typographique (1764–6), trans. and ed. by Harry Carter (London, 1930)
Legros, L.A. and Grant, J.C., *Typographical Printing-Surfaces: the technology and mechanism of their production* (London, 1916)
Loy, William E., 'Designers and Engravers of Type', *The Inland Printer*, 20 (Chicago, 1897 *et seq.*)
Warde, Beatrice, 'Cutting Types for the Machines', *The Dolphin*, 2 (New York, 1935)

Benton, Waldo & Co., *Benton's Self-Spacing Type*. Typographic specimens (Milwaukee, c. 1886)

A Hand-list of the Writings of Stanley Morison, John Carter, compiler (Cambridge, 1950)

Morison, Stanley, 'Towards an Ideal Italic', *The Fleuron*, v (London, 1926)

9: NUMERALS

Hansard, T.C., *Typographia* (London, 1825)

Wolpe, Berthold, 'Caslon Architectural', *Alphabet* (London, 1964)

10: CHARACTER SPACING

Blumenthal, Joseph, 'The Fitting of Type', *The Dolphin*, 2 (New York, 1935)

Carter, Harry, 'Monotype Van Dijck and Christoffel Van Dyck', *Signature*, 6 (London, 1937)

Rogers, Bruce, 'Paragraphs on Printing' (1943); reprinted in *Books and Printing, q.v.*

11: THE SLAB-SERIF

Gray, Nicolete, *Nineteenth-Century Ornamented types*, 2nd edn. (London, 1976)

Harling, Robert, *The Letter Forms and Type Designs of Eric Gill* (Westerham, 1976)

McLean, Ruari, 'An Examination of Egyptians', *Alphabet & Image*, 1 (London, 1946)

The Monotype Recorder, commemorating an exhibition of lettering and type designs by Eric Gill, xli, 3 (London, 1958)

Reed, T.B., *A History of the old English Letter Foundries*, ed. A.F. Johnson (London, 1952)

Vincent Figgins Type Specimens 1801 and 1815, ed. Berthold Wolpe (London, 1967)

12: THE SANS-SERIF

Beaujon, Paul [Beatrice Warde], 'Eric Gill, Sculptor of Letters', *The Fleuron*, vii (Cambridge, 1930)

Beissert, Gunter, *Jakob Erbar and the Sans-Serif*, trans. F.J. Maclean (Frankfurt, 1936)

Dreyfus, John, *Italic Quartet: a record of the collaboration between Harry Kessler, Edward Johnston, Emery Walker and Edward Prince in making the Cranach Press italic* (Cambridge, privately printed, 1966)

Gray, Nicolete, 'Sans-Serif, and other Experimental Inscribed Lettering', *Motif*, 5 (London, 1960)

Gray, Nicolete, *Lettering on Buildings* (London, 1960)

Handbuch der Schriftarten (Leipzig, 1926; with supplements to 1937)

Handover, P.M., 'Grotesque Letters: a history of unseriffed type faces from 1816 to the present day', *Monotype Newsletter*, 69 (London, 1963)

Johnston, Priscilla, *Edward Johnston* (London, 1959)

McLean, Ruari, *Jan Tschichold, Typographer* (London, 1974)

Megaw, Denis, 'Twentieth-Century Sans-Serif Types', *Typography*, 7 (London, 1938)

Miles, John, 'Some Grotesque type faces', *Motif*, 3 (London, 1959)

Mosley, James, 'The Nymph and the Grot: the revival of the sans-serif letter', *Typographica*, 12 (London, 1965)

Naylor, Gillian, *The Bauhaus* (London, 1968)

Schug, Albert, *Art of the Twentieth Century* (New York, 1969)

Tschichold, Jan, 'New Life in Print', *Commercial Art* (London, July 1930)

Tschichold, Jan, *Asymmetric Typography* (Toronto and London, 1967). (A translation by Ruari McLean of *Typographische Gestaltung*, Basle, 1935.)

The work of Bruce Rogers, catalogue of an exhibition (New York, 1939)

13: THE TYPES OF JAN VAN KRIMPEN

Carter, Harry, 'Johannes Enschedé & Zonen', *Signature*, 4, new series (London, 1947)

Carter, Harry, 'Johannes Enschedé & Zonen: postscript', *Signature*, 5, new series (London, 1948)

Dreyfus, John, *The Work of Jan van Krimpen: a record in honour of his sixtieth birthday* (London, 1952)

Dreyfus, John, 'Spectrum, designed by J. van Krimpen', *Penrose Annual*, 48 (London, 1954)

Dreyfus, John, 'Romulus', appendix in *A Tally of Types: with additions by several hands* (Cambridge, 1973)

Enschedé en Zonen, *A Selection of Types from Six Centuries in use at the Office of Joh. Enschedé en Zonen* (Haarlem, 1930)

Enschedé en Zonen, *Letterproef* (a specimen book), (Haarlem, 1932)

Enschedé en Zonen, *The House of Enschedé, 1703–1953* (Haarlem, 1953)

Glick, William J., *William Edwin Rudge*, Typophiles Chap-Book 57 (New York, 1984)

'Jan van Krimpen, Type Expert', obituary, *New York Times* (23 October 1958)

'Jan van Krimpen, noted Designer of Type', obituary, *New York Herald Tribune* (23 October 1958)

Johnson, A.F., review of the Romulus roman and italic, *Signature*, 13 (London, 1940)

Krimpen, J. van, 'Typography in Holland', *The Fleuron*, vii (London, 1930)

Krimpen, J. van, 'The House of Enschedé', *Penrose Annual* (London, 1953)

Krimpen, J. van, 'A Perspective on Design', an address to the Society of Industrial Artists and Designers in London, 1956, printed in *Printing & Graphic Arts*, v, 1 (Lunenburg, 1957)

Krimpen, J. van, *On Designing and Devising Type*, Typophiles Chap-Book, 32 (New York, 1957)

Krimpen, J. van, 'On Related Type Faces', *Book Design and Production*, i (London, 1958)

Krimpen, J. van, 'First Steps towards the Roman Letter', *Printing & Graphic Arts*, vii, 1 (Lunenburg, 1959)

Krimpen, J. van, 'A Perspective on Type and Typography', *Printing & Graphic Arts*, viii, 4 (Lunenburg, 1959)

Krimpen, J. van, *A letter to Philip Hofer on certain problems connected with the mechanical cutting of punches*. With an introduction and commentary by John Dreyfus. (Cambridge, Mass., 1972)

Morison, Stanley, review of the Lutetia roman, *The Fleuron*, v (London, 1926)

Morison, Stanley?, review of the Lutetia italic, *The Fleuron*, vi (London, 1928)

Morison, Stanley?, review of the Antigone Greek, *The Fleuron*, vii (London, 1930)

Morison, Stanley, review of the Romanée roman, *The Fleuron*, vii (London, 1930)

'Mr Jan van Krimpen, a Type Designer of Distinction', obituary, *The Times* (21 October 1958)

Ovink, G. Willem, 'Grandeurs and Miseries of the Punch-Cutter's Craft', a review of *A to Z. Een autobiografie van P.H. Rädisch, staal-stempelsnijder*. In *Quaerendo*, x (Amsterdam, 1980)

'Van Krimpen in Retrospect', *The Times Literary Supplement* (9 February 1967)

14: SOME TYPES BY FREDERIC GOUDY

BR Today. A Selection of his Books, with Comments, catalogue of an exhibition (New York, 1982)

Coggeshall, Howard, 'The Designer', *Typographer* (Rochester N.Y., 1960)

Dreyfus, John, 'The typographic heritage of Frederic William Goudy', *Newbury Library Bulletin*, vi, 9 (Chicago, 1978)

Goudy, Frederic, 'Types and Type Design', an address at Syracuse University in 1936. Printed in *Books and Printing*, q.v.

Goudy, Frederic, *A Half-Century of Type Design and Typography, 1895–1945*. Two volumes. (New York, 1946)

Goudy, Frederic, *Goudy's Type Designs*, one-volume facsimile of the above. (New Rochelle, N.Y., 1978)

Goudy, Frederic, *The Alphabet and Elements of Lettering* (New York, 1963). (A reprint of the work published in California in 1952, the two parts having first appeared in 1918 and 1942.)

McMurtrie, Douglas, *American Type Designs in the Twentieth Century*, with an
introduction by Frederic Goudy (Chicago, 1924)

Rogers, Bruce, 'An Account of the Making of the Oxford Lectern Bible', included in *The
Trade: passages from the literature of the printing craft*, selected by Ellic Howe
(London, 1943)

Stone, Herbert Stuart, Jr., 'Stone & Kimball: some personal observations', *Newberry
Library Bulletin*, vi, 9 (Chicago, 1978)

Targ, William, *The making of the Bruce Rogers World Bible* (New York, 1949)

15: THREE TYPES BY RUDOLF KOCH

Carter, Harry, 'Sans-Serif Types', *Curwen Miscellany* (London, 1931)

Guggenheim, Siegfried, 'Rudolf Koch: his work and the Offenbach Workshop', *Print*, v,
1 (New Haven, 1947)

Gebr. Klingspor Schriftgiesserei, Offenbach a-M; various specimen books

Klingspor, Karl, *Über Schönheit von Schrift und Druck* (Frankfurt, 1949)

Kühl, Gustav, *On the Psychology of Writing*, trans. John Bernhoff (Offenbach, 1905)

The Little ABC Book of Rudolf Koch, a facsimile of *Das ABC Buchlein*, with a memoir
by Fritz Kredel and a preface by Warren Chappell (Boston, London, Offenbach, New
York, 1976)

Mitchell, Breon, 'German Expressionist Art and the Illustrated Book', *Fine Print* (San
Francisco, April 1977)

Morison, Stanley, *A Review of Recent Typography* (London, 1927)

Newdigate, Bernard, 'Type Design: Germany', *Art of the Book* (London, 1938)

Rodenberg, Julius, 'The work of Karl Klingspor', *The Fleuron*, v (London, 1926)

Rodenberg, Julius, 'Rudolf Koch, Designer of Letters', *Penrose Annual*, 37 (London,
1935)

Roh, Franz, *German Art in the Twentieth Century*, trans. Catherine Hutter, ed. Julia
Phelps, with additions by Juliane Roh (London, 1968)

Standard, Paul, 'Fritz Kredel, Artist, Woodcutter, Illustrator', *Motif* 4 (London, 1960)

Whitford, Frank, *Expressionism* (London, 1970)

Windisch, Albert, 'The work of Rudolf Koch', *The Fleuron*, vi (Cambridge, 1928)

Berthold Wolpe: a retrospective survey (London, 1980)

16: THE TYPES OF W.A. DWIGGINS

Abbe, Dorothy, *Stencilled Ornament and Illustration* (Hingham, 1979)

Beaujon, Paul [Beatrice Warde], 'On Decorative Printing in America', *The Fleuron*, vi
(Cambridge, 1928)

Blumenthal, Joseph, *The Printed Book in America* (New York, 1977)

Burke, Jackson, 'Black-and-white-smith', *Penrose Annual*, 45 (London, 1951)

Dwiggins, W.A., *Layout in Advertising*, revised edition (New York, 1948)

Hofer, Philip, 'The work of W.A. Dwiggins', *The Dolphin*, 2 (New York, 1935)

Postscripts on Dwiggins, Typophiles Chap-Books 35 and 36 (New York, 1960)

Unger, Gerard, 'Experimental No. 223, a Newspaper Type Face designed by
W.A. Dwiggins', *Quaerendo*, xi, 4 (Amsterdam, 1981)

Updike, D.B., 'Designs to be used with Type: illustrated by the work of W.A. Dwiggins'.
With a note by D.B. Updike. *Graphic Arts*, 3 (Boston, 1912)

WAD. The work of W.A. Dwiggins, (A.I.G.A.) (New York, 1937)

WAD to RR: a letter about designing type (Cambridge, Mass., 1940)

17: STANLEY MORISON'S TIMES ROMAN

Dreyfus, John, 'The Evolution of Times New Roman', *Penrose Annual*, 66 (London,
1973)

Hutt, Allen, 'Times Roman: a re-assessment', *Journal of Typographic Research*, iv, 3
(Cleveland, 1970)

Lang, Penny, 'Times Roman: a revaluation', *Alphabet & Image*, 2 (London, 1946)

The Monotype Recorder, 38, 4 (London, 1942–3)

Moran, James, *Stanley Morison: his typographic achievement* (London, 1971)

[Stanley Morison], *Printing The Times: a record of the changes introduced in the issue of 3 October 1932* (London, 1932)

[Stanley Morison], *Printing The Times since 1785* (London, 1953)

Morison, Stanley, *A Tally of Types, cut for Machine Composition and introduced at the University Press, Cambridge, 1922–32* (privately printed, Cambridge, 1953)

Morison, Stanley, *A Tally of Types: with additions by several hands* (Cambridge, 1973)

Parker, Mike, 'Punches and Matrices of the Museum Plantin-Moretus', *Printing & Graphic Arts*, vi, 3 (Lunenburg, 1958)

'Related Bolds', *The Monotype Recorder*, xxxvi, 4 (London, 1938)

'*The Times* and its New Roman type', The Monotype Recorder, xxi, 246 (London, 1932)

Index

An italic figure indicates an illustration